Huxley's
Brave New World:
Essays

edited by DAVID GARRETT IZZO
and KIM KIRKPATRICK

McFarland & Company, Inc., Publishers
Jefferson, North Carolina, and London

\uden
005),
llectual
nst the
2006),
1 Vincent
Garrett

LIBRARY OF CONGRESS CATALOGUING-IN-PUBLICATION DATA

Huxley's Brave new world : essays / edited by David Garrett
    Izzo and Kim Kirkpatrick.
        p.   cm.
    Includes bibliographical references and index.

    ISBN-13 978-0-7864-3683-5
    softcover : 50# alkaline paper ∞

    1. Huxley, Aldous, 1894–1963. Brave new world. 2. Huxley,
Aldous, 1894–1963 — Political and social views. 3. Huxley, Aldous,
1894–1963 — Philosophy. 4. Dystopias in literature. I. Izzo,
David Garrett. II. Kirkpatrick, Kim, 1962–
PR6015.U9B675   2008
823'.912 — dc22   2008013463

British Library cataloguing data are available

Cover illustration ©2008 Shutterstock

Manufactured in the United States of America

McFarland & Company, Inc., Publishers
    Box 611, Jefferson, North Carolina 28640
    www.mcfarlandpub.com

Carol A. Corrody, spirit-catcher,
Laura Archera Huxley, for *This Timeless Moment*,
and Aldous Huxley for his inspiration in art and life
— D.G.I.

For the funny little man — K.K.

Contents

Introduction

DAVID GARRETT IZZO

Brave New World (1932) is perhaps the most influential novel of the twentieth century if one sees its impact as not exclusively literary. Huxley's intentions were social, political, economic, psychological, scientific, philosophical, and *then* literary. Many of the ideas in this "novel of ideas" came from his voluminous essays written in the ten years prior to its publication. The influence is wide and deep. For example, admirers of the philosophy of Horkheimer and Adorno, particularly their essay "The Culture Industry," are actually influenced by Huxley, whom Horkheimer and Adorno read. There is an academic Aldous Huxley Society with a home base in Muenster, Germany, that appreciates his impact on our world and spreads the gospel of Huxley through a book-length Huxley Annual and a conference every year so that he will not be forgotten. His friend and fellow philosopher Gerald Heard called Huxley "The Poignant Prophet" (101), and he was certainly a godfather of the New Age. With all of his accomplishments, perhaps the most enduring was how endearing he was to those who knew him and adored his wit, his kindness, and, finally, his profound humanity, which is behind his writing of *Brave New World*.

Huxley was the man in British literature in the 1920s, much more so than Eliot was, although Eliot's reputation has fared better since then. Huxley's influence was enormous, directly and indirectly. In the U.K. and U.S., undergraduates made sure to read him in the 1920s. When Christopher Isherwood was a student at Cambridge, his mid–1920s Mortmere story, "Prefatory Epistle to my Godson on the Study of History," has a Mr. Starn proclaim, sounding Huxleyesque, that "man is the sole and supreme irrelevance. He is without method, without order, without proportion. His childish passions, enthusiasms, and beliefs are unsightly protuberances in the surface of the Universal Curve." (171). Starn also warns his godson to be skeptical of the New Testament, saying: "I refer to this exploded forgery with all due reference to Professor Pillard, who has, by the Historical Method, clearly proved that it is the work of Mr. Aldous Huxley" (171 footnote).

The cult of Aldous Huxley was afoot as he dared to write down what other artists and intellectuals would have loved to have said, particularly regarding class pretension and snobbishness. Indeed, his subject matter itself was innovative — and widely imitated. Isherwood's first two novels in 1928 and 1932 are Huxleyesque attacks on the bourgeois middle and upper classes — or, as Isherwood called them, "the Others." Later, in Isherwood and Auden's 1935 satirical play, *The Dog Beneath the Skin*, it is clear from the following lines that they had read Huxley's *Brave New World*: "No family love. Sons would inform against their fathers, cheerfully send them to the execution cellars. No romance. Even the peasant must beget that standard child under laboratory conditions. Motherhood would be by license. Truth and Beauty would be proscribed as dangerously obstructive. No books, no art, no music" (167). Huxley in the 1920s and 1930s was a marked man by "the Others" who considered him the most cynical of the postwar cynics.

Aldous Huxley circa 1960 (Library of Congress, Prints and Photographs Division, NYWT&S Collection, [LC-USZ62-119153]).

Huxley's novels of ideas are always about moral dilemmas that need to be sorted out. In the 1920s his characters wallow in the philosophy of meaninglessness with sarcasm as their defense veiling a prevalent despair. The characters secretly — or openly — seek a vehicle that can give meaning to a world that has realized that science, technology, and industry are not the answers. Huxley's protagonists evolve as either upward seekers of the perennial philosophy of mysticism, or they devolve into an even greater disaffected nihilism. *Brave New World* was a warning of a future 600 years hence that is already here.

The title comes from Shakespeare:

> O, wonder!
> How many goodly creatures are there here!
> How beauteous mankind is! O brave new world,
> That has such people in't!
> *The Tempest*

How influential is Huxley's *Brave New World*? The title, while from *The Tempest*, is recognized today as being from Huxley's novel — these three words are a catchphrase for any person or idea that is cutting edge and may have a possible positive/negative duality. If one Googles "brave new world" (as of 11 May 2006) there are 953,000 hits and the majority are not about Huxley's novel. Examples: "The Brave New World of Customer Centricity," "Mental Health Review, Brave New World," "Iraq embraces a brave new world of democracy,"

"Brave New World Astrology Alive!," "The Brave New World of E-Showbiz," "Computer Intelligence: A Brave New World," "Politics in a Brave New World," "Koreans Discover Brave New World of Blog," "Brave New World Surf Shop." No other twentieth-century novel title on this planet has become such a ubiquitous term. The meaning of the phrase as Huxley intended is now both ubiquitous and threatening.

Huxley's world is already upon us. Huxley himself recognized it long before the year 2000, first in his introduction to the 1946 edition of *Brave New World*, and then in book-length form for 1958's nonfiction reevaluation *Brave New World Revisited*. This novel, the precursor for the modern genre of science fiction, is still telling the future; the threats it depicts are now more reality than fantasy. "[B]rave new man will be cursed to acquire precisely what he wished for only to discover — painfully and too late — that what he wished for is not exactly what he wanted. Or, Huxley implies ... he may be so dehumanized that he will not even recognize that in aspiring to be perfect he is no longer even human" (Kass, 52).

In Huxley's *Brave New World* the duality of reason and passion is explicitly out of balance. There is no emotional passion whatsoever. The world is run by Mustapha Mond. "John the Savage" enters this world and almost turns it upside down. To follow, the two square off. Mond: "The world's stable now. People are happy; they get what they want, and they never want what they can't get. They're well off; they're safe; they're never ill; they're not afraid of death; they're blissfully ignorant of passion and old age; they're plagued with no mothers or fathers; they've got no wives or children or lovers to feel strongly about; they're so conditioned that they practically can't help behaving as they ought to behave. And if anything should go wrong, there's soma" (220). Soma is the all-purpose, feel-good drug that fixes everything; a populace in a stupor is not inclined to be rebellious.

John the Savage: "But I don't want comfort. I want God, I want poetry, I want real danger, I want freedom, I want goodness. I want sin." "In fact," said Mustapha Mond, "you're claiming the right to be unhappy." "All right then," said the Savage defiantly, "I'm claiming the right to be unhappy" (240). John is actually claiming the right to have free will, choices, initiative, and spiritual freedom. In this world the people are conditioned to fill and accept certain roles genetically and with "educational" conditioning that amounts to brainwashing. The masses are pacified to believe they want for nothing. All is good — so they think; nothing is bad. There is no sense of comparison. They are lazy, not just of body but also of mind — their ability to think independently has nearly disappeared. While the collective body of the people is pacified, the collective mind is dying into apathy and ignorance. The world is becoming soulless, and without soul and spirit, in Huxley's vision, there will be no progress toward the evolution of consciousness — and that is much more important than being pacified by the constant, sensuous satiety of food, sex, and drugs.

If there is no dark, one cannot truly appreciate the light and think about why the light and dark need to be compared. Light and dark, strong and weak, good and evil have no meaning without contrast and it is from thinking about their meanings that the collective mind moves toward an evolving spiritual consciousness. The mystics call this the reconciliation of opposites. The friction and fission of these opposites rubbing against each other creates the energy needed for consciousness to evolve. Without a reconciliation of opposites the body may be satisfied, but the spirit knows nothing of what it means to be good, strong, heroic and noble. And without this knowledge, life has no meaning. Moreover, the reconciliation of opposites explains the force which Huxley would later call "upward transcendence," the desire to move toward the world of spirit. Downward transcendence is when one thinks too much of one's self and not for the good of the whole. If all good is given instead of chosen, there would be no effort to learn the difference and no progress toward the evolution of consciousness.

The novel opens in 2632 A.F. (which means After Ford, as in Henry Ford, the father of mass production and god of the New World), and after civilization was largely destroyed by a world war. Dictatorship by the tyrannical boot-on-the-neck approach did not work — repression through force eventually collapses under its own effort to maintain it, as it did in the Soviet Union in 1989. A second war follows and the formation of the Brave New World begins, a human society that achieves stability through pleasure instead of fear, conditioning the masses to believe they are happy. Society has a scientifically engineered and cloned caste system. Ten "Controllers" run the world, and stability is enforced by brainwashing people from infancy to accept their roles and by tranquilizing adults with the drug soma. Feelings of passion and the expiation of passion are limited to an encouraged sexual promiscuity and in no way encouraged to become strong feelings for any single individual. Independent thinking is repressed. Any sign of it means exile for the thinker. Science and "reason" exert control. Marriage and normal childbirth are not even remembered except as barbaric rites conducted by primitive savages long ago.

The novel begins with students being given a guided tour through the London Hatcheries, a facility that clones different castes. Henry Foster and Lenina Crowne, who work there, have been seeing each other regularly, which is against state rules. Emotional attachments are not in the state's best interests. Lenina's friend Fanny warns her to be careful and display a more socially acceptable promiscuity. Lenina follows Fanny's advice and decides to see Bernard Marx, who is very intelligent but a bit quirky and slightly nonconformist compared to the others of his caste. Lenina and Bernard go on a vacation to a reservation in New Mexico. There, the inhabitants live primitively and engage in the barbaric practices of marriage and childbirth. Before Bernard leaves, he is warned by Director of Hatcheries Tomakin that his eccentricities could get him exiled to Iceland.

In New Mexico, Lenina and Bernard meet Linda and her son, John the Savage. Bernard learns that long ago Linda had come to the reservation with Tomakin, who had abandoned her there. Linda, pregnant by Tomakin, knew that she could not return to the "normal" world in such a disgraced state; she stayed on the reservation and raised John. Bernard brings Linda and John back to the utopia. Tomakin, stunned, humiliated, and ridiculed, resigns. Bernard believes he has now eluded exile to Iceland.

With Bernard as his keeper, John becomes a magnetic curiosity and amusement, and Bernard enjoys the attention that John brings him along with the women who had previously not been interested in Marx. John is repulsed by the ways of the New World. He will not take soma because he knows it is a fool's cure. Lenina is attracted to John and tries to seduce him — which is normal in her world. John, who read Shakespeare on the reservation, and believes in the plays' noble ideals, particularly romantic love over sexual promiscuity, resists his sexual attraction to her and rejects her advances. This scene is replete with a then-unheard-of striptease that Huxley infers by the repetition of "zip" as in Lenina undoing her zippered up outfit.

When his mother dies from a soma overdose — she had no qualms about taking it — John rebels. He tries to convert the others to his romantic ideals and briefly causes a stir that must be repressed. Bernard and his friend Helmholtz Watson are blamed for the small rebellion. When the two of them are taken to Mustapha Mond, along with John, Bernard and Helmholtz are exiled. John is retained for further experimentation. He resists and tries to flee into solitude, but the citizens of utopia continue to hound him. In a fit of misery and depression, John hangs himself (as did Huxley's brother Trevenen when he, too, could not abide the world he lived in).

John the Savage is no more savage than Queequeg in Melville's *Moby Dick*, which Huxley had read, as noted in a 1923 letter. Amongst his supposed civilized fellow whale hunters, Queequeg, the Pacific Islander, was, in Ishmael's view, more spiritually advanced. Queequeg and John the "Savage" are both looking for a balance of passion and reason.

Huxley's dear friend D. H. Lawrence, as the character Mark Rampion, was the life force that inhabited Huxley's 1928 novel *Point Counter Point*, and Lawrence is the spirit force that suffuses *Brave New World*. Lawrence died in 1930 in the presence of his wife, Frieda, and Aldous and Maria Huxley, whom he had asked to be with him. Lidan Lin writes, in reviewing Dana Sawyer's *Aldous Huxley: A Biography*:

> Lawrence's influence contributed to the composition of the novel.... Huxley shared Lawrence's aversion for the process of industrialization that turns humans into mechanical objects. As Sawyer writes, "[H]ere we find Huxley in agreement with Lawrence who believed that 'men that sit in front of machines, among spinning wheels, in an apotheosis of wheels, often become machines themselves.' Both Huxley and Lawrence believed that work ... can cause us to shirk our first duty to life,

which is to live." Sawyer also illuminates the extent to which Huxley's disapproval of H. G. Wells's utopian novel *Men Like Gods*, and Henry Ford's autobiography *My Life and Work* spurred the composition of the novel.

In 1929 Huxley met Gerald Heard, who would replace Lawrence as Huxley's best friend. Heard was already deeply involved with his philosophy of humanity being actually a spiritual species that had gone astray from its spiritual underpinnings. Heard affirmed Huxley's deepening interest in mysticism and together they explored the potential for rejuvenating the latent spirit in human beings. Lawrence's lasting influence and Heard's living influence sustained the rest of Huxley's life.

In *Brave New World*, spirit is absent. There is no need for God.

In real life it is tragedy that is in conflict with routine, which gives everyday life its perspective about what is truly important. In a *Brave New World* of ceaseless pacification and sensual pleasure, there is no basis for comparison; stability is maintained, but the spirit's evolution toward consciousness is stalled. Only when individuals, then small groups, then larger groups, then towns, and so on, seek to renew the life of the spirit can humanity reach its destiny.

This collection updates the significance of *Brave New World* for the twenty-first century. Read now, it much more truly describes the current world than the world of 1932. This newly profound reading is both enlightening and frightening if the present trek toward nebulous complacency and scientific "progress" continues with too much humanity left out in favor of a numbing expediency. These essays will add fuel to the fire of *Brave New World*'s reinvigorated relevance.

Coleman Carroll Myron believes that in *Brave New World* Aldous Huxley responds to specific dictatorships around the globe born out of economic necessity, global warfare and social chaos by wrestling not only with the root of the issue but also with the complexities that individuals living in such societies face. Although totalitarian manipulation of the masses can take many forms, the end result is inertia that stifles both the individual and society. Whereas Huxley is not treating a new idea, for societies have placed people in chains of conformity to safeguard the nation state since the beginning of time, he is asking at what cost should systems endure in which the motives of a select enlightened, self-interested minority rule over the majority?

Gavin Miller depicts a "World State" in which sexual expression is essential to the functioning of a nonviolent totalitarian system. As with industrialized gestation, the use of non-lethal weapons, and hypnopaedic "education," the immediate gratification of sexual desire ensures a minimum of social conflict. Huxley's representation of sexuality therefore seems to oppose that found in another great twentieth-century dystopian novel, *1984*, which contains an entirely different account of the relation between sexual desire and political oppression.

Bradley W. Buchanan writes that many critics have long held the view that in *Brave New World*, Huxley tries to show that "the conditioned happiness of *BNW* cuts men off from deep experience, keeps them from being fully human" (118). This kind of analysis may well explain why, despite its continuing popularity, *Brave New World* has fallen into critical neglect in an age of "post-humanist" criticism. Yet *Brave New World* is more complex than hand-wringing humanist readings would indicate, and Huxley makes it clear that through John ("the Savage") he is exploring problems and fatal flaws within the very "human" condition he is assumed to be celebrating. The main mechanism through which Huxley does this is Freudianism, which offers, in the shape of the Oedipus complex, a self-consciously humanistic narrative that Huxley both invokes and satirizes in his futuristic utopian fiction.

Angelo Arciero compares the dystopian visions of Brave New World and *Nineteen Eighty-Four* in present terms.

Scott Peller's theme is that *Brave New World* is perceived as depicting an anti-utopia by virtue of its penchant for readymade leisure and pleasure activities, while millions of human beings are still required to perform tedious, repetitive job tasks in order for the upper castes to enjoy their infantile pleasures. Superior characters such as Helmholtz Watson and Bernard Marx garner narrative attention because they perceive themselves as different from the other sense-satisfied Alphas and end up exiled to distant islands far away from the standardized mainstream society. The pneumatic Beta, Lenina Crowne, is pretty much the lone prominent character who is seemingly unable to be anything other than a well-socialized citizen of the stable, happy society. As readers, we are meant to embrace the Savage and Watson for their self-consciousness and their nonconformist actions, while we are supposed to deride the World Controller for participating in the perpetuation of the lowbrow world, Lenina for her inability to decipher her conditioning, and Bernard Marx for failing to engage in a more rebellious course of action.

Sean A. Witters sees that *Brave New World* has the curious legacy of confirming the development of the modern dystopian genre while at the same time satirizing and critiquing its conventions. When Huxley took up the genre in 1932, it had yet to be fully realized as a modern literary stream; yet, his treatment shows remarkable insight into the features we now recognize as its hallmarks. His exploration of language and the mechanics of power in modernity foreshadow the culture theory of the Frankfurt School and Poststructuralism, and distinguish the novel from its predecessors and the majority of its descendents. This distinction owes in large part to Huxley's clever narrative structure, which imparts his critique by way of misdirection, or what can more artfully be described as narrative feints.

John Coughlin describes the relationship between *Brave New World* and Ralph Ellison's *Invisible Man*.

Paul Smethurst writes that Huxley's satiric vision of scientific utopia introduces Shakespeare as a symbol of high art that has led some critics to accuse the author of cultural arrogance. But he argues that the positioning of Shakespeare in the Brave New World envisioned by Huxley is ambivalent, especially when read from a twenty-first-century perspective. From a conventional, liberal, humanist point of view, Shakespeare is the champion of that high art which conveys the values of a free society while speaking of the ideals of truth and beauty. Low art, on the other hand, is a distraction, performing rather than discoursing on the values of free society.

Kim Kirkpatrick believes that *Brave New World*'s penultimate scene, when John kills Lenina, culminates in a Nietzschean birth of tragedy within the Brave New World society. In *The Birth of Tragedy*, Friedrich Nietzsche compares the Apollonian and Dionysian principles to the two sexes: just as both male and female, sperm and ovum, are needed for procreation to take place, so both the Apollonian and Dionysian need to merge for high art and tragedy to be created.

Angela Holzer relates the influence of *Brave New World* on the philosophy of au courant "culture industry" philosophers Horkheimer and Adorno.

Theo Garneau proves that Huxley's "musicalization of fiction" in *Point Counter Point*, his novel of 1928, is continued in *Brave New World* by expressing the inducible truths Huxley heard in Beethoven or Bach's polyphony and that the sheer aurality and musicality of *Brave New World* demand ultimately that the novel be considered as an experiment aimed at enlarging the bounds of textual signification. *Brave New World* is a literary experiment that asks first and foremost to be heard *as music*.

Katherine Toy Miller deconstructs the reservation in *Brave New World* and makes the case that D. H. Lawrence is the basis for John the Savage and that Lawrence's wife Frieda is the basis for John's mother.

Robert Combs sees Huxley as calling for individual psychological alternatives to mass behavior rather than speculating about collective political options. The crisis explored in *Brave New World* is that it is very difficult, if not impossible, to experience the self in a world driven by consumerism and its attendant narcissism. Huxley does not look to the future for some solution, but to the experience of the self in an ongoing present. The full implications of Huxley's diagnosis of the soul-sickness of modern life were not realized until 1944, with the publication of *The Perennial Philosophy*. Clearly, that work, rather than being a departure from Huxley's usual thing, satirical attacks on contemporary lifestyles, is key to bringing his vast journalistic and fictional output into focus. Bringing philosophies of Asia to bear on Western problems, *The Perennial Philosophy* makes the same kind of sense that T. S. Eliot's *Four Quartets* (1943) did after *The Waste Land* (1922).

James Fisher explores the many TV and movie versions of Brave New World and its derivatives.

ductive forward movement of society. Whether or not stopping is good or bad, the Brave New World mirrors the world view that Luther presented when he stated that citizens should not change from the professions they were born into.

To identify the stereotypical levels of society, Deltas wear khaki, Epsilons (genetically manipulated to be stupid) wear black, hard-working Alphas wear gray, and upper-caste Gammas wear green, for example. These austere colors serve utilitarian purposes and mirror clothing worn by either those living a monastic life or engaged in the armed forces, people who have made choices in their lives to negate the self in favor of the group. However, where Luther sees one's profession as an assignment from God, the civilization of *Brave New World* no longer worships Luther's God but the spirit of mass-production as founded by Henry Ford. Huxley drives this point into the minds of the reader by setting *Brave New World* society in the year A.F. 632 — 632 years after Ford created the Model T. In addition, Huxley skews the idea of Ford as god with Freud as god, so that industrial production creates human beings desiring comfort and happiness rather than truth and beauty. A society revolving around Fordian and Freudian ideas is the society that capitalism has founded and has allowed to flourish through consumerism which has led everyone to buy and sell themselves as slaves. When confronted with this worldview, John the Savage, outsider and freethinker, reacts with violent retching behind a clump of laurels. He is appalled by this mechanical control of the people into specialized classes. To force people into social-caste systems limits citizens to associate only with those of their own caste, and with capitalism society has forced people into two classes: the haves and the have-nots.

After providing an overview in the first two chapters of the current world state that emphasizes how the "World Controllers" program happiness through prenatal treatment, drugs, and hypnotic suggestions, Huxley shifts his emphasis to Bernard Marx, Helmholtz Watson, and John the Savage, three individuals who aren't doped up on soma and oblivious to the controls placed on them by society. In freeing themselves from the mind-numbing motto of the Brave New World society, "Conformity, Identity, and Stability," these nonconformists forge their own identity and selfhood apart from the state, where everyone who conforms is part of the mechanism of capitalistic society and of the Protestant work ethic run amok. Because they seek change, these individuals will face exile from this community since their mere presence and thoughts create instability.

In the character of Bernard Marx, Huxley catapults the reader further into the theme behind his novel; for in the naming of Bernard Marx, Huxley draws upon the name of Karl Marx, author (along with Friedrich Engels) of *Das Kapital* who denounces capitalist society. Whereas Karl Marx challenged capitalism from a philosophical viewpoint, Bernard Marx lashes out at the Brave New World society because it proves hostile to him. From a conversation between Lenina and Fanny, the reader learns that Bernard has a bad "reputation" because "he doesn't like Obstacle Golf" and because "he spends most of his time by himself—*alone*" (*BNW* 44). Aside from the information that other characters reveal, Marx himself admits to being disgusted with society's view of Lenina as a piece of "meat" (45), of her belonging to everyone else. In addition to these dislikes, which could possibly be attributed to the fact that "somebody made a mistake when he was still in the bottle — thought he was a Gamma and put alcohol into his blood surrogate" (46), Marx represents a failed component of the Brave New World society, in that he, an Alpha male, when in contact "with members of the lower castes always [is] reminded ... painfully of ... physical inadequacy. 'I am I, and wish I wasn't'; his self-consciousness was acute and distressing. Each time he found himself looking on the level, instead of downward, into a Delta's face, he felt humiliated ... the laughter of the women to whom he made proposals, [and] the practical joking of his equals among the men ... made him feel an outsider; and feeling an outsider he behaved like one, which increased the prejudice against him and intensified the contempt and hostility aroused by his physical defects" (64–65). The fact that Marx does not relish his membership in the society leads to his discontent with it, and, in turn, to his aloneness and appreciation for the beauty of nature. Although he makes disparaging comments and is bitter about the state of affairs, he does nothing when faced with adversity and tries to piggyback onto the efforts of others who do fight: "And suddenly there was Helmholtz at [John's] side — 'Good old Helmholtz!'—also punching ... [and] throwing the poison out by handfuls through the open window.... 'They're done for,' said Bernard and, urged by a sudden impulse, ran forward to help them; then thought better of it and halted; then, ashamed, stepped forward again; then again thought better of it, and was standing in an agony of humiliated indecision" (219–220). His reluctance to act on his ideas brandishes him as a coward and a hypocrite. Despite his reluctance to act, he is still recognized as a partner in crime with the other two heroes, which resigns him to a fate, foreshadowed earlier in the novel, of exile to Iceland.

Unlike Bernard Marx, Helmholtz Watson, his friend and fellow soul searcher, is not an outcast in society and recognizes that his mental capacity and individuality sets him apart from other human beings. He is the "Escalator-Squash champion, [an] indefatigable lover (... six hundred and forty different girls in under four years) ... [an] admirable committee man and best mixer" (67). Yet like Bernard, he recognizes all too recently his indifference to those in civilization and "sport, women, [and] communal activities were only, so far as he was concerned, second bests" (67). As he tells Bernard, "I've been cutting all my committees and all my girls. You can't imagine what a hullabaloo they've been making about it at the College. Still, it's been worth it, I think" (68–69). Aside from steering clear of his willing role as consumer of sex and sport, Helmholtz, as a lecturer at the college of emotional engineering, has been diverging from orders to write phrases that adhere to the company line in order to write ones containing "a bit of propaganda ... [that] engineer[s] [the students] into feeling as I'd felt / when I wrote the rhymes" (183–184). Specifically, Helmholtz wants to write phrases that require students to look inside themselves to discover what is within: "Did you ever feel ... as though you had something inside you that was only waiting for you to give it a chance to come out? Some sort of extra power that you aren't using — you know, like all the water that goes down the falls instead of through the turbines?" In admitting to having "a queer feeling ... that I've got something important to say and the power to say it — only I don't know what it is, and I can't make any use of the power" (69), Helmholtz shows that he has advanced more than Marx because he is able to articulate his selfhood when he joins with John the Savage in the soma incident and when he creates a poem that celebrates silence and the presence of a spiritual being. As a direct result of the incident with John, Helmholtz is exiled to the Falkland Islands, where, as the Controller explained to him earlier, "he'll meet the most interesting set of men and women to be found anywhere in the world. All the people who, for one reason or another, have got too self-consciously individual to fit into community-life. All the people who aren't satisfied with orthodoxy, who've got independent ideas of their own. Everyone, in a word, who's any one. I almost envy you, Mr. Watson" (233). For Helmholtz, his exile gives him the freedom to pursue his interests without the interference of the nation state.

Finally, in the character of John the Savage, Huxley gives the reader the outsider in civilization, the one who is to provide understanding to the situation. Not only is John the outsider to the Brave New World, but also to those on the "Savage Reservation." On the reservation, John's *persona non gratis* status is because his mother is a former inhabitant of the new world who — from the old world's perspective — prostitutes herself. His mother's amoral behavior and her present circumstances as a woman of the new world shift to her son John who is despised and chastised by his peers on the reservation. This inheritance that Linda gives to John also makes John an outsider in the new world, where natural birth by a mother is abhorrent. As an oddity in the new world, John befriends Bernard Marx who identifies in the other the great pangs of loneliness that each feels because of the way that people perceive them: "Bernard blushed uncomfortably. 'You see,' he said, mumbling and with averted eyes, 'I'm rather different from most people, I suppose. If one happens to be decanted different.... Yes, that's just it.' The young man nodded. 'If one's different, one's bound to be lonely. They're beastly to one. Do you know, they shut me out of absolutely everything? When the other boys were sent out to spend the night on the mountains— you know, when you have to dream which your sacred animal is — they wouldn't tell me any of the secrets....'" (139).

After failing to effect change by tossing out the soma, John attempts a more philosophical approach through a conversation with Mustapha Mond, the freethinking world controller. Together they discuss the price of happiness.

John focuses on the price of happiness: freedom and individual expression, while basing his argument on Shakespearean thought. World Controller Mond states that society has had to suppress feelings, beauty, and truth in order to maintain a stable, thriving society. And he says of this particular work [Shakespeare], which "people used to call high art," that the ideas it cultivates do not fuel society and are sacrificed in favor of products that "don't mean anything" but do provide immediate satisfaction: feelies, scent organs, obstacle golf, drugs, and ritual (226–227). When the conversation shifts to the absence of religion from present society, Mond points out that God has been tossed from the picture because civilization is so stable that no one has the need to reach out for a God since every need that it has is immediately provided. Through systematic control of society and the elimination of aspects of it that do not maintain stability, the Brave New World creates an immobile society where everyone is conditioned to be happy. In spite of this utopian society, John makes his decision:

> "But I don't want comfort, I want God, I want poetry, I want real danger, I want freedom, I want goodness, I want sin."
> "In fact, said Mustapha Mond, "you're claiming the right to be unhappy."
> "Not to mention the right to grow old, and ugly and impotent ..." [246].

John's decision, foreshadowed earlier by his tossing out of the soma, revolves around the idea that he would rather be unhappy than live his life superficially.

His retreat to the lighthouse marks a desire to repent for his ways; yet, even in this environment, John is hounded by the all-pervasive arm of a society concerned only with its efficiency. As John attempts to find selfhood and purge himself from the effects of civilization, Darwin Bonaparte captures his self-flagellation on film in *The Savage of Surrey,* a product of the capitalist scheme to make a product at anyone's expense. John's eventual suicide signifies to the Brave New World society that this world, which has restricted his individual freedom and dignity, is one in which he cannot live and maintain his selfhood. Although he would have relished the opportunity to be banished as his friends Bernard and Helmholtz were, it wasn't an option for him since society controls and maintains his work or position.

With the death of John and the banishment of Helmholtz and Marx, the Brave New World returns to normalcy and can continue forward while maintaining its immobility. At all levels, *Brave New World* operates to satisfy the community that wraps itself around the cog of capitalism and the Protestant work ethic that denies the self and selfhood in all manners and forms.

Works Cited

Huxley, Aldous. *Brave New World*. New York: Harper Perennial, 1989.
Lipset, S. M. "The Work Ethic, Then and Now." *Public Interest*, Winter 1990: 61–69.
Tilgher, Adriano. *Homo Faber: Work Through the Ages*. New York: Harcourt Brace, 1930.

Political Repression and Sexual Freedom in Brave New World *and* 1984

GAVIN MILLER

Brave New World depicts a "World State" in which sexual expression is essential to the functioning of a nonviolent totalitarian system. As with industrialized gestation, the use of nonlethal weapons, and hypnopaedic "education," the immediate gratification of sexual desire ensures a minimum of social conflict. Huxley's representation of sexuality therefore seems to oppose that found in another great twentieth-century dystopian novel, for *1984* contains an entirely different account of the relation between sexual desire and political oppression. Orwell's novel (on first reading, at least) presents sexual frustration, rather than expression, as the means by which the Oceanic state controls its citizens. As Blu Tirohl notes, "the Party ... reappropriates sexual energy for its own needs. As desire, or urge, would diminish after sexual intercourse the Party attempts to sustain in its members a state that permanently anticipates pleasure and then channels that energy for its own purposes" (55–56). This thesis clearly differs from that contained in *Brave New World*, as Cass R. Sunstein explains: "We might even identify a Huxley hypothesis, one that appears to compete directly with Orwell's: Sexual activity diverts people from engaging in political causes, and it ought therefore to be encouraged by a government that seeks a quiescent population" (238). This indeed is what Huxley himself claims in his 1946 foreword to *Brave New World*, where he asserts that "as political and economic freedom diminishes, sexual freedom tends compensatingly to increase" (xxxvii). Such opposing views on the political meaning of sexual freedom would not in themselves be particularly surprising, except that both these texts rely upon the same broadly Freudian account of sexuality, a model that is readily apparent in the apposite metaphors of "channeling" and "diversion" used by Tirohl and Sunstein. It is this hydraulic model of the psyche, its political vacuity, and the hints in both texts of an alternative psychology, that will be explored.

Orwell's *1984* contains a Freudian "hydraulic" account of the conversion of libido into psychopathology. Julia explains to Winston how the party exploits an underlying instinctual drive, that may either be expressed healthily in sex,

17

or, if frustrated, expressed unhealthily in state loyalty: "When you make love you're using up energy; and afterwards you feel happy and don't give a damn for anything. They can't bear you to feel like that. They want you to be bursting with energy all the time. All this marching up and down and cheering and waving flags is simply sex gone sour" (118). The narrator's voice summarizes Julia's analysis, explaining further the "sourness" of this sex: "Sexual privation induced hysteria, which was desirable because it could be transformed into war-fever and leader-worship" (118). Winston, too, agrees, wondering to himself, "How could the fear, the hatred, and the lunatic credulity which the Party needed in its members be kept at the right pitch, except by bottling down some powerful instinct and using it as a driving force?" (118).

This thesis is not merely propounded by the voices of the narration, it is also represented in the action of the story. The conversion of frustrated sexuality into aggression is exemplified by Winston's compulsive feelings of sexual sadism towards Julia during the Two-Minute Hate: "He would tie her naked to a stake and shoot her full of arrows like Saint Sebastian. He would ravish her and cut her throat at the moment of climax.... [H] e realized *why* it was that he hated her. He hated her because she was young and pretty and sexless, because he wanted to go to bed with her and would never do so" (18). The action of *1984* also connects sexual frustration to other pathologies, particularly of a psychosomatic variety. For example, Winston encounters a man in the street with a tic, which he later attributes to sexual tension, and he himself suffers from a varicose ulcer on his ankle, which heals as his sexual relationship with Julia develops. Furthermore, Katharine, Winston's state-sanctioned wife, suffers from a chronic muscular tension linked to sexual repression: "Even when she was clasping him against her he had the feeling that she was simultaneously pushing him away with all her strength. The rigidity of her muscles managed to convey that impression" (61).

Brave New World, on the other hand, usually places a quite different political construction upon sexual repression and expression. As Mustapha Mond and the director lecture the students in the gardens around the Conditioning Centre, the former explains how Freud, as well as Ford, created the template for their society. "Our Freud," explains Mustapha, was "the first to reveal the appalling dangers of family life. The world was full of fathers—was therefore full of misery; full of mothers—therefore of every kind of perversion from sadism to chastity; full of brothers, sisters, uncles, aunts—full of madness and suicide" (Huxley 33). But although Freud showed the problem, Mustapha's solution is based on a quite different, and textually anonymous, twentieth-century thinker. The Controller explains how Pacific Island culture "among the savages of Samoa, in certain islands off the coast of New Guinea" seemed to offer a different social organization: "The tropical sunshine lay like warm honey on the naked bodies of children tumbling promiscuously among the hibiscus blossoms. Home was in any one of twenty palm-thatched houses. In the Trobriands conception was the work of ancestral ghosts; nobody had ever heard of a father" (33). The unacknowledged allusion here is to Bronislaw Malinowski's anthropological research in the Trobriand Islands, published in works such as *Argonauts of the Western Pacific* (1922), and *The Sexual Life of Savages in North-Western Melanesia* (1929). The description of childhood sexual play, for example, can be found in the latter text, when Malinowski states that the children of the Trobriand Islanders "initiate each other into the mysteries of sexual life in a directly practical manner at a very early age" (*Sexual Life* 47). The Controller's comment on fatherhood, meanwhile, borrows from Malinowski's claim that the islanders are entirely ignorant of the causes of human conception, and so believe that "the only reason and real cause of every birth is spirit activity" (146).

We might profitably contrast Malinowski's description of the average Trobriand Islander with Orwell's account of the average Eurasian. The latter is a bundle of Freudian tics and compulsions. The former, however, is depicted as in exemplary psychic health: "I could not name a single man or woman who was hysterical or even neurasthenic. Nervous tics, compulsory actions or obsessive ideas were not to be found" (*Sex and Repression* 87). The Controller's account of his society intensifies the cultural pattern underlying Malinowski's analysis, for the Freudian period of sexual latency, and later proscriptions on adolescent sexuality, are entirely alien to the World State. Mustapha explains, to the hilarity of his audience, how "erotic play between children had been regarded as abnormal (there was a roar of laughter) ... and had therefore been rigorously suppressed," and how, until age twenty, no sexual expression was permitted except covert "auto-eroticism and homosexuality" (27).

The model of the psyche developed by Freud, and accepted by Malinowski, becomes clearer as Mustapha (accompanied by the narrator's voice) explains the reasoning behind the World State's prescription of sexual expression. Emotion, according to this model, appears only when a desire is unfulfilled; the bare consciousness of a striving becomes something stronger, and more distinct, in the self's failure to find immediate satisfaction.

In *1984*, totalitarianism is aided by the bottling up of sexual desire, and an exploitation of the consequent frustrated aggression. The Two-Minute Hate is the central political rite, and the sadistic O'Brien the central psychological type. In *Brave New World*, the stopper is taken out of the bottle, so that totalitarianism can exploit a passive population. The group sex of "orgy-porgy" is the concomitant ritual, and the most typical citizen is Lenina's friend, the dutifully promiscuous Fanny.

The plausibility of each novel proceeds from a common reliance upon a model of the psyche as a hydraulic system. This familiar model owes its enduring appeal to a number of features: its apparent economy of explanation, a degree of logical consistency, the plausibility of the psychological connections it offers, an analogy with natural scientific processes, an apparent consonance with sexual psychopathology, and its usage by a generation of psychoanalytic clinicians. Yet, though this model makes a great deal of sense, and seems to be clinically useful, it is far from clear whether there is indeed any reality to which it corresponds. The philosopher Ernest Gellner, for example, mocks the "pseudo-psycho-hydraulics" apparent in intuitions such as the credo "forces blocked in one way find outlets elsewhere" (106). He remarks, "One may doubt ... whether the sketchily constructed model of sluices and channels and chambers and locks and water-wheels, which translate these forces into concrete and specific directions of conduct and feeling, is in any way scientifically serious, as opposed to being mere metaphor" (107). For Jürgen Habermas, the model's distance from natural-scientific verification is more than doubtful:

> Freud sets up several elementary correlations between subjective experiences on the one hand and energy currents, conceived of as objective, on the other. Pain (*Unlust*) results from the accumulation of stimulation, with the intensity of the stimulation proportional to an energy quantum. Inversely, pleasure originates in the discharge of dammed-up energy, in other words through a decrease of stimulation. The motions of the apparatus are regulated by the tendency to avoid the accumulation of stimulation [249].

However, he concludes, "the energy-distribution model only creates the semblance that psychoanalytic statements are about measurable transformations of energy. Not a single statement about quantitative relations derived from the conception of instinctual economics has ever been tested experimentally" (253).

A further problem with the hydraulic model is that it regards social relationships as derived from the blockage of drive satisfaction. According to Freud, "Love is derived from the capacity of the ego to satisfy some of its instinctual impulses auto-erotically by obtaining organ-pleasure. It is originally narcissistic, then passes over on to objects, which have been incorporated into the extended ego, and expresses the motor efforts of the ego towards these objects as sources of pleasure" (136). As autoeroticism is repressed, so libido finds itself blocked, then diverted towards objects (persons, in effect) as the means to its satisfaction: social relationships, in other words, "lean upon" drive satisfaction. However, like libidinal economics, this conception has largely been disproved by empirical studies. Developmental psychologists such as Colwyn Trevarthen, attachment theorists such as John Bowlby, and even "object relations" psychoanalysts such as W. R. D. Fairbairn, have concluded that human beings are born with an innate social impulse that is independent of drive satisfaction. In Trevarthen's words, "the theory that 'innate intersubjectivity' is the primary motive principle of infant learning and cognitive growth has gained wide acceptance — it cannot be dismissed as a romantic fantasy" (81); "even the vegetative or physiological 'state' regulations of newborns are aided by psychological 'mind-to-mind' effects — the benefits of mothering ... are augmented by the tones of affectionate maternal speech and by eye-to-eye contact with the mother" (86).

The hydraulic model, then, is the condensation of a number of plausible psychological hypotheses, rather than a verifiable general psychology. It has the following basic scheme, which is clearly present in both *Brave New World* and *1984*. There is presumed first a dualism of conation, frequently based upon the opposition of instinctual desire: e.g., all striving is either fundamentally self-preservative, or fundamentally sexual (species-preservative). Then it is supposed that inhibition of a striving can occur only from the opposition of these two impulses. Typically, this is a matter of the self-preservative instinct opposing ("damming," "bottling up") the sexual tendency. Two distinct, but interrelated consequences, proceed from this inhibition of desire. On the one hand, inhibited impulse is supposedly converted into emotion; feeling substitutes for action, and all feeling (qua frustration) is painful. On the other hand, the painful and threatening emotion derived from a frustrated impulse may become unconscious, and so reemerge in an attenuated and qualitatively distinct form. This may be either as a symbolic sublimation (experienced as ego-internal) or as a symptom (an ego-alien automatism, such as a tic, psychosomatic disorder, or compulsion).

In order to understand how this model of the psyche is related to the dystopian visions of Orwell and Huxley, it is necessary to consider their shared political concern. Although *1984* and *Brave New World* might seem to represent very different political systems— one violent, the other nonviolent — the common anxiety in each is towards a perfectly "functional" social system. By the 1920s and 1930s, early functionalists such as A. R. Radcliffe-Brown and Malinowski had begun to analyze societies by employing an analogy with biological organisms. In his 1935 paper, "On the Concept of Function in Social Science," Radcliffe-Brown explains the primary, biological sense of "function": "the function of a recurrent physiological process is ... a correspondence between it and the needs (i.e., necessary conditions of existence) of the organism" (179). The function of digestion, for example, is to provide energy and raw material to the cells of the body, and so maintain the continuity of the organism. Something similar, believes Radcliffe-Brown, can be said for patterns of social activity: "The *function* of any recurrent activity, such as the punishment of a crime, or a funeral ceremony, is the part it plays in the social life as a whole and therefore the contribution it makes to the maintenance of the structural continuity" (180). Naturally enough, functionalism has little to say about the value of any such recurrent activity, except in so far as it is an effective means to structural continuity. This ethically vacuous conception is what haunts both *Brave New World* and *1984*, both of which postulate societies that are (or seem) immensely stable, yet are quite indifferent to the deeper welfare of the individual: "'Stability,' said the Controller, 'stability. No civilization without social stability. No social stability without individual stability'" (Huxley 36); "Can you not understand," says O'Brien to Winston, "that the individual is only a cell? The weariness of the cell is the vigour of the organism. Do you die when you cut your fingernails?" (Orwell 227).

The problem with the hydraulic model of the psyche is that both repression and expression can be regarded as functional for the subordination of the individual to the continuity of the social structure. On the one hand, "freely flowing" desire supposedly preempts self-reflection, and directly connects desire to action and fulfillment. The average citizen of the World State therefore has little capacity for self-reflection, and fewer, it would seem, of the higher or sublimated forms of sexual drive. On the other hand, the "damming" or "bottling up" of a drive leads to the repression of painful emotions which reemerge in psychic automatisms such as the compulsive sadism of the average Oceanian. Taken together, *Brave New World* and *1984* present a cruel dialectic in which the creation of self-conscious subjectivity is also the destruction and self-alienation of that same subjectivity.

The futility of this dialectic is emphasized because each text unintentionally anticipates the other, despite the "official line" in each toward sexual expression and repression. Toward the end of *Brave New World*, for example, John the Savage begins to resemble Winston Smith, as his frustrated desire for Lenina is converted into sexual sadism. This sadism he then introverts, unconsciously substituting his own body for Lenina, as he begins to flagellate himself: "'Strumpet! Strumpet!' he shouted at every blow as though it were Lenina (and how frantically, without knowing it, he wished it were!), white, warm, scented, infamous Lenina that he was flogging thus" (223). The World State soon absorbs this impulse into a giant sadomasochistic "orgy-porgy" that resembles a Two-Minute Hate turned back on itself. In *1984*, on the other hand, despite Winston's longing for sexual expression, the most carefree and promiscuous members of society seem to be the Proles, who, though they lack the World State's contraceptive technology, have found in gin, sex, and popular song, their own "soma." Moreover, one can quite reasonably view the love affair between Julia and Winston not as an expression of sexual freedom, but as an unconscious act of extended self-destruction. When they agree to rent the room above Charrington's shop, the narrator's voice remarks that "[b]oth of them knew it was lunacy. It was as though they were intentionally stepping nearer to their graves" (Orwell 124). Torture and submission to the party, believes Winston, is a "predestined horror ... fixed in future times, preceding death as surely as 99 precedes 100" (124). There seems something unconsciously compulsive in Winston's path towards O'Brien's ministrations—which have been described by Sunstein as "a series of sexually sadistic acts ... a sustained scene of rape and castration" (236).

Neither text, perhaps despite the intentions of Huxley and Orwell, presents any great faith in either sexual expression or repression as a safeguard for political dissent. But if in each text we can find an undermining of its doctrine on sexuality, what is the hydraulic model of the psyche doing in them?

The opposing poles of the hydraulic model of the psyche seem to gesture towards something that both texts have difficulty in representing and conceptualizing, precisely because of their reliance upon this model. Mustapha, for example, identifies the family as a central barrier to the free flow of instinct (35). Yet it is unclear whether the family is of concern because it "channels" instinctual drives, like a narrow-bore pipe, or whether it is a threat because it creates a domain of (innate?) intersubjectivity below the level of the entire community (31). Mustapha seems more than a little anxious as he compares a human mother to a cat, loyal to her kittens, and voices what he assumes to be her sentiments: "My baby, and oh, oh, at my breast, the little hands, the hunger, and that unspeakable agonizing pleasure! Till at last my baby sleeps, my baby sleeps with a bubble of white milk at the corner of his mouth" (32). What is of concern here? Is it the "channeling" of a drive to only one object, or the hint of a personal intimacy that is an end in itself?

From a functionalist point of view, the family is a "recurrent activity" that serves the continuation of society as a whole through reproduction and early socialization. If these functions can be replaced, as they are entirely in *Brave New World*, then the family should be an obsolete mechanism. Yet *Brave New World* seems to point, through the fog of a "psychohydraulic" rhetoric, to the family as a domain of intimate companionship that is an end in itself, rather than just a means to social stability and continuity, or a derivative of hedonistic drive satisfaction. However, the only model for familial love that the text supplies is the Oedipal upbringing experienced by John in the reservation, and with it come all the attendant jealousies, resentment, and aggression, as John and his father-substitute Popé battle for possession of Linda.

Orwell's *1984* is more open in its acknowledgement of a domain of non–Freudian love and companionship. It is clear that the family for party members in Oceania exists *only* for reproduction: the children are produced by a monogamous relationship but are socialized into a direct loyalty to the state. The destruction of such intimate intrafamilial loyalty is what haunts Winston in repressed memories of his mother's tender love for his sister. One night with Julia he has a dream set inside the glass paperweight that he earlier bought in Charrington's shop: "The dream had also been comprehended by — indeed, in some sense it had consisted in — a gesture of the arm made by his mother, and made again thirty years later by the Jewish woman he had seen on the news film, trying to shelter the small boy from the bullets, before the helicopter blew them to pieces" (142). This "enveloping protecting gesture of the arm" Winston first witnesses during his childhood when he robs his sister of a chocolate ration (144). To comfort her daughter, "his mother drew her arm round the child and pressed its face against her breast" (145). This faint memory of nonsexual intimacy leads Winston to appreciate, for the first time, that the Proles are neither a *lumpenproletariat* nor a class in itself that must one day become a class for itself: "The proles ... were not loyal to a party or a country or an idea, they were loyal to one another. For the first time in his life he did not despise the proles or think of them merely as an inert force which would one day spring to life and regenerate the world" (147).

Winston's relationship with Julia must therefore be analyzed in terms other than those that he provides for it. His sexualized view of their relationship is encouraged by Julia. Yet it is quite possible that this is "devil's doctrine," given the numerous hints that Julia is an agent of the party (for example, it would seem to be her coffee that drugs both her and Winston before their arrest; she seems surprised only by the location of the telescreen in their room, rather than its existence; and so forth). The self-conscious sexual rebellion of their relationship may well be a cover for its real meaning (to Winston at least) as a domain of private love and intimacy. In an early encounter with Julia, for example, Winston is motivated not by desire, but by an instinctive sympathy: "In front of him was an enemy ... in front of him, also was a human creature, in pain and perhaps with a broken bone. Already he had instinctively started forward. In the moment when he had seen her fall on the bandaged arm, it had been as though he felt the pain in his own body" (Orwell 95). As their relationship develops, this nonsexual sympathy and companionship increasingly rears its ugly head. When Julia refuses to meet because she is menstruating, Winston finds himself confronted with an emotion that is normally obscured by the noise and turmoil of sexual tension and release: "When one lived with a woman this particular disappointment must be a normal, recurring event; and a deep tenderness, such as he had not felt for her before, suddenly took hold of him" (124).

One could, of course, regard this tenderness as the sublimation of an abruptly aim-inhibited sexuality: but this would be, as an interpreter, to play the game demanded by the party, and played also by *Brave New World*—the game that treats intimate companionship as a manifestation of a pseudo-hydraulic sexual drive. If we mistake the party's official counter—ideology as the meaning of *1984*, then we will indeed arrive at Sunstein's conclusion that "Orwell's thesis is a crude, vaguely Freudian cliché" (241). Yet this "Freudian cliché" is certainly not all that the novel represents: the hydraulic model is a discourse undermined by others in the novel, such as Winston's repressed memories of a time when love could be neither fundamentally sexual, nor merely functional for the state.

On the other hand, *Brave New World* accepts more readily the social-scientific and psychological discourse that it employs. This is why *Brave New World* has to place its hopes elsewhere. While *1984* gestures to an instinctual need for intimate companionship as a threat to the state, *Brave New World* cannot locate so much subversive potential in the human psyche. Instead, chance and contingency make up as best they can for political dissent. From the director accidentally waking the children, to Bernard's faulty conditioning, to Linda's pregnancy, *Brave New World* locates the threat to the World State outside the minds of its characters and inside the contingencies which, however weakly, threaten the functional goals of "Community, Identity, Stability" (1).

The dialogue between *1984* and *Brave New World* is therefore a challenge to literary criticism, for it threatens the hydraulic model of the psyche that appears quite readily, almost unthinkingly, in much modern critical theory. To take just one possible example out of many: Robert Young in *Colonial Desire* claims "that the prime function incumbent on the socius has always been to codify the flows of desire, to inscribe them, to record them, to see to it that no flow exists that is not properly dammed up, channeled, regulated" (169). Despite the authority of analyses such as Young's, the use of this psychic model is a case of literary theory lagging behind both the texts it studies *and* the disciplines from which it borrows. *Brave New World* and *1984* gesture toward nonsexual companionship — a need for intimate community that can be grasped neither by an outmoded Freudian (or drive-based) psychology, nor by functionalist sociology. Taken together, these texts challenge a prejudice still common in those who, like Orwell's party members, love ideas more than people: namely, that is it is somehow more scientific, or objective, or perceptive, to deny that love is an original emotion, and talk instead of the damming and diverting of instinct and the functional value of this largely conjectural process for the stability and continuity of society.

Works Cited

Freud, Sigmund. "Instincts and Their Vicissitudes." In *On Metapsychology: The Theory of Psychoanalysis*, edited by Albert Dickson, 113–38. Penguin Freud Library Volume 11. Harmondsworth, England: Penguin, 1984. First published 1915.

Gellner, Ernest. *The Psychoanalytic Movement: Or the Cunning of Unreason*. London: Collins, 1985.

Habermas, Jurgen. *Knowledge and Human Interests*. Translated by Jeremy J. Shapiro. London: Heinemann, 1972.

Huxley, Aldous. *Brave New World*. 1932. London: Vintage, 2004.

Malinowski, Bronislaw. *Sex and Repression in Savage Society*. 1927. London: Routledge and Kegan Paul, 1960.

_____. *The Sexual Life of Savages in North-Western Melanesia*. 3rd ed. London: Routledge and Kegan Paul, 1932.

Orwell, George. *Nineteen Eighty-Four*. Harmondsworth, Middlesex: Penguin, 1954.

Radcliffe-Brown, A.R. *Structure and Function in Primitive Society*. London: Cohen and West, 1952.

Sunstein, Cass R. "Sexual Freedom and Political Freedom." In *On Nineteen Eighty-Four: Orwell and Our Future*, edited by Abbott Gleason, Jack Goldsmith, and Martha C. Nussbaum, 233–41. Princeton: Princeton University Press, 2005.

Tirohl, Blu. "'We Are the Dead ... You Are the Dead': An Examination of Sexuality as a Weapon of Revolt in Orwell's *Nineteen Eighty-Four*." *Journal of Gender Studies* 9, no. 1 (2000): 55–61.

Trevarthen, Colwyn. "Proof of Sympathy: Scientific Evidence on the Personality of the Infant and MacMurray's 'Mother and Child.'" In *John MacMurray: Critical Perspectives*, edited by David Fergusson and Nigel Dower, 77–117. New York: Peter Lang, 2002.

Young, Robert. *Colonial Desire: Hybridity in Theory, Culture and Race*. London: Routledge, 1995.

Oedipus Against Freud: Humanism and the Problem of Desire *in* Brave New World

BRADLEY W. BUCHANAN

Many critics have long held the view that, in his famous novel *Brave New World*, Aldous Huxley tries to show that (in Mark Hillegas's words) "the conditioned happiness of Brave New World cuts men off from deep experience, keeps them from being fully human" (118). The humanistic moral Hillegas draws from the book has been widely accepted; indeed, this kind of analysis may well explain why, despite its continuing popularity, *Brave New World* has fallen into critical neglect in an age of "post-humanist" criticism. Yet *Brave New World* is more complex than hand-wringing humanist readings would indicate, and Huxley makes it clear that through John ("the Savage") he is exploring problems and fatal flaws within the very "human" condition he is assumed to be celebrating. The main mechanism through which Huxley does this is Freudianism, which offers, in the shape of the Oedipus complex, a self-consciously humanistic narrative that Huxley both invokes and satirizes in his futuristic utopian fiction.

Freud's role in Aldous Huxley's *Brave New World* has been much discussed, but little consensus has emerged, partly because of Huxley's apparent ambivalence about Freud's ideas and his growing reluctance, after he had written the novel, to admit that he had ever been in agreement with Freud's conception of human nature. In a 1960 interview, Huxley said, "I was never intoxicated by Freud as some people were, and I get less intoxicated as I go on" (Meckier 37). Although some have taken this statement as an unequivocal denial of any affinity Huxley may have had for Freud,[1] it reads less as a repudiation of Freud than as a confession that Huxley was indeed intoxicated by Freud to a certain extent when he was younger, although he certainly never reached the stage of feverish zealotry achieved by some of his contemporaries.[2] Indeed, Huxley's half-hearted protestations against Freud have prompted insinuations about the motives behind them. For instance, Charles Holmes has written "that throughout his life Huxley rejected Freud, though the tone and intensity of his rejection varied. Given Freud's emphasis on sex and Huxley's near-obsession with it, the rejection implies unconscious resistance incompletely understood" (Holmes 137). Philip Thody has undertaken to explain this resistance in biographical terms: "Huxley's adoration of his mother implied feelings of intense jealousy for his father, and ... these were translated into the subconscious notion that Leonard Huxley was at least partly guilty for his wife's death.... [T]he hostility which Huxley always shows for Freud's ideas [is] an indication of the fear which he had that such a diagnosis might be true, and the fact that almost all the fathers in Huxley's fiction are caricatures would lend weight to this view" (Thody 16–17). The purpose here, however, is not to confirm or refute such descriptions of and speculations about Huxley's ambivalent attitude to Freud, but to show how this attitude manifests itself in *Brave New World*, where Freudian ideas are plainly on display. Any account of Huxley's reaction to Freud should also take into account the influence on Huxley of D. H. Lawrence, who attacked Freud's humanistic theories yet whose own life and work present clear examples of many Freudian theories.

The most prominent of Freud's ideas is his notion of the Oedipus complex, which, according to Freud, describes a male child's feelings of incestuous desire for his mother and parricidal anger towards his father. Oedipus's story is potentially every boy's, according to Freud, because all boys see their mothers as love objects and their fathers as rivals. For Freud, Oedipus (who kills his father and marries his mother) is "nothing more or less than a wish fulfillment — the fulfillment of the wish of our childhood" (*The Basic Writings of Sigmund Freud* 308). The universality of this desire is the foundation of Freudian humanism: the supposition that through a single narrative or "complex" we can know ourselves and our deepest desires.[3] This was perhaps Freud's most influential and controversial theory, one that Huxley might have been particularly eager to debunk. Yet on August 24, 1931, shortly after finishing *Brave New World*, Huxley wrote a letter to his father in which he describes his new book as "a comic, or at least satirical, novel about the future ... and adumbrating the effects on thought and feeling of such quite possible biological inventions as the production of children in bottles, (with the consequent abolition of the family and all the Freudian complexes for which family relationships are responsible)" (*Letters of Aldous Huxley* 35). This letter shows that Huxley was willing to discuss the Freudian complexes for which family relationships are responsible very seriously indeed, and with his own father, no less. If Huxley had any doubts at all about the truth of the most famous of these complexes, he would surely have assured his father that he harbored no such complex, with its attendant murderous and incestuous feelings, or at least to have palliated the unpleasant thought that his own family was to blame for imposing these emotions on him. The fact that he did not says a good deal about his opinion of the fundamental truth of Freud's theory of the Oedipus complex.

This opinion is shown even more clearly in *Brave New World*, in which the Oedipus complex is deemed such a dangerous and powerful force that it (along with the family structure that produces it) has been eliminated from civilized life, as far as possible. Children are no longer born to a set of parents but produced in an assembly-line process from fertilized eggs which are then decanted into bottles and subjected to endless chemical alteration and conditioning. By controlling all aspects of a child's birth and upbringing, and by keeping adults in a condition of infantile dependency on a larger social body, Huxley's imaginary state has taken over the role of parent and robbed the child of his or her Oedipal potentialities. Indeed, it could be argued that the active suppression of the Oedipus complex is the principal tool of social stability practiced in this future. Yet this state of affairs is really just an extension of principles that have helped to form twentieth-century life, according to Freud. After all, in *Totem and Taboo* Freud postulates that the reason Oedipus's parricide and incest shock us so much is that we have constructed civilization precisely to discourage the two crimes of which Oedipus is guilty, the "only two crimes which troubled primitive society" (*The Basic Writings of Sigmund Freud* 917). In Huxley's futuristic utopia the prohibitions against parricide and incest are simply taken to their logical extreme, so that even the unconscious energies produced by repressing such desires are dissipated. The solution to the problem of Oedipal desire is to make everyone so infantile that they still feel as if they are in the womb/decanter. A popular song expresses this pre–Oedipal state: "Bottle of mine, it's you I've always wanted! / Bottle of mine, why was I ever decanted?" (*Brave New World* 91).

Freud himself is treated as a prophet in this pseudo-paradise; indeed, he is elevated to near divinity, along with Henry Ford (the similarity of their names comes in handy), as the following passage makes clear: "Our Ford—or Our Freud, as, for some inscrutable reason, he chose to call himself whenever he spoke of psychological matters—Our Freud had been the first to reveal the appalling dangers of family life" (*Brave* 44). These dangers have to do not with incest or parricide but with "the prohibitions they were not conditioned to obey and which force them to feel strongly" (*Brave* 47). Strong feelings, of course, are unpleasant enough to the denizens of the brave new world, but the director of London's central "hatchery" supplements this already grim picture with the horrible thought of emotionally suffocating parents who once clung desperately to their children: "The world was full of fathers—was therefore full of misery; full of mothers—therefore of every kind of perversion from sadism to chastity" (*Brave* 44).

The people of Huxley's future have not read Freud, quite clearly, but they have been indoctrinated with a Freud-influenced awareness of the possibility of illicit relations between mother and child. This awareness, which manifests itself in Lenina Crowne's distaste for the "indecent" spectacle of "two young women giving the breast to their babies, the sight of which makes her blush and turn away" (*Brave* 130), is exploited to inculcate a less visceral but nonetheless strong suspicion of any private or emotionally intense relationship between two people. Indeed, any individualized, personalized sexual feelings are branded as essentially incestuous, and the language of forbidden passion is essentially a disgusting outgrowth of the obsolete love talk between mother and child (*Brave* 49). An "only love" is an incestuous love, in Huxley's futuristic world, because it tends to work against the social solidarity, which is the key to peaceful life.

Despite all this revulsion toward the very possibility of Oedipal crimes or Oedipal urges, the mythical figure of Oedipus returns to Huxley's novel with a vengeance, in the form of John Savage, a man who was born (in the traditional way) into an Indian tribe on a reservation in New Mexico. John's father is the director of the London hatchery, and leaves John to be raised by his mother, Linda, after he has impregnated her in the once-traditional but now unthinkable way. Like Oedipus, John grows up without knowing whom his biological father is, but finally, with the help of his mother, learns the truth. He also unintentionally ruins his father by embracing him publicly, kneeling before him, and addressing him as "my father," a scene that no doubt functions as Huxley's satirical rendition of Oedipus's unwitting murder of his own biological father. Yet John is more of a Freudian case study than a reincarnation of Oedipus himself; his sensibilities have been formed by a battered edition of Shakespeare he finds (rather improbably) in the squalor around him, and he identifies strongly with Hamlet's rage about his mother's marriage to Claudius. He experiences some classically Freudian Oedipal jealousy of the native man who sleeps with his mother, spurring his anger with apt quotations from *Hamlet*: "He hated Popé more and more. A man can smile and smile and be a villain" (*Brave* 156).

John's readings from Shakespeare are supplemented by his internalization of tribal values and practices, and he seems to be Huxley's attempt to distill a mixture of the stereotypical "noble savage" and the best of Western humanistic culture (via Shakespeare). Yet these mixed traditions produce an explosive situation: reading Hamlet intensifies and focuses John's anger towards Popé (*Brave* 157). Huxley implies that literary examples of human behavior—for instance, the Shakespearean representation of a son's jealousy about his mother's relations with another man in *Hamlet*, anticipate the Freudian theory of the Oedipus complex. His portrait of John shows how the Oedipus complex is produced partly through natural boyish pride and jealousy and partly through John's aesthetic appreciation of Shakespeare's language. This is no doubt a sidelong jab at Freud, and certainly adds resonance to Huxley's remark that "All that modern psychologists … have done is to systematize and debeautify the vast treasures of knowledge about the human soul contained in novel, play, poem and essay" (*Music at Night* 292).

John and his mother eventually leave the reservation with Bernard Marx, an insecure would-be intellectual, who seeks to win approval and social status by parading them as curiosities back in London. Yet even once he has encountered the many attractive and available women there, John remains obsessed with his mother. He remembers the intimate moments between him and Linda fondly, recalling those times when he sat on her knees and she put her arms about him and sang, over and over again, rocking him, rocking him to sleep (244). Linda's own behavior towards John has contributed heavily to his fixation on her; she has been neglectful, sentimental, abusive and affectionate by turns towards John. For instance, when John was little she slapped him for calling her his "mother" and then, in a matter of moments, repented and kissed him "again and again" (*Brave* 150), as if he were a suitable replacement for the lovers she has lost temporarily because of other women's jealousy. John never understands the nature of his feelings toward Linda, conflating his incestuous desires and violent impulses towards Popé with the trappings of heroism (after all, both traits are found in Hamlet). The fact that such powerful attachments are not normal any longer in a world of Malthusian belts and orgy porgies simply reinforces John's sense of tragic self-importance. Direct exposure to Freud's writings might have been able to inform John that his feelings are not symptoms of some extraordinary powers or responsibilities, but that they are normal emotions (at least in Freud's mind) to be recognized and overcome. Yet, as we can readily see, no one reads Freud anymore; or if they do, they fail to apply or explain his theory of the Oedipus complex to John, the one human being to whom it is still relevant.

John finds it difficult to renounce his mother or sever their emotional connection (as he shows throughout the novel) and this leads him to be extremely censorious of any lustful impulse in himself, since all his erotic attachments seem charged with the unsatisfied desires of his childhood love for Linda. When he calls Lenina an "impudent strumpet" (*Brave* 232) he is not only censuring her evidently promiscuous behavior (which she, ironically, seems at times to be willing to change for his sake), he is projecting his revulsion at his own lusts onto her. We get a sense of how deeply John's libido has been repressed when he attends a feely (a futuristic movie which allows spectators to feel as well as see the actions onscreen) that features scenes of sex between "a gigantic negro and a golden haired young brachycephalic Beta Plus female" (*Brave* 200). No doubt prompted by memories of Linda and Popé,[4] John is revolted by this interracial love story; he "start[s]" violently as it begins and later terms it "horrible" (*Brave* 202), though he is struck by the similarities between it and Shakespeare's Othello. Long afterwards, John's desire for Lenina becomes inextricably linked to the mixture of sexual arousal and disgust that he feels while watching the feely (*Brave* 229).

John seems to identify with the possessive (whom he links to Shakespeare's nobler Othello) just as he had once identified with Popé, and yet he reacts with predictable disgust at the depiction of his own incestuous fantasies on the screen (just as he comes to hate Popé for having sexual access to Linda). Like Linda, the heroine of the "feely" is a blonde Beta who makes love to a man from a different, darker-skinned race. Lenina, who accompanies John to the feely, is herself associated in John's mind with the brachycephalic blonde and, by extension, with Linda herself[5]; thus, as Freudians might well argue, he cannot imagine having sexual relations with Lenina before he has exorcised the unconscious incestuous demons that plague him and make him mistrust all sexual activity. These demons seem to determine his reactions to many of the everyday features of the world he has entered; for instance, he is outraged by the docile subservience of a group of identical Deltas awaiting their dose of drugs. He sees such twins as less-than-human monsters, asking them why they don't want to be free and men, and challenging them to throw off their dependence on drugged bliss: "Do you like being babies? Yes, babies. Mewling and puking" (*Brave* 254). Here Huxley's keen sense of irony is working overtime: the Savage accuses the cloned workers of the same infantilism he has only managed to confront (and only partially) through his violent and unresolved Oedipus complex. There may be more than Freudian theory at work here; however, as anthropologists have observed, twins frequently symbolize the results of incestuous activity. As René Girard writes, "Incestuous propagation leads to formless duplications, sinister repetitions, a dark mixture of unnamable things. In short, the incestuous creature exposes the community to the same danger as do twins ... mothers of twins are often suspected of having conceived their children in incestuous fashion" (*Violence and the Sacred* 75). Thus it may be that Huxley wants to indicate that John associates these twins with his own unfulfilled urges, which he must then repress all the more violently, or sublimate into radical activity (witness his act of throwing the Deltas' long-awaited soma out the window). After Linda's death, the link between her and these twins remains prominent: "He had sworn to himself he would constantly remember ... Linda, and his own murderous unkindness to her, and those loathsome twins, swarming like lice across the mystery of her death" (*Brave* 296–7).

The violence of John's reactions to the stimuli he encounters in London seems to justify, at least in part, the systematic attempts of Huxley's modern Londoners to obliterate the tensions that produce such extreme emotions. Furthermore, just as his intolerance for interracial love sours his own desire for Lenina, his repressed Oedipal desires drive him to distraction when he confronts a group of low-caste twins after his mother's death. In the same way that in D. H. Lawrence's *Sons and Lovers* Paul Morel's attachment to Clara Dawes seems to end only when his mother is close to death, Savage's flirtation with another woman seems to bring his mother ill health, and intensifies his own guilty feelings (his subsequent sense that he has killed her is predictable, given the Lawrentian-Freudian psychology drawn from by Huxley). John's uncompromising judgments of the twins and others similarly lacking in individuality are deeply at odds with the passive, hedonistic and collectivist ethos of the world around him; Mond admonishes him that "our world is not the same as

Othello's world ... you can't make tragedies without social instability" (*Brave* 263). Nevertheless, John sees individuality as an indispensable precondition of human identity; he describes the twins created by the Hatchery as "less than human monsters," asking them why they don't want to "be free and men" (*Brave* 254). Unfortunately for him, John's conception of individual responsibility gives him a powerful sense of the sinfulness of all sexual actions and thoughts; John may be the last truly "human" being, but he is far from being a true humanist, as his revulsion toward almost all forms of sexuality indicates. Dismayed by Lenina's willingness to sleep with him, John quotes *King Lear* (Act IV, Scene VI): "Down from the waist they are Centaurs, though women all above" (*Brave* 233). Sexuality makes animals out of human beings, at least in John's mind, and this is another form of hybridity that he cannot stomach (perhaps because it reminds him too much of his own mixed identity and all the anxieties it has created in him). In any case, John's disgust with Lenina's sexuality shows him to be as fatally unaware of his own capacity for sensual excess as Oedipus is that he has committed incest with Jocasta, and this blindness, once it has been dispelled in a drug-induced orgy, leads to John's suicide.

Before Nietzsche famously foresaw the replacement of humanity by "supermen," he celebrated Oedipus (in an unpublished manuscript) as "the last man" (quoted in Shapiro, *Nietzschean Narratives* 156). This prophecy appears to have come true, in a sense, in Huxley's dystopia. The Oedipal "Savage" is, in a real sense, the "last" human being (aside from the primitives on the reservation) in a world of engineered infants. The "Bokanovsky process" circumscribes the identity of each person, limiting it to the caste to which he or she belongs. Thus, although each individual is a clone of many others, there is no way to generalize about humanity anymore: the species has been fractured into incommensurable sections. All this is quite in keeping with the dogmas of the new order; as the D.H.C. rationalizes while he gives student visitors to the hatchery their tour, "particulars, as every one knows, make for virtue and happiness; generalities are intellectually necessary evils" (*Brave* 2). Hence maxims like "All men are physico-chemically equal" (*Brave* 87) only serve to reinforce Mustapha Mond's upper-caste scorn for the idea that humanity itself could be more than a "physico-chemical" category (*Brave* 55).

Because of this new conception of human nature as a "physico-chemical" phenomenon, no serious attempt is made to give the idea of the human any additional meaning by attaching it back to a divinity that might guarantee its sacredness. Mustapha Mond does contemplate the undesirable (though remote) possibility that citizens of the Brave New World might "lose their faith in happiness as the Sovereign Good and take to believing, instead, that the goal was somewhere beyond, somewhere outside the present human sphere" (*Brave* 211), but happily for him, there is no sign of any such discontent apart from that voiced by the unconditioned, obdurately Oedipal John. Mond quotes Cardinal Newman's belief that "independence was not made for man — that it is an unnatural state" (*Brave* 279), but facilely dissents, arguing that "we can be independent of God" since "youth and prosperity" (the conditions for independence, according to Newman) are enjoyed by all, until they die suddenly, of course (*Brave* 279). This argument smacks of sophistry (Newman's criteria are not the only ones that might be imagined), and to some (like Newman himself, were he to have lived long enough to read it), such a defense of this utopia might testify to the incoherence of the idea of the human once any superhuman goal or imperative is abandoned. To others, however, Mond's smug and limited humanism may simply suggest that no valid conception of the human can afford not to take death into account. Aside from the smoke from the crematoria and the early training that encourages children to treat death as they might treat a stay in a hotel, death is invisible in the London Huxley imagines; it has no emotional or intellectual force for even exceptional citizens like Bernard Marx or Helmholtz Watson. The only person in the novel for whom death has any significance is John, and he ends up affirming his difference in the only way left to him, by committing suicide, thus apparently taking humanity's last chance with him.

Still, the ever-ironic Huxley plants many hints that John is not the only one who finds himself unable to live within the parameters of Huxley's imagined society. Bernard Marx and Helmholtz Watson share a sense that they are individuals, and chafe against the conformity imposed on them, however pleasant its trappings may be. Like John, both of these heroes have a certain amount in common with Oedipus; both end up in exile, Bernard for his obstreperousness and Helmholtz for his refusal to live by the usual rules enforcing indulgence, promiscuity and sociability.[6] While Bernard's show of resistance to the permissive status quo disappears once he has gained the self-confidence to get what he wants,[7] Helmholtz's desire to impose a measure of austerity on himself, especially with respect to his sexual relationships, is genuine.

John's and Helmholtz's moral objections to the amorous goings-on around them have long been assumed to be an expression of Huxley's own disapproval of promiscuity, and understandably so. After all, a few years before writing *Brave New World*, Huxley had claimed that "nothing is more dreadful than a cold, unimpassioned indulgence. And love infallibly becomes cold and unimpassioned when it is too lightly made" (*Do What You Will* 137). In a 1931 essay, Huxley argues that "no reasonable hedonist can consent to be a flat racer. Abolishing obstacles, he abolishes half his pleasure. And at the same time he abolishes most of his dignity as a human being. For the dignity of man consists precisely in his ability to restrain himself ... to raise obstacles in his own path" (*Music at Night* 167). This view is remarkably close to that expressed by Freud in *Civilization and Its Discontents*,[8] a book translated into English and published in 1930, and which Huxley may or may not have managed to read before or during the composition of *Brave New World* (from May 1931 to August of that year). Nevertheless, Freud is certainly to be numbered among the reformers mentioned by Mustapha Mond in *Brave New World* when he addresses his charges as follows: "Has any of you been compelled to live through a long time interval between the consciousness of a desire and its fulfillment?... And you felt a strong emotion in consequence?... Our ancestors were so stupid and short sighted that when the first reformers came along and offered to deliver them from those horrible emotions, they wouldn't have anything to do with them" (*Brave* 52–3). Yet passages like these have caused some of Huxley's readers to lump Freud in with his supposed followers in the novel. For instance, Thody[9] argues that "In *Brave New World* it is ... the implied ethical teachings of Freudianism that attract his scorn, the rejection of complex and mature emotions in favor of instant gratification and the pleasure principle. His disapproval is, in fact, almost Victorian in his moral intensity" (Thody 54). Nevertheless, critical opinion on this issue has been divided; Peter Firchow points out that in *Brave New World* excessive restraint, like the Savage's, still leads to self-destruction. (Firchow 55). Firchow not only contests the claim that Freud is a spokesman for libertinism in Huxley's eyes, he even goes so far as to argue (without much evidence, it must be said) that "Freud ... is the closest the new world's science comes to having a conscience" (Firchow 47).

Another area in which Huxley and Freud have been deemed to disagree irreconcilably has to do with artistic creation. The case for their incompatibility here is a better one; we know that in Huxley's view, Freud was guilty of implying that art was (in Huxley's words) a "happy efflorescence of sexual perversity" (*Proper Studies* xvi). In an article called "Formulations Regarding the Two Principles in Mental Functioning," first published in 1911, Freud did make the somewhat insulting claim that "the artist is originally a man who turns from reality because he cannot come to terms with the demand for the renunciation of instinctual satisfaction as it is first made, and who then in fantasy life allows full play to his erotic and ambitious wishes" (*A General Selection from the Works of Sigmund Freud* 44).[10] Yet this position is a long way from the simple choice presented by Mustapha Mond (or "the Controller"), who puts the official position thus: "You've got to choose between happiness and what people used to call high art. We've sacrificed the high art" (264). Some have inferred that this passage means that in Huxley's mind Freud is the opponent of high art, since his theory of the Oedipus complex is meant to induce people to accept their lot and to be happy, rather than continue being neurotic and creative. Whatever the merits of this characterization of Freud's position, its assumption about the straightforwardness of Huxley's views does them a disservice. Huxley was deeply ambivalent about high art, especially tragedy, which he regarded as an outdated genre. In his essay "Tragedy and the Whole Truth," Huxley argues that there is something inherently false about a tragic narrative: "To make a tragedy the artist must isolate a single element out of the totality of human experience and use that exclusively as his material. Tragedy is something that is separated from the Whole Truth, distilled from it, so to speak"

(*Music at Night* 12–13). In this essay, Huxley uses *Othello* as an example of a tragedy that must exclude realistic details that would make it more truthful in order to achieve its dramatic effect. Of course, *Othello* is also mentioned prominently in *Brave New World*, where its interracial sexual themes resurface in the pornographic feely attended by John and Lenina. Mindful of John's habit of viewing everything in Shakespearean terms, Mond admonishes John that "our world is not the same as Othello's world ... you can't make tragedies without social instability" (*Brave* 263). We may infer that in Huxley's eyes the "Whole Truth" lies somewhere between tragedy and pornography, and that John's tragic vision of reality is an oversimplification of what Huxley recognizes as the complexities of modern life.

Huxley even seems to endorse one element of Freud's characterization of the artistic impulse, insofar as it is related to the Oedipal energies John represents. In *Group Psychology and the Analysis of the Ego*, Freud creates a scenario to explain the role of creativity, or more specifically, of epic narrative, in primitive society just after the parricidal crisis in which the famous band of brothers has slain the tyrannical father: "Some individual ... may have been moved to free himself from the group and take over the [dead] father's part. He who did this was the first epic poet; and the advance was achieved in his imagination.... He invented the heroic myth" (*A General Selection from the Works of Sigmund Freud* 203) This formula of original creativity is extremely tendentious, to say the least; as Richard Astle puts it in his article "Dracula as Totemic Monster: Lacan, Freud, Oedipus and History," Freud is "projecting Oedipus onto an earlier age to explain the origin of myth and, more generally, of narrative" (Astle 99). Nevertheless, Huxley seems to endorse something rather like it in his description of Helmholtz Watson's artistic difficulties. While John has no difficulty expressing his emotions (even if only through Shakespearean tags) Helmholtz, although a would-be artist, seems to be searching for an objective correlative with which to express his sense of difference and his ambitions; he has "a feeling that I've got something important to say and the power to say it — only I don't know what it is.... If there was some different way of writing.... Or else something else to write about" (*Brave* 82). He is looking for something important to say, something "more intense" and "more violent" (*Brave* 83), but he cannot countenance John's suggestion that he look to family life for his subject matter. Helmholtz refuses to see family life as a possible source of what he lacks. Helmholtz will never be a real artist, nor will he ever be able to understand his friend John, as long as he cannot accept that there is some validity to the Oedipal narrative.

Another disagreement that has been noted between Huxley and Freud has to do with their attitudes to religion. Huxley plainly deplored Freud's implication that religion and other mystical experiences were a product of neuroses or sexual repression; yet, he seems to acknowledge the reality of what Freud referred to in *Civilization and Its Discontents* as "the oceanic feeling." If Huxley had not read this book, it must stand as an extraordinary coincidence that the religious ceremonies in *Brave New World* employ much of the same vocabulary used by Freud to describe a theory propounded by one of his correspondents (who turned out to be none other than the French writer Romain Rolland):

> I had sent him my small book that treats religion as an illusion, and he answered that he entirely agreed with my judgment upon religion, but that he was sorry I had not properly appreciated the true source of religious sentiments. This, he says, consists in a peculiar feeling, which he himself is never without, which he finds confirmed by many others, and which he may suppose is present in millions of people. It is a feeling as of something limitless, unbounded — as it were, oceanic. This feeling, he adds, is a purely subjective fact, not an article of faith; it brings with it no assurance of personal immortality, but it is the source of the religious energy which is seized upon by the various Churches and religious systems, directed by them into particular channels, and doubtless also exhausted by them. One may, he thinks, rightly call oneself religious on the ground of this oceanic feeling alone, even if one rejects every belief and every illusion [*Civilization and its Discontents* 11].

The quasi-spiritual rituals of "atonement" in *Brave New World* rely heavily on imagery very close to Freud's here; one song which features in these moments of group celebration is called a "Solidarity Hymn" and contains these lines: "Ford, we are twelve; oh, make us one, / Like drops within the Social River" (*Brave* 94–5).[11] Each participant drinks from a "loving cup" of soma after reciting a pledge of self-effacement — "I drink to my annihilation" (*Brave* 95)— in a ceremony that seems like a parody of Christian self-abnegation.

This kind of water imagery is very much a part of everyday life in Huxley's dystopia; yet, as if to register his awareness that this kind of mindless bobbing on the ocean's surface is not quite what Freud meant by the "oceanic feeling," he shows Bernard contemplating the ocean after participating in one of these liquefying moments. Bernard takes comfort in the ocean's inhuman wholeness, and feeling that his tenuous individuality has been strengthened somehow: "It makes me feel as though.... I were more, if you see what I mean. More on my own, not so completely a part of something else. Not just a cell in the social body" (*Brave* 106). While Bernard's testimony of what this oceanic feeling means to him does not quite fit Rolland's description of a vague spiritual awareness, it does correspond rather well to Freud's judgment on the sources of such a feeling. Freud writes: "We are perfectly willing to acknowledge that the oceanic feeling exists in many people, and we are inclined to trace it back to an early phase of ego feeling" (*Civilization and Its Discontents* 19).[12]

Yet another accusation made by Huxley against Freud is the not terribly original claim that the latter's emphasis on sexuality was "monomaniacal," as Huxley wrote in 1927 (*Proper Studies* xix). Yet Huxley himself reconsidered this verdict very publicly, in a newspaper article published on March 11, 1933. In this brief piece, Huxley editorializes about the relative nature of Freud's insights about human nature, claiming that "it is only in the more prosperous sections of civilized urban communities that hunger loses its preeminence. Freud, who gives the palm to sex, worked in Vienna ... Love, as a wholetime job, has only been practiced by the more prosperous members of civilized societies" (*Huxley's Hearst Essays* 161). Huxley admits that Dr. Audrey Richards is right to point out that sex does not assume the same importance in Bantu society as Freud claims it does in all human civilizations, but he goes on to say something that those who see Huxley as an unflinching anti–Freudian ought to find rather surprising: "That the psycho analysts should be wrong about savages is not particularly important. The significant fact is that they are probably right about civilized people" (*Huxley's Hearst Essays* 161). Huxley implies that Freud's pleasure principle is likely to triumph wherever social and technological efficiency prevail,[13] and he shows no signs of regarding this likelihood as anything to be lamented. In this respect, we may well wonder whether all the promiscuity he portrays in *Brave New World* is to be regarded as the inevitable manifestation of otherwise desirable advances in human civilization.

Huxley was more than capable of making up his own mind about the relative merits of psychoanalysis, but around the time he began to write *Brave New World* he was still very much under the influence of D. H. Lawrence, whose anti–Freudian, anti–humanistic views were impossible for Huxley to ignore entirely. Huxley first met Lawrence in December of 1915 but did not become a close friend of Lawrence's until 1926, when he and his wife Maria saw a good deal of the Lawrences in Italy. In 1920, Huxley had referred to Lawrence as a "slightly insane novelist" who had been "analysed for his complexes, dark and tufty ones, tangled in his mind" (*Letters of Aldous Huxley* 187). As a result, Huxley cattily writes, "The complexes were discovered, and it is said that Lawrence has now lost, along with his slight sexual mania, all his talent as a writer" (*Letters* 187). Huxley soon changed his mind about Lawrence, but his conviction that literary talent cannot survive psychoanalytic scrutiny or successful therapy remained. Lawrence was a very important figure for Huxley during the years just before *Brave New World* was written[14]; Huxley visited Lawrence in Italy during the latter's final illness, and as his letters testify, he was profoundly moved by Lawrence's courage and his uncompromising (albeit frequently irrational) views about sex, social life and the artistic vocation. Huxley was with Lawrence when he died on March 2, 1930, and witnessed his final struggles with great emotion, calling Lawrence "the most extraordinary and impressive human being I have ever known" (*Letters* 332). In memory of his friend, Huxley put together an edition of Lawrence's letters and even contemplated writing a biography of him, though the freshness of the memory and his own contractual obligations prevented him from writing a full-length work devoted to Lawrence.

Lawrence's deep attachment to his sensitive mother and his hostility to his crude father, a Nottinghamshire coal miner, might well have showed Huxley that at least one aspect of Freud's writing (i.e., the basic conception of the Oedipus complex) was very likely true, or at least very plausible. It must be said, however, that Lawrence himself differed vigorously with Freud about incestuous desire, claiming there was in fact a natural antipathy between parents and children where sex was concerned, and that "the incest motive is a logical deduction of the human reason, which has recourse to this last extremity, to save itself" (*Fantasia of the Unconscious, Psychoanalysis and the Unconscious* 206). Indeed, the differences between the two thinkers are profound and thoroughgoing: whereas Freud saw in the sexual urge a "victory of the race over the individual," Lawrence was to reject both Freud's conception of the growth of the individual as a recapitulation of the history of the human species (*On Sexuality: Three Essays on the Theory of Sexuality and Other Works* 341). Lawrence extends his conception of "the individual" to make it a microcosm of all "life" whether human or not (*Fantasia* 13). Lawrence even goes a step further, rejecting the very concept of humanity; in a famous letter sent by Lawrence to his agent, Edward Garnett, in 1914 (and quoted by Huxley), he declares: "That which is ... non-human in humanity, is more interesting to me than the old-fashioned human element.... I only care about what the woman is—what she is inhumanly, physiologically, materially" (quoted in Huxley, *The Olive Tree* 222).

Such anti-humanistic rhetoric found a faint but distinct echo in Huxley's writings, which admittedly take a more scientific view of what humanity consists of: "Man is a multiple amphibian who lives in about twenty different worlds at once" (quoted in Bedford 642). At any rate, Lawrence's concerns were central to Huxley's work between the time Huxley renewed his acquaintance with Lawrence in 1926 and Lawrence's death in 1930. During these years Huxley published *Point Counter Point, Proper Studies, Do What You Will,* and *Music at Night,* all of which contain references to Freud and/or psychoanalysis. Furthermore, while Huxley was writing *Brave New World* between May and August of 1931, he was still looking at Freud largely through Lawrentian lenses. Lawrence's own passionate engagement with Freudianism, and his dogged but rather confused attempts to refute Freud's theory of the universality of the Oedipus complex certainly made an impression on Huxley. In his essay on Lawrence, Huxley addresses the question of Freud's relevance to Lawrence only once, and rather defensively: "Explanations of him [Lawrence] in terms of a Freudian hypothesis of nurture may be interesting, but they do not explain. That Lawrence was profoundly affected by his love for his mother and by her excessive love for him, is obvious to anyone who has read *Sons and Lovers.* None the less it is, to me at any rate, almost equally obvious that even if his mother had died when he was a child, Lawrence would still have been, essentially and fundamentally, Lawrence" (*The Olive Tree* 206). Huxley is no doubt reacting against the crudely Freudian analysis of Lawrence's writing contained in John Middleton Murry's book *Son of Woman,* which in the same essay Huxley dismisses as "destructive" and "irrelevant" (*The Olive Tree* 205).

Huxley deemed Lawrence "a great man" (*Letters* 88) and although he found Lawrence "difficult to get on with, passionate, queer, violent" (*Letters* 288) he was generally very loyal to him, and especially so after Lawrence's death.[15] In September of 1931 Huxley was making notes for a short study of Lawrence to serve as introduction to the letters, a study which, as Huxley says, "cannot be specifically a retort to Murry" but will "try to undo some of the mischief that slug has undoubtedly done" (*Letters* 355). The main symptom of Murry's mischievous "cleverness" is his exploitation of "the psycho analytical rigamarole" where Lawrence was concerned (*Letters* 355). Addressing this aspect of Murry's book, which Huxley (showing an uncharacteristic taste for oxymorons) terms a "vindictive hagiography," he admits that Murry's views into Lawrence's psyche are often accurate; Murry's Freudian analysis of Lawrence as a man in love with his mother and in violent rebellion against his father is able and in parts very true (*Letters* 353). *Son of Woman* was published in April 1931, and as a friend of Lawrence's as well as a man of letters, Huxley might well have read it in time for it to affect his perspective. Whether this was in fact the case, we may draw a number of analogies between John the Savage and Lawrence himself, with whom Huxley was undoubtedly still preoccupied regardless of his reaction to Murry's book. As a visionary (at least in Huxley's mind) who remained true to his beliefs to the bitter end, Lawrence would have provided an excellent model for John the Savage, whose ultimately self-destructive moral absolutism is as unusual in the London he visits as Lawrence's was in his own bohemian circle (which included the notorious womanizer Bertrand Russell, his wife Dora, Lady Ottoline Morrell and Gerald Heard). While John's apparent prudery seems to be fundamentally opposed to Lawrence's worship of the phallic principle and emphasis on the regenerative aspects of sexual activity, these two figures both share an important common trait in Huxley's eyes: they cannot countenance sex as a meaningless form of recreation. Both are convinced that sex bears a tremendous significance and that the purely recreational, hedonistic promiscuity of people such as Lenina and Bernard is deeply obscene.

The Oedipal themes in Lawrence's own life resonate deeply with John's struggles in *Brave New World*; Huxley's decision to have John direct his parricidal aggression towards Popé, a Native American, may have been inspired by Lawrence, who (having spent many years living among the native people of America) muses in a later essay about the notion of having a "dusky lipped tribe father" who, like many an old father with a changeling son ... would like to deny me" (*Phoenix: The Posthumous Papers of D. H. Lawrence* I, 99).[16] Moreover, Linda's capricious, yet ardent affection for John is entirely in keeping with Lawrence's pronouncements about mothers' culpability in the development of incestuous desires in their sons. The over-affectionate mother, in Lawrence's eyes, "has not the courage to give up her hopeless insistence on love, and her endless demand for love" (*Fantasia of the Unconscious, Psychoanalysis and the Unconscious* 126) and therefore "she provokes what she wants. Here, in her own son who belongs to her, she seems to find the last perfect response for which she is craving. He is a medium to her, she provokes from him her own answer. So she throws herself into a last great love for her son" (*Fantasia* 122). Other familial situations found in Lawrence's work crop up in *Brave New World*; for instance, in Lawrence's *Sons and Lovers*, Paul Morel's aborted parricidal impulse seems to have been diverted and to have attached to Mrs. Morel. As her cancer worsens, Paul wishes she would die, and even goes so far as to administer a large dose of morphine to speed up the process. Huxley's John does not actually administer the gradual overdoses of soma that kill Linda, but, pressured by doctors, he agrees to allow her to take as much as she wants, which leads to her demise (and to his crippling feelings of guilt).

Before he wrote *Brave New World*, Huxley denied having portrayed Lawrence in his own fiction, claiming that Mark Rampion, the Lawrence-like character in *Point Counter Point* was "just some of Lawrence's notions on legs" (*Letters* 340). Huxley felt that Lawrence was "incomparably queerer and more complex" than the dogmatic Rampion, whom Lawrence himself referred to as a "gas-bag" (*Letters* 339). Despite Huxley's diffidence about his fictional renditions of Lawrence, we cannot avoid suspecting that his portrayal of John in *Brave New World* is heavily indebted to his friend. For one thing, Huxley repeatedly describes Lawrence's sense of humor as "savage": his "high spirits" are "almost terrifyingly savage" and his "mockery" is "frighteningly savage" (*The Olive Tree* 238–9). In both cases, Huxley remarks upon Lawrence's satirical intelligence (one of Lawrence's less-well-known traits) and testifies to its power; it is therefore not surprising that he chooses a Lawrence-like hero like John to be the explicitly savage vehicle of his own most biting satire. Although John does not display a terribly sophisticated sense of humor himself, his naïveté, intense earnestness and plainspokenness make for a number of mordant scenes in *Brave New World*. For instance, when John falls to his knees in front of the D.H.C. and hails the horrified bureaucrat as "father," a word which is so "comically smutty" to the onlookers that they break into "hysterical" laughter (*Brave* 181), Huxley is making a sardonic point about how completely traditional family-based values have been turned on their head in his utopia.

Furthermore, like John opposing Mond, Lawrence stands in Huxley's mind for the integrity of the artistic impulse, and for the belief that it must be permitted to express itself even if the result is disastrous; as Huxley claims, "Lawrence was always and unescapably [sic] an artist" (*The Olive Tree* 203).[17] In describing the difficulties of being an artist, Huxley quotes Lawrence's complaint that "at times one is forced to be essentially a hermit. I don't want to be. But everything else is either a personal tussle, or a money tussle; sickening… One has no real human relations — that is so devastating" (quoted in *The Olive Tree* 226). Huxley echoes this lament after quoting it: "One has no real human relations: it is the complaint of every artist. The artist's first duty is to his genius, his daimon; he cannot serve two masters" (*The Olive Tree* 226). Huxley's remarks here imply that he finds there to be a split between the artist's task and his or her relationships, and that the true genius must finally lose faith in the social setting that others depend on. We recall that, after making the rounds in London (visiting the self-declared intellectuals, much as Lawrence once did, to his own great disgust), the Savage tries to live as a hermit in the woods, and Helmholtz Watson decides that exile will serve his own artistic ambitions better than continuing to live in London.

Huxley realized that Lawrence had his shortcomings; as he says, "I never understood his anti intellectualism.... His dislike of science was passionate and expressed itself in the most fantastically unreasonable terms" (quoted in Bedford 192). In this respect, once again, Lawrence is very like John, who dismisses the scientific and technological advances of civilized London with quotations from Shakespeare or some other irrelevancy. Moreover, despite his sympathy for Lawrence, Huxley felt that his friend's illnesses, both physical and psychological, were "unnecessary, the result simply of the man's strange obstinacy against professional medicine" (quoted in Bedford 215). As we see, Huxley was deeply ambivalent about Lawrence's attitudes to Freud; while he felt a great loyalty toward and admiration for Lawrence, he could not suppress his feeling that Murry was in fact right about the complex that afflicted Lawrence, and that the latter could have been happier and healthier, though not necessarily a better writer, if he had accepted Freud's insights to a greater extent. This feeling is perhaps reflected in *Brave New World*; indeed, it could well be argued that John desperately needs Freud to explain his own urges and hostilities before they destroy him. However, while Lawrence knew of Freud, and disagreed strenuously (and perhaps mistakenly, in Huxley's eyes) with Freud's assessment of the incestuous subtext of human sexuality, the real problem in Huxley's *Brave New World* as far as John is concerned is perhaps not that Freudianism has taken over the social structure, but that no one is able to properly explain, remember or apply Freud's theories any longer, since the family structure they assumed has been abolished in "civilized" circles.

Clearly, Huxley's distrust of Freud was by no means the typical antagonism felt by an artist toward a scientist who is treading on his or her toes; Huxley's own ancestry (his grandfather was T. H. Huxley, the father of so-called "Social Darwinism") made him rather more receptive to scientific principles than most novelists would be. Indeed, Huxley was often dismayed at what he took to be Freud's lack of real scientific rigor; as he once exclaimed, "How incredibly unscientific the old man [Freud] could be!" (*Letters* 837). Furthermore, although *Brave New World* seems to imply that the conflicts within human nature are worth preserving, since they make us interesting, heroic and tragic, Huxley himself was committed to treating mental and emotional illness by any means necessary. He was a firm supporter of the use of drugs in psychotherapy, and despite the fact that he derided Freud's insistence on the value of his famous talking cure,[18] he shared Freud's urge to help individual people survive their psychological disturbances. What *Brave New World* shows us, however, is that Huxley was willing to mock his own (and Freud's) drive to define and delimit something like the universal human condition in order to eliminate suffering from human existence. *Brave New World* may still be read as a parable about the difficulty of understanding or preserving anything we can recognize as "human" even if and when Freud's theory of the Oedipus complex is taken seriously and acted upon by an authoritarian political system. Nevertheless, given Huxley's own documented assent to many of Freud's views on the subject of infantile desire and repression, it is difficult to disagree with Robert Baker's claim that "the Freudian family romance, despite Huxley's repeatedly expressed misgivings concerning Freud's emphasis on erotic behavior, is one of the principal satirical conventions of his social satire. *Brave New World* is no exception to this practice" (Baker 141–2). In other words, Huxley seems to have been using the Oedipus complex in *Brave New World* not as a target for mockery but as a weapon in his satirical (and Lawrentian) attack on the mores of modern life and on its hubristic, humanistic and utopian fantasies.

Notes

1. Foremost among these scholars is Jerome Meckier, who argues that Huxley's novel is a rejection of Freud's theories. Meckier's article, while intriguing, is unsatisfactory, mainly because it dogmatically asserts that Huxley satirizes Freudianism for being part of what Meckier calls a behaviorist conspiracy that dominates Western thought, which Meckier deems mechanistic and materialistic (41). Of course, as Peter Firchow points out, "Huxley knew very well [that] mechanistic psychologists ... were adamantly opposed to Freud; for them, consciousness was the last refuge of the soul" (47). Furthermore, as we shall see, Huxley was often more of a materialist than Freud ever was, recommending drugs and behavioral modification therapy rather than Freud's talking cure in cases of mental illness.

2. According to an oft-repeated anecdote, Huxley mocked these Freud worshippers at a psychoanalysts' convention by crossing himself whenever their hero's name was mentioned.

3. There is an irony in this Freudian supposition, since Oedipus himself has been seen as hubristically claiming the same power: his solution to the riddle of the Sphinx is itself a would-be universal statement about human development, as thinkers such as G. F. Hegel, Friedrich Nietzsche and Jean-Joseph Goux have argued. Needless to say, Oedipus's apparent insight into the human condition doesn't save him from violating basic human taboos, which suggests that any attempt to define or understand the human is doomed to disaster. Richard Kuhns makes the case for a kinship between Freud and Oedipus in his book *Tragedy*: "When Freud was fifty years old he was honored by his colleagues with the presentation of a medallion on which was engraved Oedipus confronting the Sphinx; on the reverse was Freud himself" (Kuhns 59). The inscription on this medal was a quotation from Sophocles' *Oedipus the King*: "He who answered (as if through divination) the famous riddle and was indeed a most mighty man." Kuhns remarks that it is "tiresome" to "link Freud with Oedipus," yet as he points out, the link has a "private significance" for Freud, who according to Kuhns, was deeply "moved — even shaken" by the inscription on the medal, which "states that which Freud thought about himself: that he was the solver of a riddle, the deepest that was ever put to humankind, by humankind, and that his solution was the inevitable outcome of genius that had foreseen its destiny, since Freud had marked that very sentence from the tragic drama ... when he was a gymnasium student. That in itself is perhaps an Oedipean fate" (59).

4. John has memories of "white Linda and Popé almost black beside her, with one arm

under her shoulders and the other hand dark on her breast, and one of the plaits of his long hair lying across her throat, like a black snake trying to strangle her" (*Brave* 157).

5. The link between Lenina and Linda remains strong in John's mind, even after Linda dies from an overdose of soma: "He tried to think of Linda, breathless and dumb, with her clutching hands ... Poor Linda whom he had sworn to remember. But it was still the presence of Lenina that haunted him. Lenina whom he had promised to forget" (302). John seems to have successfully transferred his love from his mother to Lenina, but instead of congratulating himself on his more adult object choice (as Freud would likely have told him to do) he feels guilty for forgetting Linda, especially since he still blames himself for her death. It is difficult to avoid the suspicion that reading a bit of Freud might have helped John accept his adult sexuality.

6. Oedipus exiled himself after discovering he was guilty of incest and parricide. While Helmholtz's genius with words and metaphors seems to recall Oedipus's facility in solving the riddle of the Sphinx which depends upon a metaphorical interpretation of the word "legs," Bernard's bodily defects— he is abnormally short — bear a resemblance to Oedipus's deformed feet. Both Bernard and Oedipus are forced to make their minds their most powerful asset; as Huxley's narrator remarks of Bernard, "a physical shortcoming could produce a kind of mental excess" (81).

7. Bernard claims to want to delay his own gratification, telling Lenina that he wishes that their date had not ended with going to bed (109), but (unlike Helmholtz) he lacks the willpower to impose real obstacles on himself.

8. Freud makes it quite clear that in his view all pleasure is only the release of tension, or the overcoming of obstacles and impediments; without the unpleasant uncertainty of anticipation or fear, there is no real enjoyment: "What we call happiness in the strictest sense comes from the (preferably sudden) satisfactions of needs which have been dammed up to a high degree.... When any situation that is desired by the pleasure principle is prolonged, it only produces a feeling of mild contentment" (*Civilization and its Discontents* 23). There is no essential contradiction between Freud's view and that expressed by Huxley: "Love is the product of two opposed forces— of an instinctive impulsion and a social resistance acting on the individual by means of ethical imperatives justified by philosophical or religious myths. When, with the destruction of the myths, resistance is removed, the impulse wastes itself on emptiness" (*Do What You Will* 137).

9. Thody is eager to make Freud the main villain of the novel, as his analysis makes plain: "In *Brave New World* it is the declared aim of the authorities to translate into the sexual behaviour of adults the total irresponsibility and immaturity which supposedly characterize a child's attitude to its own body.... The Freudian idea that we should avoid repressions and frustrations, that the way to happiness lies in the satisfaction of those primitive, instinctual, sexual drives which previous societies have been compelled to inhibit, is thus criticized first and foremost for the effect that it has on people's emotional life" (Thody 54–5).

10. Freud goes on to mitigate this slight against artists: "But he [the artist] finds a way of return from this world of fantasy back to reality; with his special gifts he molds his fantasies into a new kind of reality, and men concede them a justification as valuable reflections of actual life. Thus by a certain path he actually becomes the hero, king, creator, favorite he desired to be, without pursuing the circuitous path of creating real alterations in the outer world" (*A General Selection* 44).

11. "Twelve" here refers to an idea of Gerald Heard's who was Huxley's closest friend after Lawrence and for a lifetime. Heard was a philosopher who believed humanity needed to be made over, one mind at a time, as an educative process that would work most effectively in groups no larger than twelve.

12. Characteristically, Freud denies that this feeling is truly the source of religious emotions, which he attributes directly to one's relationship (or lack thereof) with a paternal figure: "I cannot think of any need in childhood as strong as the need for a father's protection. Thus the part played by the oceanic feeling, which might seek something like the restoration of limitless narcissism, is ousted from a place in the foreground" (*Civilization and its Discontents* 19).

13. Huxley concludes his essay with the following remarks: "Men and women under high biological pressure arrange the pattern of their life in one way; under low pressure, in another way. With every increase in the efficiency of social organizations, more individuals will come to live under low biological pressure" (*Huxley's Hearst Essays* 161).

14. As Huxley's biographer Sybille Bedford argues, Huxley was very much under Lawrence's influence when he was writing *Do What You Will*, a collection of essays published in October of 1929: "Much of *Do What You Will* was a continuation of ideas turned up in *Point Counter Point* [that] Mark Rampion is talking on. The impression of the Lawrentian ship was still upon the water" (Bedford 219).

15. After Lawrence died, Huxley visited Nottingham to see some of Lawrence's relatives, then in January of 1931 he went to the coal fields in Durham, trying to understand more about Lawrence's background as the son of a miner, and researching the problem of unemployment. By May 18, 1931, he had begun writing *Brave New World*, which he at first described in a letter as a "revolt" against "the Wellsian Utopia" (*Letters* 348).

16. Lawrence continues: "I know my derivation. I was born of no virgin, of no Holy Ghost ... I have a dark faced, bronze voiced father far back in the resinous ages. My mother was no virgin"(*Phoenix* I 99).

17. Huxley is clearly directing this remark at Murry, who deemed Lawrence a kind of prophetic, almost messianic figure, but refused to call him an artist because of the intensely personal and occasionally didactic nature of Lawrence's work.

18. Huxley enunciates his dissent from Freud on this point in no uncertain terms: "Freud — although he did himself say that finally all nervous disorders would turn out to be organic — he did say that in the meanwhile ... we could treat them successfully by purely psychological means — I think this is absolutely untrue" (quoted in Bedford 641). Thus in *Brave New World* Freud's verbal therapeutic technique has been replaced entirely with drugs and Pavlovian systems of punishment and reward. Interestingly, in 1949 Huxley wrote a letter to George Orwell, congratulating him on the publication of *1984*, but explaining why he felt that his own vision of dystopia was more likely to prevail than Orwell's. He wrote: "Freud's inability to hypnotize successfully ... delayed the general application of hypnosis to psychiatry for at least forty years. But now psychoanalysis is being combined with hypnosis.... Within the next generation I believe that the world's rulers will discover that infant conditioning and narco hypnosis are more efficient, as instruments of government, than clubs and prisons" (*Letters* 605).

Works Cited

Astle, Richard "Dracula as Totemic Monster: Lacan, Freud, Oedipus and History." *Substance: A Review of Theory and Criticism* XXV (1980): 98–105.

Baker, Robert S. *The Dark Historic Page: Social Satire and Historicism in the Novels of Aldous Huxley 1921–1939*. Madison, WI: University of Wisconsin Press, 1982.

Bedford, Sybille. *Aldous Huxley: A Biography*. London: Chatto and Windus, 1973.

Firchow, Peter. *The End of Utopia: A Study of Huxley's Brave New World*. Lewisburg, PA: Bucknell University Press, 1984.

Freud, Sigmund. *The Basic Writings of Sigmund Freud*. Translated by James Strachey. New York, NY: Random House, 1938.

_____. *Civilization and Its Discontents*. Translated by James Strachey. New York, NY: W. W. Norton, 1989.

_____. *A General Selection from the Works of Sigmund Freud*. Edited by John Rickman. Garden City, NY: Doubleday. 1957.

_____. *A General Introduction to Psychoanalysis*. Translated by Joan Riviere. New York, NY: Washington Square Press, 1962.

_____. *On Sexuality: Three Essays on the Theory of Sexuality and Other Works*. New York, NY: Basic Books, 1975.

_____. *Sexuality and the Psychology of Love*. Translated by Philip Rieff. New York, NY: Macmillan, 1993.

Girard, René. *Violence and the Sacred*. Baltimore, MD: Johns Hopkins University Press, 1979.

Goux. Jean-Joseph. *Oedipus, Philosopher*. Stanford, CA: Stanford University Press, 1993.

Hillegas, Mark. *The Future as Nightmare: H. G. Wells*. New York, NY: Oxford University Press, 1967.

Holmes, Charles. *Aldous Huxley and the Way to Reality* Bloomington, IN: Indiana University Press, 1970.

Huxley, Aldous. *Brave New World*. New York, NY: Harper & Brothers, 1946.

_____. *Do What You Will*. London: Chatto & Windus, 1956,

_____. *Huxley's Hearst Essays*. Edited by James Sexton. New York: Garland, 1994.

_____. *Letters of Aldous Huxley*. Edited by Grover Smith. London: Chatto & Windus, 1969.

_____. *Music at Night*. London: Chatto & Windus, 1970.

_____. *The Olive Tree*. New York, NY: Harper & Brothers, 1937.

_____. *Proper Studies*. London: Chatto & Windus, 1933.

Kuhns, Richard. *Tragedy: Contradiction and Repression*. Chicago, IL: University of Chicago, 1991.

Lawrence, D. H. *Fantasia of the Unconscious, Psychoanalysis and the Unconscious*. Markham, Ontario: Penguin, 1975.

_____. *Phoenix: The Posthumous Papers of D. H. Lawrence*. Vols. I and II, New York: Viking, 1964.

_____. *Studies in Classic American Literature*. New York, NY: Thomas Seltzer, 1923.

Meckier, Jerome. "Our Ford, Our Freud and the Behaviorist Conspiracy in Huxley's *Brave New World*." *Thalia: Studies in Literary Humor* 1, no. 1 (1978): 35–59.

Shapiro, Gary. *Nietzschean Narratives*. Bloomington, IN: Indiana University Press, 1989.

Sophocles. *Oedipus Tyrannus* in *The Theban Plays*. Translated by Robert Fagles. New York, NY: Viking, 1982.

Thody, Philip. *Huxley: A Biographical Introduction*. New York, NY: Charles Scribner's Sons, 1973.

Some Kind of Brave New World: Humans, Society and Nature in the Dystopian Interpretations of Huxley and Orwell

Angelo Arciero

(translated into English by Gianna Fusco)

In a letter dated 21 October 1949, thanking Orwell for sending him *1984*, Aldous Huxley did not fail to express some perplexities about the novel. The praise for a work that he judged fine and profoundly important, in fact, is balanced by his doubts with regard to the ways in which the Inner Party had gained its power, Huxley being convinced that the recent developments of psychoanalysis, together with the techniques of hypnotism, would have offered the "world rulers" more reliable and effective instruments of governance than those described by Orwell. These considerations led Huxley to affirm: "I feel that the nightmare of *1984* is destined to modulate into the nightmare of a world having more resemblance to that which I imagined in *Brave New World*" (1969: 605). A few years later, in *Brave New World Revisited*, after having defined *1984* as "a magnified projection into the future of a present that contained Stalinism and an immediate past that had witnessed the flowering of Nazism" (online), he claimed again the closer adherence of his dystopia to the social and political developments of the second postwar period.

On the other hand, although he assigned such a prominent role to *Brave New World* during the planning process of *1984* as to include it in the chain of utopia books together with London's *The Iron Heel*, H. G. Wells's *When the Sleeper Wakes*, and Zamyatin's *We*, Orwell had previously and repeatedly distanced himself from a vision of the future that, according to him, lacked any satisfactory explanation of power relations. Moreover, evincing his preference for London and Zamyatin, he had gone so far as to put forward the suspicion that Huxley had consciously drawn his inspiration from *We*.[1] Actually, beyond any mutual ideological incomprehension between the two authors, their

46

dystopias, although deriving from a common root,[2] offer a political scenario undeniably informed by opposite hypotheses.

At the beginning of his career and up to the 1930s, Orwell had manifested his admiration for Huxley, and in his first novel, *Burmese Days*, we can discern many affinities with *Brave New World* that, although probably unintentional,[3] confirm a commonality of interests and concerns. John Flory's emotional isolation, his estrangement from the colonial world to which he however fully belongs, and his attraction for the inaccessible Burmese culture are reminiscent of both Bernard Marx's controversial relations to the system he belongs to and the sense of alienation experienced by John the Savage in his contact with the civilization of the "new world," while the latter's tormented relationship with Lenina Crowne recalls the bond between Elizabeth Lackersteen and the protagonist in *Burmese Days*. John Flory's characterization, in particular the social complex caused by his birthmark, evoke moreover the accident undergone by Bernard during the phase of prenatal treatment, with the consequent alteration of his psychophysical condition and the other Alphas' prejudices against him; both, finally, before their definitive expulsion from their native environment, experience a short-lived popularity that further emphasizes their subsequent marginalization.

Equally significant are the analogies in the approach by the members of the advanced societies to the surrounding primitive world and consequently the interpretative and literary directions in which this encounter is developed. Just as the description of the Burmese landscape —characterized by the combination of the recurring presence of death and the melancholic gratification excited by the flowing of seasons— expresses a "tragic" conception of time as contrasted to the farcical repetition of the rituals of the colonizers' circle, so the natural dimension of life in *Brave New World* is completely antithetical to the aseptic existence ruled by scientific criteria that subvert the normal course of human activities. The dynamics of Bernard and Lenina's visit to the pueblo of Malpais, moreover, are similar to those informing the episode in which John and Elizabeth watch the performance of a Burmese dancer in a club in Kyauktada. The two men's passionate response to the body's symbolic movements— a synthesis evocative of the complex of collective traditions stratified through time — is balanced by the two women's impatient reaction that foregrounds, although with different meanings, an irremediable opposition between culture and civilization. In *Brave New World*, nature is actually devoid of that regenerative function that constitutes one of the predominant features of Orwell's production and, while in *Burmese Days* even Elizabeth, attracted by death, gets to give herself up to the rhythm of the Burmese jungle, in Huxley's novel Lenina is able to escape the disturbing effect of the panorama of the Indian reservation only when, by depriving it of any alterity, she reduces its forms to those of standard modern cities: "The top of the Mesa was a flat deck of stone. 'Like the Charing-T Tower,' was Lenina's comment. But she was not allowed to enjoy her discovery of this reassuring resemblance for long" (93). Finally, ending with the protagonist's suicide, a solution Orwell would however irrevocably deny to Winston Smith, both novels depict convergent alternatives to the tensions between the individual, society, and nature, as further demonstrated by the gin's sedative action in *Burmese Days* paralleling, although approximately, the "anesthetic" function of soma in *Brave New World*.

What in *Burmese Days* could be considered simply as an assonance becomes an explicit reference to Huxley's novel in *Keep the Aspidistra Flying* (1936). The setting of Gordon Comstock's vicissitudes (the London of the 1930s) represents in fact a degraded version of the consumeristic society of the "new world," a place dominated by rough, yet pervasive advertising, and by offensive class divisions, lacking the social usefulness and yielding approval that are necessary to the stability of the world of A.F. 632. And the only, unacceptable alternatives the protagonist of Orwell's novel is able to oppose to the corruption and the degradation emanating from the city of London are suicide, the conversion to Catholicism, and a version of socialism as stereotyped as to be immediately assimilated to Huxley's fictive construction: [Ravelston:] 'But what *would* Socialism mean, according to your idea of it?' [Gordon:] 'Oh. Some kind of Aldous Huxley *Brave New World*; only not so amusing. Four hours a day in a model factory, tightening up bolt number 6003. Rations served out in grease-proof paper at the communal kitchen. Community-hikes from Marx Hostel to Lenin Hostel and back. Free abortion-clinics on all the corners. All very well in its way. Only we don't want it' (IV: 97).

The polemic juxtaposition of the version of socialism opposed by Gordon Comstock and Huxley's dystopian model is actually one of the numerous narrative devices to which Orwell resorted in *Keep the Aspidistra Flying* in order to represent his progressive ideological evolution that, in the complex play of identification with and distancing from his character, resulted in a political conception in which the economic instances of Marxism were reconnected to the instinctual values of the working class and deprived at the same time of those abstract theoretical elements feeding the "easy" optimism of communist intellectuals in the 1930s. In this sense, the reference to *Brave New World* does not represent a distancing from socialist ideas, nor does it imply a questioning of Huxley's satirical intentions, but rather imposes itself as a privileged path for a critical revision of utopian ideals. Just one year later, in fact, in *The Road to Wigan Pier*, Orwell expressed his most thorough and, under certain aspects, conclusive appreciation for the contents of *Brave New World* that he defined as "the paradise of little fat men" (V: 180). Although he recognized the limits of Huxley's futuristic hypotheses— openly drawing for this on Strachey's analyses in *The Coming Struggle for Power*[4]— Orwell opposed them in fact to Wells and praised them for questioning the idea of progress, "the tendency of the machine to make a fully human life impossible" (V: 188–189).

During the second half of the 1930s, following the participation in the

Spanish Civil war, Orwell's attention to contingent historical events temporarily overwhelmed theoretical reflections, resulting in a close parallel between fascism and capitalism and in a temporary pacifist stance that, although devoid of any deep ideological consent, led him nonetheless to support Huxley in his polemic with Romney Green in May 1938 (XI: 152–154). Yet, at the beginning of the Second World War, the revaluation of democratic ideals, the rediscovery of his own patriotic feelings, the final espousal of a democratic socialism animated by strong revolutionary instances, and the growing attention to the danger of totalitarianism — an attention stimulated by the reading of such authors as Russell, Lyon, Salvemini and Borkenau — determined a resolute change in his perspective. Even the previous interpretation of the utopian category, anchored in *The Road to Wigan Pier* to the classic model of a bright world shining with steel and concrete, gave way to a representation of the future marked by a depressing, gloomy atmosphere, based on a regression of society to an almost primitive condition, and characterized by power relations inspired by the cult of strength and violence. During this phase, which extended itself uninterruptedly until the publication of *1984*, Huxley still constituted, although in a polemical spirit, one of the main references of Orwell's interpretations, although his attention was turned almost exclusively to *Brave New World*.[5]

A supporter of a conception of the novel based on the prominence of ideas, Huxley had himself impressed meanwhile a turn to his production that had been characterized up to then by social reflections already interwoven with themes that would inform his later activity (aversion to death, a tendency to mysticism, the interest in religion) and in which it is possible to trace the two main elements of his 1932 utopia, namely the criticism of both the Bolshevik revolution and the U.S. mass culture. Therefore, beginning with *Eyeless in Gaza* (1936), a work animated by the pacifist instances recurring in the majority of his essays (*What Are You Going to Do about It?*, *Ends and Means*, *An Encyclopaedia of Pacifism*), and up to *Ape and Essence* (1949),[6] Huxley undertook an ideological evolution in which the denunciation of the political irrationality of his era joined the quest for an almost metaphysical ideal aiming at the "recovery of the person as totalizing principle" (Runcini 659).[7] Clearly, these positions were utterly incompatible with Orwell's conceptions, since the latter, in his search for a balance between the individual and the social dimension, had identified the sphere of action as the real meaning of human life, thus preserving the integrity of his hope for a revolutionary progress that could virtually affect both the individual conscience and political structures[8] and thus realize a better, although not perfect, society. Indeed, the open criticism of pacifist positions, the disapproval of the cosmic pessimism of the authors of the 1920s, the condemnation of the exponents of a reactionary ideology first propounded by T. E. Hulme, often involved Huxley's name,[9] to whom Orwell ascribed, in August 1948, a deep-rooted distrust of life: "Mr. Huxley's mystical pacifism is

simply a kind of death wish based on a sense of futility ... and the teaching of
D. H. Lawrence had no permanent effect upon him" (XIX: 416–417).

These diverging opinions determined and broadened the ideological break
between Huxley and Orwell. The latter, in a review dated 1940, extending to
other utopian works (London's *The Iron Heel* and Ernest Bramah's *The Secret
of the League*) the confrontation previously drawn in *The Road to Wigan Pier*,
defined *Brave New World* as "a post-war parody of the Wellsian Utopia"[10] and,
besides recognizing in Huxley's work an amplification of the flaws of *The Sleeper
Wakes*, reduced its value to the mere parodic perception of the dangers of its
time, denying to it any capacity to relate to the future. Resuming an opinion
already expressed in "Notes on the Way," in fact, Orwell identified the hedonistic nature of the political system described by Huxley as the main cause for
the inefficacy of *Brave New World*, further confirming these assumptions in
"Wells, Hitler and the World State" (1941) and, above all, in "Freedom and
Happiness" (1946), where, after having emphasized the analogies between Huxley's dystopia and Zamyatin's *We*, he identified in the Russian novel a more
marked presence of "a political point" and, appreciating particularly its "intu-
itive grasp of the irrational side of totalitarianism — human sacrifice, cruelty
as an end in itself, the worship of a Leader who is credited with divine attributes," he manifested again his reservations about *Brave New World*: "In Huxley's book the problem of 'human nature' is in a sense solved, because it assumes
that by pre-natal treatment, drugs and hypnotic suggestion the human can be
specialized in any way that is desired.... At the same time no clear reason is
given why society should be stratified in the elaborate way that is described.
The aim is not economic exploitation, but the desire to bully and dominate does
not seem a motive either. There is no power hunger, no sadism, no hardness
of any kind. Those at the top have no strong motive for staying at the top, and
though everyone is happy in a vacuous way, life has become so pointless that
it is difficult to believe that such a society could endure (XVIII: 14).

Actually, in a letter to S. Moos dated 16 November 1943, Orwell declared
that the danger of a "completely materialistic vulgar civilization based on hedonism" was made an anachronistic hypothesis by the slave connotation of modern dictatorial regimes: "Such a state would not be hedonistic, on the contrary
its dynamic would come from some kind of rabid nationalism and leader-worship kept going by literally continuous war, and its average standard of living
would probably be low" (XV: 308). It was exactly under the pressure of this
anti-hedonistic tendency that the eclectic configuration of totalitarianism, a
doctrine based on ideological instability, tended to resolve into a univocal direction, favoring the return to primordial practices and to the sort of irrational
activism propounded by Hitler in the raving proclamations of *Mein Kampf*, but
characterizing also the political praxis of the Soviet Union, defined by Orwell
as a "militarized version of Socialism" (XII: 118).[11]

These interpretative coordinates were destined to converge directly in *1984*, a novel that imposes itself throughout, in the wide range of its conceptual references, as a reversal of the dystopian canons propounded by Huxley. The efficiency of the gloomy but well-organized buildings exhibited in *Brave New World* is immediately replaced by the gaunt sight of the Victory Mansion houses, while the caricatural sound of the "Big Henry" ("Ford, Ford, Ford") is turned into the thirteen alienating strokes of the clocks of 1984, where the only space for the survival of the utopian imagery is relegated to the architectural structure of the four ministries, perversely echoing Wells's and Huxley's prefigurations and thus consecrating its ultimate degradation.[12] Even Orwell's most tangible reference to *Brave New World*, that is the allusion to Shakespeare as an element connecting the present to the past, has a perturbing oppositional function. The pervasive (beginning with the title) presence of Shakespearian quotations in Huxley's novel is dissolved in *1984* in Winston's isolated fragment of a dream, only to become later the center of a complex, presumptive web of evidence emphasizing the meaning of his unconscious complicity with the power and amplifying the effect of simulation produced by a political system whose main feature is the complete expulsion of the sense of tragedy from human life.[13] These and other devices of analogy and divergence between Huxley's and Orwell's dystopias, a contraposition many scholars have dwelled upon,[14] coalesce into a wider effect of reversal in which the innocuous attainment of an imperturbable happiness is substituted with the cruelty of a political universe dominated by the Ingsoc's paroxystic logic of a combination of opposites, as exemplified in the radical difference between the psychedelic ritual of the Orgy-porgy — a grotesque deformation of the Eucharistic liturgy ("the approaching atonement and final consummation of solidarity, the coming of Twelve-in One, the incarnation of the Greater Being") (75) — and the schizophrenic ceremony of the Two Minute Hate.

In this perspective, if the real utopia, as stated by Wells in 1905, had to be "kinetic" and structured "not as a permanent state but as a hopeful stage, leading to a long ascent of stages" (5), then *1984*, as compared to *Brave New World*, asserts itself as the perfect fulfillment of the dystopian principles. The ideal of unchangeability proclaimed by the motto "Community, Identity, Stability" and the invalidation of the normal articulation of time to which Lenina gives voice in Huxley's novel ("'was and will make me ill,' she quoted, 'I take a gramme and only am'") (89), are subjected by Orwell to a process of systematic revision that by relativizing their most intimate contents, intensify the dynamic connotation of his last work, in a perfect coincidence with the dialectic structures of the Ingsoc. The absolute interchangeability of the binary oppositions of the party's slogans and, more significantly, the dogma ("Who controls the past controls the future: who controls the present controls the past"), exhibit a shameless destructuring of objective reality achieved through the continuing rewriting of history[15] and through an alteration of the sensorial perception that finally ends up influencing the individual's social function itself and his relation of dependence from power, a relation no longer informed by the principles "Thou shalt not" and "Thou shalt," imposed by past dictatorships and by previous totalitarian regimes respectively, but by the much more conditioning demand "Thou art" (IX: 267).[16] The formal coincidence with which in both novels the individual is isolated in a perpetual present is counterpoised in *1984* by the unscrupulous ideological annihilation of human faculties, an annihilation that is not attenuated even by the comparable consciousness with which Winston Smith and Helmholtz Watson acknowledge the present impossibility for writing to impose itself as an element of connection between present, past, and future. Even the way the inhabitants of the "new world" automatically resort to formulas derived from advertising and acquired during their formative treatment is different from the stereotyped aphorisms of the citizens of Oceania. The latter in fact, although they are deprived of any intellectual autonomy, must continually conform to the variability of the party's dogmas and to the sophisticated procedures of approach to external reality imposed by the doublethink and based on a simultaneous contamination between consciousness and unconsciousness.

There is actually a diametrically opposed process of "immunization"[17] going on in the two novels, a process aimed in *Brave New World*, a globally pacified world, at preemptively eliminating any external danger (history, nature, international conflicts) and at definitively neutralizing the risks of internal disintegration, while in *1984*, the setting of an instrumental and fictive interplanetary conflict, the power's defensive strategy hinges on mechanisms of inclusion and exclusion: on the one hand, the "controlled" creation of an artificial opposition that penetrates into the web of power itself in order to incessantly refine its efficacy and, on the other hand, the incorporation of any potential alternative into the evolutionary compactness of the Ingsoc. Thus, while in the civilization of the "new world" God "manifests himself as an absence; as though he weren't there at all" (188), and religion, supplanted by the benevolent secular theocracy of the world's controllers (see Firchow 126), is subjected to a harmless removal exemplified by the iconographic decapitation of the cross (the "T" of the Ford model); in Oceania the party assumes the function of a Berkeleian god (see Besançon 181), assimilated in the same logic of power that reproduces its attributes of omnipotence and eternity. In *Brave New World* Huxley limits himself to a proposal of an idea of community which represents the negation of his own individualistic beliefs,[18] and makes it into a mechanicalist agglomerate order comprising the different social classes within its productive apparatus, while in *1984* Orwell radically changes his own organicistic beliefs, presenting the people of Oceania as rigidly divided into castes and the organization of the party as a real living body, the expression of a paradoxical collective solipsism. The consequence is a syncopated regulation of the functioning of the community, both on the national and on the international plan (the sexual repression, the atmosphere of mutual suspicion, the deterioration of interpersonal relationships, the manipulation of individual deviances, the isolation from the rest of the world, the alternation of military alliances), and a cautious replacement of the dominant elite through a co-optative form of recruitment independent from family connections or class position.

The relation between the sphere of human action and that of nature is also characterized by antithetical ideological lines in the two novels. Although it is not completely dominated, the nature of the "new world" — where the residual primitive space of the reservations (inexplicably survived to the advent of post–Fordist civilization) is relegated behind electric barriers that allow the entry of visitors, but not the going out of natives[19] — is however deprived of its conditioning force and subjected to human will: "What man has joined, nature is powerless to put asunder" (129). Coming out of the realm of mere slavish imitation of nature into the much more interesting world of human invention" (1922), the civilization of A.F. 632 has realized in fact a sort of mimetic continuity between its technological constructions and the surrounding habitat.[20]

Although the reproductive functions are altered by genetic standardization practices, the individuals generated through the Bokanovsky process are able to adapt themselves to any sort of environmental condition; a person's death becomes useful to the growing of plants; the movie pictures reproduce the tactile and olfactory feelings of real objects; the recreational activities are turned into consumeristic instruments; and the "soma," "Christianity without tears" (190) improves the effects of natural hallucinogens removing their side effects. Even the dance of the pueblo of Malpais— before its achieving differentiation through the spontaneous co-penetration between bodily gestures and religious syncretism — reminds Lenina of the choreography of the Orgy-porgy, while the atmospheric phenomena are completely substituted by scientific devices: "It was a night almost without clouds, moonless and starry; but of this on the whole depressing fact Lenina and Henry were fortunately unaware. The electric sky-sign effectively shut off the outer darkness" (68). In *1984*, instead, Oceania's climatic condition itself tends to conform to the political atmosphere of the regime, symbolically assuming its condition of sterility, while the blooming London countryside, the only place — apart from the dreamlike Golden Country — endowed with a natural vitality and incorporated into human habits, finally turns out to be complementary to the machinations of the party that, using hidden microphones, records Julia and Winston's early meetings in order to use them during the protagonist's reeducation process. And it is exactly during this phase that, through O'Brien's words, the whole physical structure of the universe yields to the schizophrenic logic of doublethink, thus becoming an instrument of totalitarian control, without completely losing however its alterity that allows the party to preserve the dimension of deliberate unpredictability that is indispensable to its ludic dimension.

While Orwell's career ended prematurely after the publication of *1984*, Huxley's continued up to the early 1960s, when he published *Island* (1963), a "kind of reverse *Brave New World*," in which the reproposition of utopian canons was turned into a potential harmonic recomposition of the relation between humans, science, and nature,[21] a relation doomed to be defeated, however, by the irruption of the external world in the idyllic community of Pali,[22] in conformity to the more realistic analysis of *Brave New World Revisited*, a critical reconsideration of his 1932 dystopia. Firmly believing that the foreseen transition from "too little order" to "the nightmare of total organization" of the year A.F. 632 had been cancelled by the decline of freedom and, more significantly, by the waning of the desire for freedom, Huxley insisted in this work in showing a social control based on the mechanisms of reward and scientific manipulation, supporting his theses with the research of authors like Charles Wright Mills, Eric Fromm, and William Whyte; thus, positing biology as the propulsive foundation of any social aggregation, he identified "over population" and over organization as the main impersonal forces that could lead to a renewed form of totalitarianism. The imbalance between needs and resources, together with the complexity of technological innovation and the ceasing of a natural genetic selection, tended to favor, in fact, both the formation of a political-military elite and an impoverishment of individuals' psychophysical faculties that, exposing the norms of democracy to a risk, raised a hardly resolvable "ethical dilemma." The will for order, an essential precondition for scientific and artistic activities, represented a degenerative factor on the social plan, where the "theoretical reduction of unmanageable multiplicity to comprehensible unity" was the equivalent of a reduction of human singularity to "subhuman uniformity," a transformation of responsible freedom into slavery, a predominance of cultural factors over the hereditary and physiological ones.

These considerations utterly validate Huxley's claims that he had been able to offer a more realistic vision of the future[23] through his presentation of a model of state that, hinging on a close connection between genetic techniques and consumeristic impulses—"The principle of mass production at last applied to biology" ("Foreword" 18)[24]—is not far from Baudrillard's and Eco's analyses of the "hyperreality" of consumeristic society, nor from the current political and social scenarios opened by technological and scientific innovations.

At the same time, however, it should be remarked how, in the essays preceding the publication of *1984*, Orwell had himself offered an extremely lucid diagnosis of these tendencies. The ambivalent character of mass production, favored at the beginning by economic and political interests, but soon turned into an instinctive impulse; the alienation induced by the desire for possession as an end in itself; the degradation of taste: these are the themes that recur at every new stage of his production and, acquiring a specific ideological relevance already in *The Road to Wigan Pier*, are then fully deployed in the analyses devoted to the evolution of the English society which repeatedly hint at the influence of psychoanalytic theories, the role of advertising, and the difficult balance between politics and science. Equally relevant are the remarks on the growing importance attributed to physical appearance that, although wrongly considered a passing phenomenon, are connected with extreme accuracy to that neutralization of the body that we can recognize also, in amplified and satirized forms, in the pages of *Brave New World*. Thus, for instance, in the "Wartime Diary" of 13 April 1941 and in "The Art of Donald McGill," Orwell mentioned the premature aging of the working class and, having identified the indifference about a younger appearance and the adherence to Christian values as its causes, stigmatized the middle class need to improve one's appearance through cosmetics, physical exercise, and childlessness, this need being originated by an individualistic and hedonistic impulse bound to cease with the lowering of the standard of living and the increase in the demographic rate.[25] To quote just one of the articles immediately preceding *1984*, in his "As I Please" editorial of 8 November 1946 he criticized American fashion magazines for their choice of an excessively stylized model of femininity expressing a decadent mentality confirmed by the complete absence of any allusion to death or birth, the disinterest toward work-related issues and the infrequent presence of pictures of children. All these assumptions, however, did not prevent Orwell from expressing his awareness of the potential positive effects of progress (an irreversible process to be accepted with diffidence) and from regarding history as a non-predetermined process, whose evolution could nonetheless be fathomed.

These are just the assumptions that make it possible to frame the "paradoxical" pessimism of *1984* in the right perspective and that, restoring to this novel its most authentic admonitory meaning, allow one to reduce the gap between Orwell's and Huxley's futuristic scenarios, without completely attenuating their conceptual differences. Placing the complex relations between instinct and reason at the center of his last work, and including the physical sphere of humanity in a network of plural relations with power and nature, Orwell aims at foregrounding the most perturbing questions raised by the biopolitical implications of totalitarianism. Although the mutual conditioning between body, mind, and politics occupies an equally relevant space in Huxley's dystopia, in this case too there is a complete interpretative divergence between the two works.[26] In *Brave New World,* the abolition of any postponement between the insurgence of desires and their satisfaction results in a painless suppression of people's emotional sphere, while their dependence from nature is untied by the removal of old age and illness, but not of death. In *1984*, O'Brien's old face, a testimony to the lasting conditioning of biological processes, becomes utterly insignificant in comparison with the party's "immortality," the Big Brother's virtual "eternity," the "perpetuity" of power and the "cyclicity" of its procedures, while Winston's revolt is invalidated by an action that is addressed to the intellectual sphere through physical suffering, but can be fully realized only by involving his affective dimension and by severing his ties with the whole, both spatial and temporal, universe. However, the relative lucidity with which the Ingsoc purposes to exert its power just on the intersection point between body and mind, thus implicitly perceiving the unity of the human being, constitutes a valid hypothesis only within a world characterized by the undisputed power of totalitarianism and is thus inapplicable to the actual authoritative regimes of the 1930s and 1940s whose inability to penetrate the mind of ordinary people had been repeatedly highlighted by Orwell himself.[27] For this reason he had decided not to insist in his last novel on the inherently totalitarian character of hedonistic conceptions, and to propound not only a synthesis of fascism and communism, but also—just as stated by Huxley in *Brave New World*—a projection of their possible developments, yet in a form as extreme as to assume a post-totalitarian conformation, in the sense discussed by Irving Howe (251). Huxley's interpretative approach, instead, had remained anchored to an evolution of the convergence in progress between western industrial societies and a "tame" totalitarianism, whose actual rise he could witness in post–Stalinist Russia, from which he drew the impression that the hybrid conditioning means still in use in dictatorial regimes of his time (the combination of violence and psychological manipulation) were simply a sign of the passage from the tradition of *1984* to that of *Brave New World*.[28] The dissimilarity between the two dystopian projections, when isolated from the purely narrative context of the respective works, allows one to establish some points of convergence between Huxley's and Orwell's positions. Both of them being critical observers of the capitalistic thrusts toward conformism and of the alienating effects of industrial civilization, on whose models the organizational structure and bureaucratic apparatus of new dictatorships tended to embrace, the two authors had constantly condemned all those systems of thought, either philosophical or scientific, that because of their dogmatic connotation, expressed a totalitarian conception of life. Opposing with equal vigor any attempt at subordinating means to ends, they had always made a deep ethical instance aiming at defending human freedom the cornerstone of their analyses. So that the admonitory message addressed by Orwell to common people in 1944 —"they will have to take their destiny into their own hands" (XVI: 227)— is echoed by the final exhortation of *Brave New World Revisited*:

> Meanwhile there is still some freedom left in the world. Many young people, it is true, do not seem to value freedom. But some of us still believe that, without freedom, human beings cannot become fully human and that freedom is therefore supremely valuable. Perhaps the forces that now menace freedom are too strong to be resisted for very long. It is still our duty to do whatever we can to resist them (online).

In the light of the comparison between *Brave New World* and *1984*, and bearing in mind what Marx, one of the first commentators of the crisis of modernity, had stated —"In our days, everything seems pregnant with its contrary" (500)— it is therefore necessary to continue to consider with equal attention the diverse dangers identified by these two authors who, although focusing on different realizations of totalitarian power, identified the will to integrally remold the concept of humanity as its main purpose. Indeed, beyond their opposite ideological stances and their different aims, and, above all, beyond any evaluation based on the degree of realization of futuristic hypotheses inevitably subject to the risk of sudden alterations because of their dependence of the unpredictable developments of human action, the relations between *1984* and *Brave New World* seem not to be interpretable in terms of mutual incompatibility or strict exclusivity. Rather the two novels constitute two perspectives that can alternate, superimpose or integrate each other, both diachronically and synchronically, especially when they are related to their main object of investigation. A compound and multiform phenomenon, totalitarianism, because of its innovative character and of its connotation as "extreme event" in twentieth-century history is susceptible, as underlined by Hannah Arendt and by Orwell and Huxley themselves,[29] of presenting itself in different and unexpected forms, a consequence of its aptitude to assimilate and incorporate multiple and even contradictory instances and to combine them in a coherent system, according to that "logic" of the "peculiar linking-together of opposites" that is a fundamental axis of *1984* and had been immediately perceived by early critics of fascist and communist regimes. It does not seem misleading or hazardous then to imagine a totalitarian system so pervasive as to combine heterogeneous techniques of control, exhibit its most cruel face while at the same time leaving its darkest recesses untouched, subject itself to the most daring interpretation and still preserving its enigma, a system, finally, that is able to transfigure its own repressive connotation under a surface of respectability and to be unconsciously accepted exactly for these characteristics.

After all, accustomed, or better, addicted to living in some kind of Aldous Huxley *Brave New World*, we keep representing our society according to Orwellian interpretative categories, although, unfortunately, in the restricted meaning this word has acquired in common language under the suggestive pressure exerted by the apocalyptic scenery of *1984*.

Notes

1. The veiled allusion in the review of *We* (1998 XVIII: 14) was followed by explicit statements in the letters to Fredric Warburg dated 22 November 1948 and 30 March 1949. Orwell himself, on the other hand, would be charged by Isaac Deutscher (120) with having plagiarized Zamyatin's novel, an interpretation firmly rejected, however, by George Woodcock (171–172).

2. Several studies have stressed how closely related *We, Brave New World*, and *1984* are to Dostoevsky's dialogue between Christ and the Grand Inquisitor, an episode of *The Brothers Karamazov* whose conceptual nucleus can be traced also in *The Possessed* and in *Crime and Punishment*. With regard to this, it is noteworthy how Orwell praised Dostoevsky in his review of *The Brothers Karamazov* and *Crime and Punishment* (7 October 1945) for having been able to operate "the breakdown of the hero-villain antithesis" (XVII: 296–297), while

on 26 April 1940 he had compared Richard Wright's *Native Son* to *Crime and Punishment* because of their analogous achievement of making a crime credible while comprehending "the *internal* necessity that drives a man into seemingly meaningless actions" (XII: 153). These remarks directly bear on Winston Smith's latent complicity with the totalitarian regime of Oceania and to his complex relation of identification with O'Brien. For a more detailed investigation of these aspects, among others, see Bulla.

3. The first draft of *Burmese Days* (published in 1933) dates back to the years of his stay in Burma (1926–30).

4. Strachey criticized Huxley for not having offered a satisfactory explanation of the economic relations in the utopian society and for having limited himself to a projection into the future of the features of the capitalistic system. He further specified: "[A]t the level of scientific knowledge which Mr. Huxley depicts, the necessity for anything like this amount of manual labor would have long ago disappeared. It would be far more economical to produce mechanical automata to undertake these tasks than to breed, by the elaborate and expensive process, which he describes, these prenatally (or, pre-'decantingly') conditioned, and highly perishable, workers. Again, of course, what Mr. Huxley is really thinking of is the mental and physical deformation of its manual workers which capitalism perpetrates here and now. And if he had said this, and shown that no degree of scientific advance under capitalism would ameliorate this state of affairs, but would rather tend to make it worse and worse, he would have written a clear and valuable book. But for Mr. Huxley, it is not science in the hands of a profit-making class, which must deface the mind and bodies of the workers; it is science in general. For he has never conceived of the possibility of another form of society. He has never applied his mind to the question of in what manner, and to what extent, the particular method adopted for organizing the social production necessary to life, conditions the character of life itself" (220–221). Among the most known critical assessments of Huxley's dystopia, cf. Adorno (1981) and Horkheimer (1972).

5. Huxley's other works were in fact made the object of incidental comments, this witnessing however to Orwell's enduring interest, as already manifested at the beginning of the 1930s when he suggested the reading of *Antic Hay* to Brenda Salkeld (X: 308).

6. Orwell did not appreciate this novel, as witness the letter to Richard Rees of 3 March 1949, in which he shared his correspondent's negative evaluation ("it is awful"), an opinion later repeated to Michael Meyer (XX: 52; 61).

7. For a wider reconstruction of Huxley's intellectual and narrative evolution, among the Italian contributions, see Manferlotti (1987) and Guardamagna. The latter, in particular, maintains that *Eyeless in Gaza* marks "the shift from a negative and disenchanted vision of the world — that we can identify as Huxley's point of view in the first phase — to a project of commitment towards an active pacifism and an almost mystic contemplation that includes and requires however the relation with the world" (110).

8. In "Pacifism and Progress," Orwell maintained: "In his earlier pacifist writing, such as 'Ends and Means,' Huxley stressed chiefly the destructive folly of war, and rather overplayed the argument that one cannot bring about a good result by using evil methods. More recently he seems to have arrived at the conclusion that political action is inherently evil, and that, strictly speaking, it is not possible for society to be saved — only individuals can be saved, and then only by means of religious exercises which the ordinary person is hardly in position to undertake. In effect this is to despair of human institutions and counsel disobedience to the State, though Huxley has never made any definite political pronouncement" (XVIII: 68).

9. Beside the references in "Inside the Whale" and in the "As I Please" editorial of 24 December 1943, an implicit criticism of Huxley's positions can be traced in the episode of *1984* in which Winston fantasizes about raping Julia, a passage that can be interpreted perhaps as a literary transposition of what Orwell states both in a letter to Richard Rees dated 3 March 1949 and in his *Last Literary Notebook: Aldous Huxley*. "The more other-worldly & 'non attached' he becomes, the more his books stink with sex. Above all he cannot keep off the subject of flagellating women. It would be interesting to know whether there is a connection between this & his pacifism. (Perhaps that is the solution to the problem of war —

i.e., if we could develop an interest in individual sadism we might work off our surplus energy in that way instead of by waving flags & dropping bombs.)" (XX: 203).

10. Huxley himself, on the other hand, had expressed this intention in a letter dated 18 May 1931 ("I am writing a novel about the future — on the horror of the Wellsian Utopia and a revolt against it") (348); writing to G. Wilson Knight on 15 September 1931, instead, he defined *Brave New World* as "a Swiftian novel about the Future, showing the horrors of Utopia and the strange and appalling effects on feeling, 'instinct' and general *weltanschauung* of the application of psychological, physiological and mechanical knowledge to the fundamentals of human life. It is a comic book — but seriously comic"(353).

11. An interpretation indirectly confirmed in a radio program broadcast 5 March 1943: "Outside Soviet Russia left-wing thought has generally been hedonistic, and the weakness of the Socialist Movement spring partly from this" (XV: 6).

12. On the metaphorical meaning of the Ministries of Oceania, see Arciero (2003); on the socio-political implications of Orwell's urban imagery, see Collina (2006).

13. The same theme can be found in *Brave New World* where, however, the stress, as compared to Orwell's novel, is on the incompatibility between tragedy and social stability, on the eudaemonistic finalities of power, and on the painless removal of individual emotions.

14. Among the main Italian contributions, see Manferlotti and Runcini.

15. On the issue of the manipulation of history and memory in Orwell, see Ceretta.

16. In "Politics vs. Literature," Orwell had in fact dwelled upon the totalitarian implications of anarchical conceptions, the latter being based on a system of interiorized prohibitions far more conditioning than the one ("thou shalt not") imposed by law obedience. In "Lear, Tolstoy and the Fool" and in "Reflections on Gandhi," he had extended these remarks to the pacifist ideology, a further demonstration of his distance from Huxley's theories.

17. This refers here to Esposito's theories (2002).

18. See, for example, this passage from *Brave New World Revisited*: "Biologically speaking, man is moderately gregarious, not a completely social animal; a creature more like a wolf, let us say, or an elephant, than like a bee or an ant. In their original form human societies bore no resemblance to the hive or the ant heap; they were merely packs. Civilization is, among other things, the process by which primitive packs are transformed into an analogue, crude and mechanical, of the social insects' organic communities. Needless to say, the ideal will never in fact be realized. A great gulf separates the social insects from the not too gregarious, big-brained mammal; and even though the mammal should do his best to imitate the insect, the gulf would remain. However hard they try, men cannot create a social organism, they can only create an organization. In the process of trying to create an organization they will merely create a totalitarian despotism" (online). A completely opposite position is instead expressed by Orwell in "Notes on the Way;" for example, he maintained: "Man is not an individual, he is only a cell in an everlasting body, and he is dimly aware of it" (XII: 126).

19. The use of electric barriers as an element separating human society from the surrounding world calls to mind the ecologic conceptions of Thomas Huxley who had often connected the opposition between human civilization and natural anarchy to the image of the Garden of Eden surrounded by a wall protecting it from the threats of environmental forces.

20. It is not a case that in his foreword to *Brave New World* (1946) where Huxley identified the unacceptability of the alternatives he had offered to John the Savage as "the most serious defect in the story, an insane life in Utopia, or the life of a primitive in an Indian village, a life more human in some respects, but in others hardly less queer and abnormal," in other words, a choice between insanity on the one hand and lunacy on the other (7).

21. A position clearly stated in the following passages from *Island*: "'Whereas we,' said Dr Robert, 'have always chosen to adapt our economy and technology to human beings— not our human beings to somebody else's economy and technology'"; and again: "Treat Nature well, and Nature will treat you well. Hurt or destroy Nature, and Nature will soon destroy you" (1976: 164; 248). These statements, moreover, are widely consistent with those expressed in the 1946 foreword to *Brave New World*: "Between the utopian and the primitive horn of

his dilemma would lie the possibility of sanity — a possibility already actualized, in some extent, in a community of exiles and refugees from Brave New World, living within the borders of the Reservation. In this community economics would be decentralist and Henry-Georgian, politics Kropotkinesque and co-operative. Science and technology would be used as though, like the Sabbath, they had been made for man, not (as at present and still more so in Brave New World) as though man were to be adapted and enslaved to them. Religion would be the conscious and intelligent pursuit of man's Final End.... And the prevailing philosophy of life would be a kind of High Utilitarianism in which the Greatest Happiness principle would be secondary to the Final End Principle" (8–9).

22. In a letter to Dr Humphrey Osmond (14 May 1956), Huxley identified the shocking effects of the English colonial rule in Burma as the source of his inspiration for the dramatic end of *Island* and, on 19 January 1962, proposed to Ian Parsons the reproduction on the book's jacket of Van Gogh *Fields under Storms-clouds*, a work that, according to him, symbolized "very forcibly the precariousness of happiness, the perilous position of any Utopian island in the context of the modern world" (928).

23. See, for example, Runcini's position: "Orwell's nightmares, his desperate exorcization of the future, are certainly darker and more violent than Huxley's, but less realistic. The force of Orwell's denunciation wanes just in the contact with 'its' future in our approach to year 2000. Actually, in the programmatic horizon of our time, the future never comes: what does come is the present. And this is something Huxley had perfectly understood" (161–162).

24. It is not by chance that the name "Freud" is often mistaken by the inhabitants of the "new world" for the legendary "Ford."

25. The concern over the progressive decrease in birth rate within the English nation, repeatedly expressed by Orwell in his production, is the exact opposite of Huxley's positions, the stability of the utopian society of Pali in his *Island* resting on "the road of applied biology," "the road of fertility control," and "the limited production and selective industrialization" (247).

26. Analyzing Orwell's and Huxley's novels in the light of the interpretative categories delineated by Foucault in *Il faut defendre la société,* it is possible to identify on the one hand, the presence of a "disciplinaire" mechanism in *1984* that bears on a "corps individualisé, comme organisme doué de capacities," and on the other hand, the presence of a technology "de securité" in *Brave New World* directed toward the people and in which the bodies are placed within biological and socially complex processes (see Foucault 221–222).

27. Actually, even in *1984*, there is a residual space for the survival of individual thought, since O'Brien's ability to penetrate Winston's "intellectual" mind is counterposed by the party's inefficacy to intervene on Julia's intimate sphere other than with surgery. For a more detailed analysis of the biopolitical implications of *1984*, see Arciero (2005, 428–443).

28. Indeed, in *1984* as well, the advent of the final version of the Newspeak seems to prefigure the end of totalitarian terror, in conformity with the position expressed in "Politics vs. Literature," where Orwell, referring himself to Swift, had identified the destruction of language and the consequent annihilation of the emotive and intellectual sphere of individuals as the final stage of a totalitarianism as perfect as to make any material repression of dissidents superfluous.

29. In his review of *Order of the Day* (September 1943), Orwell stated: "Possibly totalitarianism has sufficiently discredited itself by the massacre to which it has led, possibly it is simply going to reappear in new forms and different places" (XV: 243). Similar considerations were expressed by Huxley in his foreword to *Brave New World*: "There is, of course, no reason why the new totalitarianisms should resemble the old" (12).

Works Cited

Adorno, Theodor: "Aldous Huxley and Utopia." In *Prisms*, 95–118. Cambridge, Mass.: MIT Press, 1955.

Arciero, Angelo. "La città reale e la città distopica nell'immaginario politico di George Orwell," in *Metamorfosi della città. Spazi urbani e forme di vita nella cultura occidentale*, edited by M. Rocca Longo and T. Morosetti, 142–158. Roma: Edizioni Associate, 2003.

_____. *George Orwell: Contro il Totalitarismo e per un Socialismo Democratico*. Roma: FrancoAngeli, 2005.

_____. "George Orwell: Il Senso Storico e la Possibilità Della Tragedia," in *George Orwell. Antistalinismo e critica del totalitarismo*, edited by Manuela Ceretta, 103–121. Firenze: Olschky, 2006.

Besançon, Accueil. *La Falsification du bien: Soloviev et Orwell*. Paris: Julliard, 1985.

Bulla, Guido. *Il muro di vetro. 1984 e l'ultimo Orwell*. Roma: Bulzoni, 1989.

_____. "Introduzione." In *L'ultima utopia*, a George Orwell, *Romanzi e Saggi*, xi–lix. Milano: Mondadori (I Meridiani), 2003.

Ceretta, Manuela. "Potere dell'oblio e fragilità della memoria. Orwell e l'elogio della storia." *Igitur* 6, no. 1 (2005); nuova serie, *La memoria e l'oblio*, C. Solivetti, ed., 35–157.

Collina, Vittore. "L'immaginario urbano di G. Orwell," in *George Orwell. Antistalinismo e critica del totalitarismo*, edited by Manuela Ceretta, 91–102. Firenze: Olschky, 2006)

Deutscher, Issac. "*1984* and the Mysticism of Cruelty," in *George Orwell. A Collection of Critical Essays*. Englewood Cliffs, edited by R. Williams, 119–132. New Jersey: Prentice Hall, 1974.

Esposito, Roberto. *Immunitas. Protezione e negazione della vita*. Torino: Einaudi, 2002.

Firchow, Peter. *Aldous Huxley: Satirist and Novelist*. Minneapolis: Univ. of Minnesota Press, 1972.

Foucault, Michel. *Il faut défendre la société*. Paris: Seuil-Gallimard, 1997.

Guardamagna, Daniela. *La Narrativa di Aldous Huxley*. Bari: Adriatica Editrice, 1989.

Horkheimer, Max. *Eclipse of Reason*. New York: Seabury, 1972. First published 1946.

Howe, Irving. *Politics and the Novels*. New York: Horizon Press, 1957.

Huxley, Aldous. *Letters of Aldous Huxley*. Edited by Grover Smith. New York: Harper & Row, 1969.

_____. *Brave New World*, London: Triad/PantherBooks, 1981. First published 1932

_____. "Foreword." *Brave New World*. London, Triad/Panther Books, 1981. First published 1946.

_____. *Brave New World Revisited*. Microsoft Reader eBooks, 2006 (www.ebookmall.com/ebook/69261-ebook.htm). First published 1957.

_____. (1976) *Island*. London: Triad/Panther Books (1962), 1976.

Manferlotti, Stefano. *Anti-utopia: Huxley, Orwell, Burgess*. Palermo: Selleria, 1984

_____. *Invito alla lettura di Huxley*. Milano: Mursia, 1987.

_____. "Distopie contemporanee: Zamjàtin, Huxley, Orwell." In *Utopia e Distopia*, edited by A. Colombo, 35–45. Milano: Angeli, 1987.

Marx, Karl. "Speech at anniversary of the *People's Paper*." In *Selected Works, I*. By K. Marx and F. Engels Moscow: Progress Publishers, 1969.

Orwell, George. *The Complete Works of George Orwell*. Vol. XX. Edited by Peter Davison. London: Secker and Warburg, 1998.

Runcini, Romolo. "Aldous Huxley." In *I Contemporanei. Letteratura Inglese*, edited by V. Amoruso and F. Binni. Roma: Lucarini, 1977.

_____. *I cavalieri della paura. Crisi dei valori e crisi di identità nella cultura europea tra le due guerre*. Cosenza: Luigi Pellegrini Editore, 1989.

Strachey John. *The Coming Struggle for Power*. New York: Modern Library, 1935.

Symons, Julian. "Review, *1984*." In *George Orwell. The Critical Heritage*, edited by J. Meyers, 275–281. London and Boston: Routledge & Kegan, 1975.

Wells, Herbert George. *A Modern Utopia*. Lincoln, NE: University of Nebraska Press, 1967. First published 1905.

Woodcock, George. *The Crystal Spirit. A Study of George Orwell*. London, Fourth Estate, 1984.

"Laboring for a Brave New World: Our Ford and the Epsilons"

SCOTT PELLER

While *Brave New World* is readily perceived as depicting an anti-utopia by virtue of its penchant for readymade leisure and pleasure activities, millions of human beings are still required to perform tedious, repetitive job tasks in order for the upper castes to enjoy their infantile pleasures. These stupid lower castes appear throughout the novel, but for the majority of the time the action focuses on the top castes of Alphas, a world controller, and a classically (by nineteenth-century European standards) educated Savage. Moreover, superior "decanted" characters such as Helmholtz Watson and Bernard Marx garner narrative attention because they perceive themselves as different from the other sense-satisfied Alphas and ultimately end up exiled to distant islands far away from the standardized mainstream society. The pneumatic Beta, Lenina Crowne, is pretty much the lone prominent character that is seemingly unable to be anything other than a well-socialized "decanted" citizen of the stable, happy society. As readers, we are meant to embrace the Savage and Watson for their self-consciousness and their nonconformist actions, while we are supposed to deride the World Controller for participating in the perpetuation of the lowbrow world, Lenina for her inability to decipher her conditioning, and Bernard Marx for failing to engage in a more rebellious course of action.[1]

Yet, whatever the function of these prominent, upper-caste characters, the future world is founded on the rather nondescript Bokanovski groups of multi-twin Gammas, Deltas, and Epsilons upon whose decanting the Alphas enjoy and/or question their existence.[2] One is not supposed to identify with these faceless, nameless worker castes but rather marvel like the Savage does at their insufferable obedience and docility. However, the presence of these working caste nonentities serve the novel more than as a dumb contrast to the educated castes; the worker castes are meant to represent the working class being ameliorated, or at least the attempt of the working class to be ameliorated, within the mass-production factory system of automobile giant Henry Ford.

Huxley's novel exposes the foundation of Fordist economics as necessitating the maintenance and reproduction of workers engaged in repetitive job tasks.[3] The goals of happiness and contentment for workers through their enjoyment of their labor serve to ensure security, peace, and stability for the ruling Alpha elites. While Huxley's satire takes Fordism to task for reducing the intellectual aspirations of the Alphas to the banality of dancing to the music of the Sexophonists and participating in the Orgy-porgy, his novel also reveals the exploitation of the toiling masses in achieving this secure world for the elites. In World Controller Mond's model of the perfect society, the eight-ninths of the population living below the water are required in order for the one-ninth to remain on top of the iceberg (*Brave New World* 268). For Mond, the eight-ninths are the stupid masses that are content and happy while the top one-ninth are supposed to be the ones whose superior breeding must be kept in check by the controllers.[4]

By the end of the 1920s, American industry and consumer culture had come to dominate the Western world: "THE FUTURE OF AMERICA is the future of the world. Material circumstances are driving all nations along the path in which America is going" (Huxley, "Outlook for American Culture" 186). Huxley's critique of the "material circumstances" embodied in 1920s America appears in *Brave New World* through the depictions of a society predicated on abundance, mandatory guilt-free sexual relations, a caste system based on knowledge limits, and the ongoing insipid music, dancing, and sense-appealing entertainments. Huxley locates this drive toward conformity and the banality of mass culture in the mass-production manufacturing and assembly process fathered by Henry Ford and expressed in the development of the Model T automobile. For Huxley, the America driving the material circumstances is an economic, social, and cultural phenomenon identified as Fordism.[5]

Fordism is a capitalist method for securing uninterrupted production. Through the initiatives of the $5/day, eight-hour workday, means such as the Sociological Department, English school and Americanization program meant to control the lives of workers inside and outside the factory, Fordism addressed the requirements of the market for the reproduction of laborers and the fulfillment of steady production. *Brave New World* is a critique of this streamlining process, of its all-too-pragmatic father Henry Ford, and finally of the Fordist workers whose lives of repetitive labor and goals of material comfort appeared to have triumphed over notions of intellectual inquiry and self-reflection.

Fordism is named for automobile manufacturer Henry Ford. Ford appears in *Brave New World* in the dominating form of Our Ford, the father and Holy Ghost of the decanted world. Henry Ford is credited as one of the inventors of the automobile and was certainly the pioneer in the promotion of the automobile as a commodity available for the masses as opposed to its remaining solely a luxury item for the wealthy.[6] The Model T was Ford's great success; its affordability and durability enabled it to remain in production and virtually unchanged for nearly twenty years. The development of the Model T and Ford's commitment to reducing the cost of the vehicle throughout the late teens and twenties directly led to the mass consumption of a universal car. Ford achieved his cost reductions through the constant addressing of waste and unnecessary steps in the automobile production process. Most importantly, Ford consistently reduced the price of the vehicle to consumers while also raising the wages of his workers.

The affordability of the Model T coupled with the so-called high wages paid to his employees ($5/day) propelled Ford into the public eye as a genius inventor and benefactor for the public good. Ford was also seen in his day as an economic leader and social critic; he was enormously popular, and his opinions mattered or at least he made them available through many media outlets.[7] "An indigenous folk hero, Ford appealed to millions of his countrymen because, in their view, he succeeded through his own creativeness and hard work and by supplying a product to meet the public's desires rather than by manipulating money or people. He also was admired, despite his great wealth, for having retained the common touch" (Lewis 11).

Ford cultivated his image as homespun philosopher in the Ford-owned and -operated newspaper *Dearborn Independent*, ghostwritten books such as *My Life and Work* (1922), and the *Ford Almanac* series. Huxley had read *My Life and Work* and thought it important enough to have it appear in *Brave New World*. The Savage finds the text in the controller's study and he sees that it "had been published at Detroit by the Society for the Propagation of Fordian Knowledge" (261). In *Jesting Pilate*, Huxley commented on Ford's book and on the success of Ford's production methods: "When Ford started to apply common sense to the existing methods of industry and business he did it not in a book but in real life. It was only when he had smashed and rebuilt in practice that he decided to expound in a book the theory of his enormous success" (526).

The common theme in Ford's pronouncements that most irked Huxley was the idea that the arts and intellectual endeavor were unnecessary and wasteful. Ford's infamous remark that history was more or less bunk prompted Huxley to write: "The saint of the new dispensation has no choice but to hate history. And not history only. If he is logical he must hate literature, philosophy, pure science, the arts— all the mental activities that distract mankind from an acquisitive interest in objects. 'Bunk' was the term of abuse selected by Mr. Ford for disparaging history. Bunk: for how can even serious and philosophical history be enlightening? History is the account of people who lived before such things as machine tools and joint-stock banks had been invented" (*Music at Night* 131–2).

Imagination and intellectual endeavor not employed for the betterment of the human race through improved efficiency and business practices was considered wasteful. Irrational thoughts, artistic endeavors, the search for philosophical truth and poetic beauty, prove worthless in the business world promoted and dominated by Ford.

During the nineteenth-century, tool making in the United States was evolving into an ever-more-systematic process. Beginning with advances in the manufacturing of firearms by Colt and Springfield, parts production in the United States became more systematic and standardized.[8] The American system of manufacturing, as it was defined by British observers during the 1850s, involved the step-by-step repetition of operations performed on successive special-purpose machines that manufactured easily interchangeable parts.[9] The reduction in the steps of production was an ongoing process during the second half of the nineteenth century leading to Ford's advances in mass production.

By the turn of the century, the systemization of production had become the province of a former mid-level engineer named Frederick Winslow Taylor. In Taylorized production the worker's knowledge or craft experience become more an obstacle than a requirement for performing the job task. The job task is reduced to the point of one or two steps performed repeatedly by the worker throughout the day. Taylor's ideal worker needed to be strong as an ox and as stupid as one.[10]

At the Highland Park factory, Henry Ford implemented many of Taylor's production initiatives such as the time study used to determine how much time and how many workers were required to perform a certain task.[11] Ford's factories became the definitive example of rationalized labor in terms of the reduction of unnecessary physical movement by workers as well as unnecessary mental activity: "The essence of scientific management was systematic separation of the mental component of commodity production from the manual. The functions of thinking and deciding were what management sought to wrest from the worker, so that the manual efforts of wage earners might be directed in detail by a 'superior intelligence'" (Montgomery 252).

Ford's installation of the moving assembly line represented the monotonous and fast-paced job tasks of the twentieth-century factory. The incentive of high wages, nearly double the going wage by 1914 standards, was meant to solve Ford's employee turnover problem and to produce social stability through which employees would see themselves less as workers and more as consumers.[12] Thus, through Ford's efforts, a universal car, the Model T, was mass-produced by a consistent workforce at an ever-faster rate and for sale at an ever-lower price.

Ford challenged other employers to adopt his business practices, especially the creation of a company profit-sharing plan in order to broaden the economic pie. Because of the affordability and availability of the Model T, Ford led the way in the growth of mass-produced goods.[13] Through high wages and the affordability of mass-produced goods, workers were to desire commodities and to identify their interests as those of consumers rather than as workers or their ethnic group.[14]

Another important component to Ford's $5/day announcement was the simultaneous implementation of the eight-hour workday. For Ford these shorter hours conformed to his theoretical aim of maintaining well-conditioned work-

ers by limiting their breakdown through excessive amounts of fast-paced, repetitive labor. Another goal of Fordism is the idea of peace and harmony on the
shop floor between management and labor, what has been termed "work discipline."[15] Work discipline is a capitalist expression describing stable relations
between management and labor. Work discipline means the achievement for
capitalists of uninterrupted production. Ford saw himself and his production
methods as mediating social strife and solving the traditionally antagonistic
relationship between owner and worker. He strongly opposed organized labor
and craft unions but also questioned existing management methods for attaining productivity and industrial acquiescence. Employers and employees, as well
as the middle and upper classes, benefit because, "productive and well-paid
workers make for a prosperous community which will sustain sales of manufactured goods such as automobiles" (Rupert 65).

Ford capitalized on this intellectual raw material and manufactured a labor
relations premised on the "natural rights" of workers to use their hard-earned
wages to purchase and consume. The corresponding high wages and the pro-
liferation of mass-produced and hence affordable goods suggest that workers
accepted and participated in this dazzling world of commodities and consumption.[16] In literary outlets such as the Ford-owned *Dearborn Independent*, Ford
spoke on behalf of workers, claiming (and constructing) their aims and interests: "Labor doesn't want more money, but more of those things which money
represents. Money to Labor is interpreted strictly in terms of food, house, garden, maybe an automobile, a summer vacation, a piano, schooling for the children and so on" ("The Melting Pot" 1).

In order to facilitate the advancement of his workers into the new world
of consuming, "those things which money represents," Ford instituted a Sociological Department, English school, and Americanization program.[17] Most of
Ford's workers had been European immigrants who flooded the small city of
Highland Park eager to work for $5/day. However, in order to receive the full
wage, the workers were required to learn how to be proper "Americans" and
as such had to meet the requirements of the Sociological Department inspec-
tors and attend the English school. The school program included education in
what Ford deemed as proper citizenship; this included an Americanism
premised on the management and labor relations espoused by Ford. The conclusion to the English course for those graduates was the infamous parade of
nations in which immigrant workers marched dressed in their native garb cul-
minating in their transference into their new clothing and identity as transformed American workers. "This material is passed through the assembly line
of the American School for male wage earners, the final product dipped quite
literally into a giant 'melting pot' on graduation day" (Banta 213).

Ford's intention was to turn immigrant laborers from diverse backgrounds
into a like-minded workforce with repetitive lifestyles to match the repetitive
labor on the assembly line.

As with Ford's attempts at manufacturing a dependable, reproducible workforce, Huxley's novel provides its own version of Fordism. We see the manufacturing of embryos on an assembly line, the constant drive at improving efficiency, the regulation of future workers through a version of the English school and Sociological Department, and a maintaining of worker stability through the leisure-time pursuits of consumer culture.

In the first three chapters of *Brave New World*, Huxley presents the manufacturing process of embryos through a guided tour of a reproduction factory. It is on this tour that the Bokanovsky Process for the mass reproduction of workers is explained:

> Standard men and women; in uniform batches. The whole of a small factory staffed with the products of a single bokanovskified egg. 'Ninety-six identical twins working ninety-six identical machines!' [6–7].

Within the hatchery the physical reproduction of workers has become the commodity for rationalized production on the assembly line. The laborers are no longer even required to participate in the physical reproduction of themselves as the old-fashioned method of conception through physical exchange has been replaced with a reproducible formula of biological determinism. This biological determinism has been developed to the point that embryonic laborers are reproduced based on the job tasks required. Through their predetermined biological mixtures these embryos are conditioned to belong to one of five castes: Alpha, Beta, Gamma, Delta, or Epsilon. The Alpha embryos have been produced and will in turn be educated to assume the highest leadership positions within the World State. The Beta, Gamma, Delta, and Epsilon embryos will be segregated and educated to be contented in accordance with their respective lots in life.

Each of these castes is produced and conditioned to be slightly less physically and intellectually enamored by degrees than their superior class or classes. The Epsilons, at the bottom of the system, are stunted and stupefied by oxygen deprivation and chemical treatments. They have been produced to perform the lowest menial job tasks and to be contented with their position. The Epsilons are the epitome of the ideal Taylorized worker (15). The future lower-caste workers are manufactured with attributes for specific job tasks, climates, and hazardous environments. Some are produced to withstand the heat of mines and steel plants while future chemical workers are "trained in the toleration of lead, caustic soda, tar, chlorine" (18). Other future Epsilons are manufactured in a hoist in order to be able to live and work comfortably on space jets while they are in flight: "They learn to associate topsy-turvydom with well-being; in fact, they're only truly happy when they're standing on their heads" (18–9).

As individual units the Epsilons are as easily replaceable as a lug nut, but as a collectivity engaged in job tasks they are indispensable. By virtue of their decanting they are not seemingly capable of realizing the dangers of their physical labor nor are they able to desire a more fulfilling existence. The triumph of the biological determinism in *Brave New World* is the acceptance, by all castes, of the intentional production of dumb and expendable workers. "Huxley's Deltas and Epsilons are the equivalents of Taylor's gorillas and human oxen. They are deliberately bred to be just intelligent enough to do the job they are predestined for, and to be too stupid to understand or want to understand anything else" (Firchow 108).

The tour of the hatchery also reveals the drive of Fordism to continually look for ways of eliminating waste and improve the efficiency of the reproduction factory. The following exchange between the director of hatcheries and conditioning and Henry Foster reveals this agenda:

> "The lower the caste," said Mr. Foster, "the shorter the oxygen." The first organ affected was the brain. After that the skeleton. At seventy per cent of normal oxygen you got dwarfs. At less than seventy eyeless monsters. "Who are no use at all..." [15].

The comment by Foster that the eyeless monsters "are no use at all" demonstrates the endgame for human reproduction — use value. One suspects that if eyeless monsters could be used in some menial application that they too would be mass-produced. As with the time-study engineers at the Ford Highland Park factory, the director and Foster strive for and marvel at the efficiency of streamlined production. One senses in the above discussion the constant drive for improving the process through the reduction in time as Foster beams at the prospect of shortening the maturation process.

As with the process for the physical reproduction of workers, ideological methods of education and indoctrination are applied to growing children to confirm and maintain their respective social identities. During the tour of the hatchery, examples of the educational conditioning are manifested. In the nursery the students observe a group of Delta infants being educated to dislike books and flowers. This aversion therapy, the director maintains, helps to reduce thinking by the Deltas and enforces the values of the Delta children to become pleasant consumers. The students then observe the methods used to instruct children in the proper morals of the New World as they sleep. They enter a room in which older children are asleep; a whispering voice is heard repeating a lesson in "Elementary Class Consciousness." "Oh no, I don't want to play with Delta children. And Epsilons are still worse" (30–1).

With a similar purpose as the Ford Sociological Department, Americanization program, and English school, the Elementary Class Consciousness program is meant to educate workers in their future roles as workers and consumers. This conditioning does not stop once the children are adults. The lower, non-Alpha castes are modeled on Ford's productive terms in that they labor for seven hours a day and then are provided pleasures during their leisure time. While World Controller Mond contends that they like it ("it's light, it's childishly simple"), the necessity for "soma" and the "feelies" reveals that the lower castes are not completely content but still require ideological control. The entertainments and media are constructed to dispense the proper ideological content for the targeted group. As such, each group reads the newspapers that are made available for them and listens to *their* radio programs. The presence of these lifelong methods of conditioning suggests that indeed even biologically produced workers require ideological maintenance.

Brave New World is a world dominated by Fordism in which workers have achieved permanent happiness through biological conditioning, job security, and leisure time to purchase commodities and pleasures. The dystopia is based on providing uninterrupted production, which is for the most part maintained not through the violence of a repressive apparatus but rather through biological conditioning and steady ideological reinforcement. The mass conformity being constantly reinforced in Huxley's novel is Huxley's fear of Fordism run amok. It is the attainment of the perfect product (the human being) as per the requirements of the job tasks that have themselves become perfected and are unchanging.

Postscript

One of the ironies involving the publication of *Brave New World* was its appearance during the depths of the Great Depression. As Granville Hicks questioned in his 1932 review of the novel for *New Republic*: "With war in Asia, bankruptcy in Europe and starvation everywhere, what do you suppose Aldous Huxley is now worrying about? ... He is worrying about the unpleasantness of life in the utopia" (219).[18] Indeed, the prospect of attaining mass happiness and social stability through mass production and consumer culture seemed a distant memory and cruel joke for the millions of unemployed people starving in Hoovervilles across the United States.

The Model T had long since gone out of fashion, replaced by a variety of new models made available by automakers besides Ford. The notion of permanent stability achieved through commodity satisfaction had proven illusory. Ford learned this the hard way when he refused to alter or scrap the Model T in favor of new models and cars available in colors other than black. By the time he acknowledged that the Model T was not the only automobile desired by the mass consumer, his company had lost its position as number one automobile manufacturer.

When *Brave New World* appeared in 1932, the Ford Motor Company Rouge Factory complex was operating under far different circumstances than the automotive heyday of the 1920s. Through massive job cuts, limited hours for those few left employed, and a Sociological Department that had devolved into a Service Department bent on busting (literally and figuratively) union organizing attempts, Henry Ford had become like the evil capitalists he once derided.[19] On March 7, 1932, the last vestiges of harmonious work relations promised by the Fordism of the Model-T era were left bleeding on the streets near the gates of the Ford Rouge Factory in Dearborn. Four young unemployed men died from gunshot wounds fired by members of the Dearborn police force and by armed employees of the Ford Motor Company.[20] The victims had participated with fellow recently laid-off Ford workers in a hunger march to Ford's Rouge Plant with the intention of submitting a list of grievances and demands to owner Ford. What workers refer to as Bloody Monday provided a moment in Detroit history where class division became brutally visible and the failure of mass automobile production to deliver its advertised promise of financial security for workers was made clear.[21] Henry Ford's simple answer to the question of what an employer's responsibility was to worker unemployment: none.

Notes

1. Firchow 21.
2. World Controller Mond makes this point (*Brave New World* 265–6).
3. "Huxley never showed much understanding of or sympathy for the working class" (Baker 85). [Editor's note: There is much evidence to dispute Baker's assertion in Huxley's fiction, nonfiction, and biography both before and after *Brave New World*. One example: in his 1928 novel, *Point Counter Point*, Huxley valorizes the working class through his D. H. Lawrence character, Mark Rampion.]
4. "The problem is only with the alphas, that one-ninth of the population, left with the capacity to think for themselves" (Ramamurty 70).
5. I am limiting my analysis of Fordism to the period preceding and influencing Huxley's work, namely the Model-T era of the 1920s. For information on the locating of Fordism as a post–World War II development, refer to Nick Heffernan, *Capital, Class and Technology in Contemporary American Culture: Projecting Post-Fordism* (London: Pluto, 2000) and Nelson Lichtenstein, *Walter Reuther: The Most Dangerous Man in Detroit* (Urbana and Chicago, IL: University of Illinois Press, 1995).
6. Brinkley 21.
7. Lewis 129.
8. These adventures were documented in John Burroughs's *Under the Maples* (1921). According to Brinkley and Lewis, the expeditions had more publicity and less rustic and rough conditions.
9. Howe 108.
10. Hounshell 15.
11. That combination of stupidity and brute force is embodied in the worker on whom Taylor modeled his representation of the worker, a little Pennsylvania Dutch man called Schmidt. However, as Martha Banta points out, "No such person as Schmidt existed to be taught 'the science of shoveling' pig iron. Taylor made up his story based on a very different kind of worker, one Henry Noll, but the imaginary Schmidt furthered Taylor's thesis: getting the right man 'to handle 47 tons of pig iron per day and making him glad to do it.' A mix of pleasantries and tough talk accomplishes what *the boss* wants (more goods produced at lower costs) and what *the worker* wants (higher wages)" (Banta 114–5).
12. "The epitome of mass production was the Detroit-area Highland Park plant. There, unlike the older vertical production structures marked by skilled workers assembling cars in teams by hand, a modern horizontal plant layout allowed workers to remain stationary while the parts and componants moved around them" (Pietrykowski 385).

13. While Taylor's theories on scientific management became well-known and publicized, the full extent of Taylorism, especially the carrot of high wages, remained unimplemented even in the steel factories he discusses. Fordism, on the other hand, extended Taylorism through its sheer numbers of employees involved and the length of the moving assembly line and of course the increase in production rates. Ford for a time did more than merely flaunt the carrot of high wages, though with the stipulations of the Sociological Department and Americanization program. David Montgomery, *The Fall of the House of Labor: The Workplace, the State, and American Labor Activism, 1865–1925* (New York: Cambridge University Press, 1987) and Clarence Hooker, *Life in the Shadows of the Crystal Palace, 1910–1927: Ford Workers in the Model T Era* (Bowling Green, OH: Bowling Green University Press, 1997).

14. Certainly, factors other than Ford's initiatives contributed to the construction of "the consumer" and "consumer culture." The new "virtue" of spending money, the acceptance and exploitation of commodity desire, however, are inseparable from the homogenization of the workforce. For this development refer to Richard Fox and T.J. Lears, editors, *The Culture of Consumption: Critical Essays in American History 1880–1980* (New York: Pantheon Books, 1983), Stuart Ewen, *Captains of Consciousness* (New York: McGraw-Hill, 1976), and Andrew R. Heinze, *Adapting to Abundance: Jewish Immigrants, Mass Consumption, and the Search for American Identity* (New York: Columbia University Press, 1990).

15. For more on the goals of status and affluence for immigrant workers, see Otto Feinstein, "Why Ethnicity?" in *Immigrants and Migrants: The Detroit Ethnic Experience*, edited by David W. Hartman (Detroit: New University Thought P, 1974) and David Montgomery, *The Fall of the House of Labor: The Workplace, the State, and American Labor Activism, 1865–1925* (New York: Cambridge University Press, 1987).

16. For further discussion on Ford and other employers' methods for achieving work discipline, see Douglas Brinkley, *Wheels for the World: Henry Ford, His Company, and a Century of Progress, 1903–2003* (New York: Penguin, 2004), Stephen Meyer III, *The Five Dollar Day: Labor Management and Social Control in the Ford Motor Company 1908–1921* (Albany: State University of New York Press, 1981), and Mark Rupert, *Producing Hegemony: The Politics of Mass Production and American Global Power* (Cambridge: Cambridge University Press, 1995).

17. "During the twenties, the rewards of middle-class consumer society were extended to more workers than ever before. Working-class culture in some communities began to change partly as a result of leisure-time consumption patterns" (Green 104).

18. "The lessons intended to make the immigrant worker a consumer of American goods and services from American merchants" (Meyer 157).

19. "What, Granville Hicks wondered out loud, was the point of publishing an anti-utopian novel at a time like this? A novel set in a future so remote that it had virtually nothing to do with the present crises and whose only political concern was something so irrelevant as stability? Surely there were other and more important things to write about than this? In the bleak decade that followed, others took up Hicks' reproach: *Brave New World*, for all its brilliance, had precious little to offer anyone seeking political instruction" (Firchow 78).

20. "Ultimately, Ford paternalism failed. It failed for a number of different reasons. Most important was the failure to achieve its principal objective — the control of workers" (Meyer 195). For a synopsis of the Bennett-led Ford Service Department, see Stephen Norwood, "Ford's Brass Knuckles: Harry Bennett, The Cult of Muscularity, and Anti-Labor Terror, 1920–1945," *Labor History* 37, no.3 (1996): 365–91.

21. It has been disputed whether Detroit police were also involved in the shootings. Felix Marrow, "Class War in Detroit." *New Masses*, May 1932.

22. Robert Cruden, *Bloody Monday at Ford's* (New York: Labor Research Association, 1932).

Works Cited

Baker, Robert S. *"Brave New World": History, Science, and Dystopia*. Boston: G. K. Hall, 1990.
Banta, Martha. *Taylored Lives: Narrative Productions in the Age of Taylor, Veblen, and Ford.* Chicago: University of Chicago Press, 1993.

Brinkley, Douglas. *Wheels for the World: Henry Ford, His Company, and a Century of Progress, 1903–2003.* New York: Penguin, 2003.

Cruden, Robert. *Bloody Monday at Ford's.* New York: Labor Research Association, 1932.

Firchow, Peter. *The End of Utopia: A Study of Aldous Huxley's "Brave New World."* Cranbury, NJ: Associated University Press, 1984.

Ford, Henry, and Samuel Crowther. *My Life and Work.* 1922. North Stratford, NH: Ayer, 2001.

Green, James R. *The World of the Worker: Labor in Twentieth-Century America.* 1980. New York: Hill and Wang, 1991.

Hicks, Granville. "Review in *New Republic.*" 1932. In *Aldous Huxley: The Critical Heritage,* edited by Donald Watt. Boston: Routledge and Kegan Paul, 1975.

Howe, John. "Vehicle of Desire." *New Left Review* 15 no.3 (2002): 105–117.

Hounshell, David A. *From the American System to Mass Production 1800–1932: The Development of Manufacturing Technology in the United States.* Baltimore: Johns Hopkins University Press, 1984.

Huxley, Aldous. *Brave New World.* 1932. New York: Harper & Brothers, 1946.

_____. *Jesting Pilate.* In *Aldous Huxley: Complete Essays Vol. II, 1926–1929,* edited by Robert S. Baker and James Sexton. Chicago: Ivan R. Dee, 2000. First published 1926.

_____. *Music at Night.* In *Aldous Huxley: Complete Essays Vol. III, 1930–1935,* edited by Robert S. Baker and James Sexton. Chicago: Ivan R. Dee, 2001. First published 1931.

_____. "The Outlook for American Culture: Some Reflections in a Machine Age." In *Aldous Huxley: Complete Essays Vol. III, 1930–1935,* edited by Robert S. Baker and James Sexton. Chicago: Ivan R. Dee, 2001.

Lewis, David L. *The Public Image of Henry Ford: An American Folk Hero and His Company.* 1976. Detroit: Wayne State University Press, 1987.

Marrow, Felix. "Class War in Detroit." *New Masses,* May 1932.

"The Melting Pot." *Dearborn Independent: The Ford International Weekly.* March 8, 1919.

Meyer, Stephen, III. *The Five Dollar Day: Labor Management and Social Control in the Ford Motor Company 1908–1921.* Albany: State University of New York Press, 1981.

Montgomery, David. *The Fall of the House of Labor: The Workplace, the State, and American Labor Activism, 1865–1925.* New York: Cambridge University Press, 1987.

Pietrykowski, Bruce. "Fordism at Ford: Spatial Decentralization and Labor Segmentation at the Ford Motor Company, 1920–1950." *Economic Geography* 71, no.4 (1995): 383–401.

Ramamurty, K. Bhaskara. "Aldous Huxley: A Study of His Novels." 1974. In *Aldous Huxley's "Brave New World" Bloom's Notes,* edited by Harold Bloom. Broomall, PA: Chelsea House, 1996.

Rupert, Mark. *Producing Hegemony: The Politics of Mass Production and American Global Power.* Cambridge: Cambridge University Press, 1995.

Taylor, Frederick Winslow. *The Principles of Scientific Management.* Mineola, NY: Dover, 1998. First published 1911.

Words Have to Mean Something More: Folkloric Reading in Brave New World[1]

SEAN A. WITTERS

Brave New World has the curious legacy of confirming the development of the modern dystopian genre while at the same time satirizing and critiquing its conventions. When Huxley took up the genre in 1932, it had yet to be fully realized as a modern literary stream; yet, his treatment shows remarkable insight into the features we now recognize as its hallmarks. His exploration of language and the mechanics of power in modernity foreshadows the culture theory of the Frankfurt School and poststructuralism, and distinguishes the novel from its predecessors and the majority of its descendents. This distinction owes in large part to Huxley's clever narrative structure, which imparts his critique by way of misdirection, or what can more artfully be described as narrative feints. These feints draw the reader into narrative trajectories structured by cultural mythologies or folklore that underpin the conventions of the dystopian genre. The core of this genre is the operation of power and the contest between free will and coercion. Accordingly, Huxley's narrative suggests a traditional confrontation between power and its discontents. The reader is led to anticipate a narrative that climaxes in a confrontation with power, but, through a series of reversals, the author undermines this expectation. Thus, this satire of conditioning addresses both the conditioning of the subjects of *Brave New World*'s Fordian state and the reader.

The implied dramatic tension produced by Huxley's feints anticipates reading through narrative sequences about moral dilemmas commonly found in myths and folktales. This is, of course, the irony of the dystopian form — while it deals largely with complexity and modernity, the simple causal binaries that tend to drive its narratives — subject/power, free will/coercion, truth/ lies — betray its primitive narrative infrastructure. One can term this mode of reading "folkloric" because it suggests structurally transposable narrative forms, and connotes a mode of romantic idealism, since the folktale gives expression to the desire for justice or heroic restoration. This term also offers a means for moving back through the critical genealogy, from Roland Barthes' myth to Structuralist Vladimir Propp's folktale. Propp's morphological approach to the folktale proposes a transposable sequence of "narratemes" through which we can perceive the evolution of a narrative form. His effort to map the narrative landscape of the Russian folktale was an important influence on the semiological insights of Barthes' *S/Z*, which, in turn, transformed this mode of narrative analysis from a sociological study to an ideological critique.

Taking up Barthes' considerations implicit in this discussion, myth and folklore are difficult to distinguish in terms of narrative and ideological function, in the sense that both represent referential codes. We, as readers within a culture, enter into the narrative through these codes, which render the text legible to us. The codes referenced in *Brave New World*, and which structure Huxley's narrative feints, are made legible through myths of dissent based on the role of literature and language (or *the word*) and heterogeneous sexuality in relation to power. Since we are apt to rely on these myths, we are vulnerable to Huxley's feints.

The Dystopia as Folktale

If we map the dystopian fiction as it coalesced over the course of the twentieth century, as a kind of folktale about modern culture or mass society, we discover a common narrative thread that structures the genre's drama. This thread is constituted by predictable and generalizable sequential elements that can be observed in most any storytelling form. As in the folktale, the dystopian narrative takes shape by moving the hero from a journey to a test to a return. The climax of the dystopian narrative is the confrontation with power — the test at the end of the journey. This narrative is always keyed to the introduction of a magical subversive element that precipitates the final confrontation between the subject and power. Huxley's novel rests in a field of narratives that share this common structuring. Across a century of dystopian texts, this form is *consistently* discernable from H. G. Wells's *When the Sleeper Wakes* to the Wachowski Brothers' *The Matrix*.

Perhaps *the* major cinematic dystopia, rivaled only by Fritz Lang's *Metropolis* and *The Matrix*, Terry Gilliam's *Brazil* offers a particularly illuminating example of the operations of this narrative structure. There are two versions of this film: Gilliam's final cut and Universal Studios President Sid Sheinberg's "Love Conquers All" cut.[2] These competing visions illustrate the persistent aesthetic and ideological desires operative within the genre that *Brave New World* satirizes. Named for its guiding premise, Sheinberg's "Love Conquers All" cut is a classic expression of the narrative of rebellion, ending with the destruction of the Ministry of Information, the erasure of protagonist Sam Lowry's subjecthood, and a romantic escape that ratifies the idea that love subversively eludes the interdictions of power. Though the unsentimental conclusion of Gilliam's final cut insists on difference, with a deluded Lowry strapped down in a torture chamber, humming the tune "Brazil" while he envisions his escape, it simply transports the subject's liberation to another plane.

In "The Undergrowth of Enjoyment," Salvoj Zizek argues that by humming the title song, Lowry enacts a kind of banal rebellion. The song anchors him to a "residue of the Real" that pulls him out of the state's socio-symbolic order (Zizek 16). Thus, Gilliam maintains postmodern creative integrity by eschewing the notion of an individual rebellion that *actually* collapses the dystopian state but enacts a dualistic version that redeems Lowry's consciousness, though his body remains under state control. In this way, Lowry is victorious in both versions: Sheinberg frees his body and Gilliam frees his soul. The latter victory is not the destruction of the state but the denial of power's internal hegemony.

Whether the hero's journey produces a real or moral victory, this narrative form, shaped around a final confrontation with power, constitutes of the core structure of the dystopian genre as it preceded *Brave New World* and, largely, as follows it. Huxley's narrative feints invite reading within the folkloric confines of the dystopian genre, but he appropriates this structure and the ideology it reproduces, in order to generate a narrative reversal. This reversal is *Brave New World*'s paradigmatic achievement.

Language and Dystopian Narrative Tradition

In his exploration of the role of language in the dystopian genre, David Sisk endorses the idea that language is the focal point of a discourse on power within the genre writing that, "twentieth-century dystopian novels in English universally reveal a central emphasis on language as the primary weapon with which to resist oppression, and the corresponding desire of repressive government structures to stifle dissent by controlling language" (2).

The retrograde logic of this is that, because language must be controlled, it must have equal power to liberate the subject. Sisk's observation confirms common knowledge: we grant *the word* (whether in speech or literature) inherent subversive power in the dystopian narrative. This premise is borne on the shoulders of the Enlightenment humanist tradition in which mastery of language, vis-à-vis literacy, is the path out of subjugation (as in *Narrative of the Life of Frederick Douglass* in which literacy is the end and means of liberation). At the center of this system of belief, we find persistent faith in the natural power of *the word*. As *Brave New World*, and the critical work of those it influenced, particularly Max Horkheimer and Theodor Adorno, makes apparent, the operations of post-industrial mass culture belie this conception of literature or speech, within the parameters of mass society, as being *inherently* subversive or anti-totalitarian.

What Horkheimer and Adorno, and later poststructuralism, set out to counter was the persistence of this faith in the Enlightenment narrative wherein culture, the arts or literature, is supposed to be a vehicle of sweetness and light. As such, literature is treated as a natural force, inevitable in its power, but the experience of post-industrial mass culture shook this concept to its very foundation. Yet, because of modernism's construction of authorship as a self-authenticating act of transcendence, and because of critics, like Huxley's great uncle Matthew Arnold, whose notion of "sweetness and light" helped sustain the link between modernism and the Enlightenment, the conception of *the word* as liberator persists. The narrative structures in Huxley's novel are dependent on the reader's reflexive supposition that literature *necessarily* propagates the flourishing of knowledge that liberates. Accordingly, the function of *the word* within the folklore of rebellion in the dystopian genre can be distilled into a general narrative flow. This structure fits comfortably into a five-act schema:

> I. The Interdiction: Totalitarian power systematically chokes off the free intellectual life of the individual. This process establishes the conditions under which access to literature is proscribed and acts of writing and reading (and thereby thinking) are subject to control. This interdiction produces the sense of lack or harm that occasions "the Journey."
>
> II. The Journey: The protagonist begins a journey of dissent as a result of alienation, questioning, or disaffection.
>
> III. Magical Helper: The magical discovery of subversive knowledge, vis-à-vis *the word*, leads to conflict. The presence of *the word* is an anathema in a totalitarian system and is the catalyst of a profound crisis.
>
> IV. The Test: The protagonist, now carrier of *the word*, is subject to a test or trial in which the state (power) mistakes his or her presence for the greater influence of *the word*.
>
> V. Justice: In spite of the state's action against the protagonist, *the word* persists, operating in the manner daylight does in a gothic novel, wherein the light of the real penetrates the enshrouded illusions of power.

This schema simplifies typical folkloric morphology, merging it with dramatic convention, to describe features of the dystopian narrative as it appears in a range of works. If we look to early examples of the genre for the dynamic Sisk describes, and for the features of this narrative pattern, the merger of *the word* as speech-act and as literature becomes apparent.

As a key component in the genealogy of the modern dystopia, Jack London's *The Iron Heel* (1909) solidifies the function of literature within the genre. The novel is prefaced with Alfred Lord Tennyson's "The Play," casting the novel's dystopian conflict as a five-act play penned by a playwright-god. This Prospero-like deity promises restoration or justice in the fifth act.

> Act first, this Earth, a stage so gloomed with woe
>   You almost sicken at the shifting of the scenes.
> And yet be patient. Our Playwright may show
>   In some fifth act what this Wild Drama means. (Tennyson 555)

This classic meta-dramatic (or meta-literary) conceit validates *the word*'s transcendent power within the narrative it foreshadows.

London's novel purports to be a centuries-old manuscript, depicting the United States' descent into totalitarian horror under a capitalist oligarchy, written and hidden away by the wife of an assassinated socialist politician. Composed in 1932, coincidentally the year of *Brave New World*'s publication, the text explains the "wild drama" of a totalitarian past to readers in a future society. Thus, *The Iron Heel* is based on the preservation of historical truth in a manuscript that arises from the past, returning, like Arthur, from its slumber in an ancient oak. *Iron Heel* replaces the literal sleeper of H. G. Wells's *When the Sleeper Wakes* (1899), in which the protagonist returns to *speak* his word, with a literary text that embodies the anti-authoritarian resistance of *the word*. This narrative, wherein *the book* subverts the state's hegemonic power, becomes a core dystopian narrative, shaping the drama of the genre's other major works: *Nineteen Eighty-Four* and *Fahrenheit 451*. Huxley's narrative feint invites us to read *Brave New World* through just such a structure, but, as becomes evident via Huxley's reversals, ultimately challenges the celebration of literature as a natural catalyst of rebellion.

The Conditions

Brave New World opens with the director guiding a group of trainees through a decanting facility as they scribble furiously in notepads. From the very first page, there is high value placed on the acquisition of knowledge or, more specifically, a technical vocabulary; however, as the director emphasizes, the bulk of knowledge acquired is general knowledge and not comprehensive. It is precisely this contradictory condition, of possessing a technical vocabulary or jargon while lacking substantive knowledge that defines the technocratic hierarchy, and which Adorno describes in *The Jargon of Authenticity* when he writes, "whoever is versed in the jargon does not have to say what he thinks, does not even have to think properly. The jargon takes over this task and devalues thought" (9). In Fordian society, jargon affects a linguistic conditioning while affirming class divisions that are structured by levels of technocratic specialization. The contrast also establishes for the reader a suspicion that there is an esoteric set of knowledge denied to all but the mandarin class.

In the portrait of the conditioning system that the director provides the trainees, we are shown the neo-Pavlovian response training that goes on in the nursery, which purportedly ensures that the children grow up "with what the psychologists used to call an 'instinctive' hatred of books and flowers" (*Brave New World* 22). The trainees are unsurprised to witness children being given electric shocks by books, for the logic of the conditioning is readily apparent to them. One student observes that there is an obvious threat that citizens could "read something which might undesirably decondition one of their reflexes" (*BNW* 22). The fear of reading is given special attention to ensure that it is subject to a set of "reflexes unalterably conditioned" (*BNW* 22). Our attention is directed to the anxieties of this society about the power of literature to undermine social control, putting into play the idea that, if it can alter what is meant to be unalterable, the very act of reading must be subversive.

The neo-Pavlovian conditioning of the children is not targeted solely at reading; it also encompasses nature. While they readily intuit the threat from books, the students are not certain why the children are conditioned against nature. The director offers an explanation based on production and consumption necessities, but nature's pairing with reading offers another perspective to the reader. The alignment of reading and nature reinforces the idea that there is an inherent freedom that comes with reading: that acts of reading, like nature, provide unfettered access to an aesthetic world that resists politics and grants access to reality that falls outside the artifice of the present regime.

The citizens' experience of nature is always mediated by technologies; thus, they encounter nature only through helicopter tours, electro-magnetic golf, and Centrifugal Bumble-Puppy—recreation that reinforces conditioning by redirecting pleasure through the society's culture of production. The removal from nature is just one part of an entire system that denies humans the opportunity to act individually and which separates them as much as possible from information and experience. In this, we discover the reason for linking the book and the flower. Under neo-Pavlovian conditioning, the infantilized citizen is denied access to complete systems of knowledge. As with the logic of jargon, localized knowledge is endorsed while comprehensive knowledge is denied. The individual may have intricate knowledge of discrete technologies, but no insight into the workings of that technology or any creative abilities to modify it. Thus, individual knowledge and creation is reliant on social cohesion.

Within this order, pleasure is entirely an act of consumption, as we discover in Huxley's depiction of the cinematic "feelies" which so aptly anticipates the plotless pleasure of pornographic movies. The book and the flower are synecdoche for the Enlightenment tradition in which truth and beauty intertwine in art and literature. In the essay "Words and Behavior," Huxley writes that "words form the thread on which we string our existence ... the dumb creature lives a life made up of discreet and mutually irrelevant episodes" (*Collected Essays* 245). The neo-Pavlovian conditioning we encounter in the nursery is essential to cutting the future citizen's connection to his or her autonomous potential and any narrative which might afford of its discovery (thus, establishing the sense of lack that drives Huxley's narrative feints).

The author uses the relationship between Bernard Marx and Helmholtz Watson to drive home the impression that there is a growing tension situated in the nexus of language and individualism that will find expression in these two characters. Both are plagued by a sense of alienation and uncertainty, and seem to be complicit in a protean conspiracy. Hence, it is observed that "what the two men shared was the knowledge that they were individuals" (*BNW* 69). They are in the awkward position of having a sense of themselves outside of the collective. For Bernard, this sense derives in large part from his stature and resultant rumors of a "decanting error," but also from a longing for meaning. Helmholtz has a different feeling. He seems plagued by a kind of cognitive difference or a sense of election. He tellingly asks Bernard, "did you ever feel … as though you had something inside you that was only waiting for you to give it a chance to come out? Some sort of extra power that you aren't using?" (*BNW* 69).

For Helmholtz this sense of difference intertwines with what we read as a desire for literary expression — the natural irruption of a writer. In spite of his opportunity to work with words in his professional life, he finds the prescribed possibilities stifling, longing for "some different way of writing…. Or else something else to write about" (*BNW* 69). He struggles to find an outlet for his feelings and is plagued by an inchoate sense that words have the power to tell the truth or "something hynopaedically obvious" (*BNW* 69).

If language is a way of remembering, a way of recording subjective impressions and holding onto ideas, it is subversive in this Fordian society where "history is bunk." Individual memory and consistent consciousness (outside of conditioning) are antisocial qualities under this regime. There is no hell in the average citizen's imagination, only the "bottomless past" of memory. Regular soma use shores up the threat brought about by unpleasant cognitive states or dissonant memories. Solitude and reflection are subjugated to communal activities and the indulgence of empty pleasure.

The narrative builds toward Bernard and Lenina's journey into the New Mexico reservation where they meet John the Savage (a move underpinned by both folkloric structure and the tragicomic adventure of *The Tempest,* wherein nature is a stage for magical correction). Observing John carrying his ragged copy of *The Complete Shakespeare,* we wonder if the Savage is our Prospero, Ariel, or Caliban. According to our expectations, this journey, and the appearance of the Shakespeare-toting Savage, promises the reader that Huxley's drama has begun to move toward the inevitable conflict with power; yet, this is precisely the point at which the author's carefully constructed narrative feint begins to become legible as a manipulation.

Shakespeare and The Word

John the Savage seems to be the embodiment of the lost power of literature. In the spirit of Eliot's longings in *The Wasteland,* the Savage brings the book back from the ancient past to give greater meaning to the fragmentary and shallow present. For Huxley, Shakespeare is a high-culture fetish, a bringer of "sweetness and light." It is of particular import that Huxley uses Shakespeare, whom Samuel Johnson called "the poet of nature, the poet that holds up to his readers a faithful mirror of manners and of life" (301). In Shakespeare, we find the vessel of the mythology of the transcendent power of literature as a window into a sharper reality. Here is our good father Prospero, who emerges from the wilderness with his books to show us "what this Wild Drama means" and set the world in order; thus literature is simultaneously a power over nature and a natural force.

Shakespeare, in this sense, is not merely a poet or playwright; he is a ready signifier of an instance of the perseverance of the truth, a natural Copernican dissident. In the Savage's hands, Shakespeare is a secular shorthand for the struggle of the Protestant tradition wherein literacy is part of the mythology of a move from premodern servitude under an esoteric faith to an individual relationship with ultimacy (or, if you will, power) based on a new ability to access and interpret the canon. As magic-helper, bringer of *the word*, within the folkloric structure, the Savage is anticipated to shatter the esoteric knowledge that sustains totalitarian power.

Sexuality and Anti-Authoritarianism

In parallel to the folkloric structure based on the liberating power of *the word*, Huxley plays with our expectations regarding the relationship between sex and power through multiple narrative inversions of the sexual behaviors and ideologies in *Brave New World*. Here again, any preordained assumptions about narrative trajectory prove problematic. In this novel authoritarianism is not marked by Victorian prudery. To the contrary, social cohesion is ensured through a collection of nonprocreative sexual and erotic practices. The longing and disaffection that we encounter suggests desire for a "natural" sexual order: procreative monogamy. The highest practice of Fordian society is "orgy-porgy," a childishly named ceremony in which, at the height of a quasi-religious ritual, the practitioners enter into a communal state of erotic ecstasy. This is a compulsory practice within Fordian culture, for it stabilizes the hierarchy and reasserts citizenship. Orgy-porgy solidifies the connection between the state's Fordian/Freudian ideology and pleasure. The orgy is a process for co-opting individual pleasure. All acts that generate pleasure are interpolated through the state, so this orgy, which under normative Western values seems wild, is in no way subversive.

As the rhyme tells us, the bodies of the participants transform into one through the orgy. By engaging in this collective erotic act, the differentiated individuals are mapped onto a single body: the Fordian state. Just as procreative monogamous sex under Victorianism (and subsequent value systems insistent on a "traditional" family unit) affirmed citizenship by enacting the physical landscape imagined by such value systems, orgy-porgy replaces individual pleasure with acts of allegiance. In his lessons to a group of initiates, the Controller declares that there can be "no civilization without social stability. No social stability without individual stability" (*BNW* 40). The orgy is the vehicle by which these two interests are bound together through public pleasure.

This communal sex ritual is part of a matrix of public sexual behavior into which citizens are initiated from the earliest stages of their lives. Subjects are brought up, and brought into, the normative model of behavior by a training process. Controller Mustapha Mond explains that this system of indoctrination replaced an emphasis on repressive force, noting in his historical account that "in the end ... the controllers realized that force was no good" (*BNW* 50). They opted instead for "slower but infinitely surer methods" (*BNW* 50). Citizens of the state were hence subject to ecto-genesis, neo-Pavlovian conditioning, and hynopaedia. These medical treatments are reinforced by cultural institutions like orgy-porgy and elementary erotic play like "hunt-the-zipper." Huxley's emphasis on conditioning as the primary means of maintaining state control brings us to the same conclusion at which Foucault arrived in *Discipline and Punishment*: "The chief function of the disciplinary power is to 'train'" (178).

These socio-sexual rituals are part of a system of observable training that extends all the way from the playground into adult lives, maintaining conditioning through a self-reinforcing culture that shapes everything from concepts of health to modes of entertainment to clothing. The clothing, for example, reinforces early erotic play lessons with a preponderance of zippers that echoes the game "hunt-the-zipper." Citizens are reconditioned by everyday encounters; thus, social habits and fashion supplant enforcement.

Within this culture, promiscuity is de rigueur. Any hint of a long-term monogamous commitment risks both social stigma and intervention by the state. When we first meet Lenina Crowne, she has been in an unconsciously monogamous relationship with coworker Henry Foster for four months. Huxley shows her engaging in locker room gossip that outlines the dilemma facing the average woman of Lenina's standing. Though she is content, she is subject to increasing social pressure to move on to the next man. This is a crucial moment in Huxley's effort to establish our narrative expectations in relation to the characterization of monogamy as a revolutionary act. For Lenina, her commitment to Henry Foster is surprising and difficult to explain, since it is outside of her sociolinguistic abilities. What she does describe is a sensation that she has not had the desire for others—monogamy by default. Why does Huxley treat monogamy in this manner? Why does he treat it as a surprising, almost unconscious irruption?

Given the narrative form of the typical dystopian fiction, it would seem more logical to place a realized and declared love (as in the romance between Winston and Julia in *1984*), rather than this monogamy by default, in conflict

with power. In Lenina's case, her long-term relationship with Henry Foster is
left to seem self-deludedly unaware. In Huxley's schema, this is a way of nat-
uralizing monogamy, or rather, indulging the notion that the desire for long-
term individual commitment is innate. For Lenina, it seems an instinctual
behavior that emerges against her will. It denies her conditioning and the state's
power to undo what nature has built.

This is, however, another feint. In Lenina's world, the normative values
regarding monogamy and sexual behavior inherited from Victorian England
are considered deviant and even subversive. For the readers this is, of course,
a substantial reversal of narrative expectations, particularly for Huxley's contemporaries. The kinds of sexual practices the state normalizes in *Brave New
World* would have been, and continue to be, read as anti-authoritarian or subversive. The behaviors Huxley describes are readily associated with "free love,"
but that term is wholly inappropriate for describing the conditions within his
novel. Free love is a standard component of experimental lifestyles, utopian
visions, and bohemianism. In common association, free love is set in opposition to orthodoxy, establishing a binary in which there must be unfree or
enforced modes of love. Although from our present perspective, the hyper-
charged and promiscuous lifestyle of the average citizen in Huxley's novel conforms to the modes of behavior we associate with free love or sex liberation, *in
situ* the term is entirely inappropriate and illegible.

The kind of sexual behavior that is truly shocking, that which we might
call free love for the *Brave New World*, is heterosexual procreative monogamy.
Monogamy is not just considered distasteful and gauche; it is viewed as absurdly
antisocial to even entertain the notion. Why does the state resist monogamy
in particular? Quite simply, because it is regarded as an unmediated form of
allegiance. Individual pleasure only exists as a correlative of a larger group pattern. Thus, any form of allegiance that bypasses the state as an intermediary is
contrary to its model of stability. The state's rationale for the prohibition of
monogamous relationships, and indeed any intimate relationship which claims
permanence on a one-to-one basis (in particular motherhood), is that such
connections engender feelings of possession and jealousy that induce the sublimation of desire. According to Controller Mond's Freudian logic, "*impulse
arrested spills over*" (*BNW* 45). In these terms, we are led to see monogamy as
a subversive act of unmediated free will, and, ultimately, as a natural behavior, and thus, as Zizek said, a "residue of the Real" that undermines artificial
state authority.

Of course, all of this is analogous to the folkloric narrative schema I've
described for *the word*. We imagine, even if the sexual practices in the novel
are conventional in our own eyes, that such practices will have a subversive effect
and produce a confrontation with power. Just as the Savage's commitment to
Shakespeare, and the liberating power of *the word*, invites us to interpret the
narrative in a certain manner, so too does this inversion of sexual practices.

We expect Bernard's longing for monogamy, or Lenina's seemingly natural participation in it, to be part of a story of resistance.

The Inversion

As we discover, John the Savage is not Prospero. He does not set the world straight with his books. His presence does not set in motion a final conflict with the totalitarian state. Though Huxley invites us to think in this manner, to assume that such a conflict would inevitably result, requires commitment to essentialist truths about the nature of power and resistance that the text actively undermines. As biographer Dana Sawyer notes, by the 1920s Huxley considered himself a Pyrrhonist, distrusting philosophies founded on essential truths (71). Yet, in *Brave New World,* Huxley asks us, again and again, to read the text through Enlightenment traditions and myths that elevate the notion of transcendent, essential truth. He asks us to read from a distinct cultural perspective and then dashes our expectations for conflict. Huxley upsets our expectations because the conditions of language changed drastically in the twentieth century. *The word* was no longer the truth for Huxley. This consideration distinguishes Huxley's novel within the dystopian genre and recognizes the transformation of the subversive in the twentieth century under the encroaching pressures of fascism, communism, modern commodity capitalism, psychoanalysis, mass culture, and a rapidly developing culture industry: all phenomena that deploy language and mythology to condition. If language, the signifier itself, has no inherent moral content, continuing to believe that words alone have a moral valance, is, as Huxley presents it, a dangerous capitulation to the mechanisms of power in mass culture.

Knowledge and Understanding

The central problem in *Brave New World* is the disconnection of knowledge from understanding — or the difference between basic literacy and comprehension — that is the prerequisite to moral agency. The director's behaviorist fable about Little Rubin, the Polish boy who absorbed English radio broadcasts while he slept, best illustrates this distinction. Little Rubin awakens one morning parroting complete lectures by George Bernard Shaw; yet, he has no insight into the words he utters. He can mimic, but he does not understand. He exemplifies the gap between *connaître* and *savoir*. As in Adorno's critique of jargon, simply knowing words does not constitute understanding.

John the Savage's knowledge of Shakespeare is, in its essence, the same. He is not armed with a critique of the world based on the narrative models *in* Shakespeare; he is, instead, equipped to *rename* the world. The Savage can rename Lenina "whore" but he cannot see Othello's folly. Even more importantly, he no more can see Lenina as an individual behaving in accordance with a conditioned value system than he can see himself. He may have literature in his possession, but he is functionally illiterate. He is, thus, unable to fulfill the folkloric narrative of rebellion.

In "Words and Behavior" Huxley writes, "Politics can become moral only on one condition: that its problems shall be spoken of and thought about exclusively in terms of concrete reality; that is to say, of persons" (*Collected Essays* 255). Politics, and its expressive vehicle, language, are bound up in the problem of mediating individuality and collectivity. The failure of all parties within Huxley's novel lies in their insistence on reading the world through aggregate, rather than individual, identities, masking concepts over faces.

Though the close of the novel is ultimately ambiguous, the Savage seems to come to a kind of tragic recognition, but it is unsatisfying. In the orgy of atonement in which the Savage attacks Lenina with a whip to satiate the crowd's desire for a new form of collective affirmation, the Savage demonstrates how he sees the girl switch to "woman." In his eyes, Lenina is not an individual, but rather, a signifier for an entire class of libidinous female transgressors. As he lashes out at her trembling form, he cries out, "fry, lechery, fry!" (*BNW* 258). In this line, we discover the manner in which Lenina has been denied individual identity throughout the novel. She has always been the fickle Cressida, exciting the Savage's jealousy and amorous desire at the expense of his higher moral love. When the Savage strikes her body, he is striking at a concept, not a person. He is engaging in what Huxley decries as the failure of politics.

In this manner, Huxley also reveals how literature is itself a source of peril. For as we encounter here, though Shakespeare's characters have realistic depth, they are not human, and their examples cannot adequately describe moral choices of free will, especially when they are read without a developed critical consciousness. The choice of *Troilus and Cressida*, a lesser work, shows the breadth of the Savage's reading, but his actions betray the emptiness of a reading without critical insight. Even the rarified words of Shakespeare may transform into demagoguery when tainted by what Huxley calls herd poison — the fever-inducing vector of a mob — the precursor to fascism. Words, in Huxley's critique, have a different kind of power; they are the signs of our conditioning. *The word* is not, as Enlightenment mythology would suppose, freedom. It does not carry the understanding and moral insight that constitutes our freedom. It is, in fact, a device: a system of signs that enrolls us in a cultural hierarchy, referencing the codes that prescribe and proscribe our judgments. Huxley feared that "language is, among other things, a device which men use for suppressing and distorting the truth" (*Collected Essays* 255). Power, in the Fordian state, works through language by limiting discursive horizons. There is little direct physical repression within the text. Indeed, the one depicted act of repression is more custodial than punitive. This is the most commonly sited distinction between *Brave New World* and *1984*: Huxley's dystopia is sustained by pleasure where Orwell's is sustained by force.

The power of the World State is exercised through conditioning and social engineering that circumvents the need to interact critically with words, ideas, or feelings. In this society, the power of literature has not been suppressed so much as it has simply withered away. Does this mean that Huxley has forgone hope for literature's ability to precipitate sweetness and light, to impart understanding?

In his musings on language and poetry, Helmholtz declares, "words can be like x-rays if you use them properly" (*BNW* 70), but of whom may we assume are the x-rays? Do they cut through the reader or do they reveal the interiority of the writer? Huxley seems acutely aware of the manner in which words can cut both ways. *This awareness is what precedes the subversive narrative strategies of this novel.* Contrary to the Enlightenment myths, Huxley's feints invite us to indulge what we discover is a narrative designed to expose their failure. Once Huxley has established a narrative trajectory, based on seemingly natural readings, he dashes our hopes and establishes a heterogeneous and uncertain state for *the word.*

This crisis is not simply limited to language, for as we discover through Huxley's feint regarding monogamy, the same contest with naturalized liberating power is being played out for sexuality as well. In this regard, Huxley's effort aims to link two distinct streams of thought to demonstrate the dynamic of power that operates through them. The best affirmation that there is a connection between these two elements lies in the Savage's reading of *Romeo and Juliet* to Helmholtz. The play is a capsule for both the elements we expect will produce conflict. As the Savage reads the play aloud, Helmholtz is at first impressed, declaring the play "a superb piece of emotional engineering" (*BNW* 184). This suggests that his encounter with Shakespeare might decondition Helmholtz, but his laughter quickly shatters this impression. Within his understanding, Shakespeare's narrative is not a tragedy. It is a farce. His response to the play evidences the disjuncture between culture and language: "The mother and father (grotesque obscenity) forcing the daughter to have some one she didn't want! And the idiotic girl not saying that she was having some one else (whom for the moment, at any rate) she preferred. In its smutty absurdity the situation was irresistibly comical" (*BNW* 184–185).

The language and sentiment of this tragedy are fundamentally illegible — beyond his comprehension. He is moved by neither the language nor the humanity of the situation. Helmholtz, who has been cultivated as a protean dissident, reveals how thoroughly distant he is from our expectations. This encounter with Shakespeare cannot undo his cognitive or sexual conditioning. Though he seems vulnerable to deconditioning, he is not moved to value monogamy; he cannot even fathom it. We are led to anticipate that one or the other element will move the characters into a direct conflict with power, but,

as this moment with Helmholtz reveals, our grounds for believing this are subject to our own commitment to a reading through the folkloric desires that
structure the standard dystopian narrative. It is in this realization that we
glimpse Huxley's purpose for leading us astray.

The narrative feints in *Brave New World* highlight the manner in which
one might gain the ability to contest power and to resist the culture industry's
tyrannical resolution of the unique to the orthodox, in the twentieth century
and beyond. Things like language and sexual practices, in and of themselves,
are devoid of any ability to define. They are themselves subject to definition.
Language, sex, art, the whole range of human practices, are assessed through
a process of reading and writing. They are subject to a system of understanding, and understanding is arrived at through a process of comparing existing
narratives and assumptions. Huxley's dystopian narrative disrupts, but relies
upon a whole set of codes for legibility. It is what Barthes called *scriptable* or
writerly. Huxley foregrounds the text's narrative structure and its manipulation of the reader, and, thus, incites the reader's participation in production of
the text. Huxley asks us to put the writing/reading process itself, not its language or its moral content, but the cognitive processes of constructing a text,
under observation. In this way, Huxley sustains a role for literature as a means
of contesting power, while extirpating it from the messianic implications of
Arnold's "sweetness and light."

The primary difference between the society in *The Island*, Huxley's utopia,
and in *Brave New World*, is that the culture of the former teaches critical distancing. Art and literature are granted no intrinsic value on the island. The culture of the island, which appears to be a utopia, is, in fact, critical of
end-of-history narratives. Its utopia is a continuously renewed state of critical awareness. The mechanisms of its culture, the practices that condition its
citizens, exhort reflection and awareness—being "here and now" (*The Island*
7).

In the essay "Knowledge and Understanding," Huxley writes, "Knowledge
is always in terms of concepts and can be passed on by means of words or other
symbols. Understanding is not conceptual, and therefore cannot be passed on.
It is an immediate experience, and immediate experience can only be talked
about (very inadequately), never shared" (*Collected Essays* 378). It would seem
that Huxley was true to his insistence that understanding cannot be explained.
The narrative feints in this novel do the only thing possible under such a belief:
they invoke the problem of the text to offer the reader a reflective critical experience, for that is the only manner in which Huxley's designs can be commu-
nicated. This narrative structure is the illusion or storm that Huxley conjures
to impart understanding through experience.

Notes

1. An earlier version of this paper was presented at the April 2004 Society for the Study of Narrative Literature Conference, University of Vermont/Middlebury College, Burlington, Vermont.

2. The battle between Gilliam and Sheinberg/Universal Studios is itself mythologized as a narrative of anti-authoritarian subversion, casting Gilliam as a heroic artist-insurgent. Though Gilliam's black-comic cut had been released internationally, it was Sheinberg's judgment that his own version, which is eleven minutes shorter and concludes with a "happy ending," would be more profitable in the American market. Sheinberg and Universal Studios attempted to bar Gilliam from screening his version in North America. Gilliam, famously, responded by screening "clips" (constituted of his film in its entirety) for critics and film students, resulting in a press war and, ultimately, a public victory for the director. See Jack Matthews, *The Battle for Brazil: Terry Gilliam v. Universal Studios in the Fight to the Final Cut* (New York: Applause Books, 2000).

Works Cited

Adorno, Theodor. *The Jargon of Authenticity*. Translated by Knut Tarnowski and Fredric Will. Evanston, IL: Northwestern University Press, 1973.

Barthes, Roland. *S/Z: An Essay*. 1974. Translated by Richard Miller. New York: Hill and Wang, 2000.

Foucault, Michel. *Discipline and Punishment: The Birth of the Prison*. 1979. Translated by Alan Sheridan. New York: Vintage, 1995.

_____. *The History of Sexuality: An Introduction*. Vol 1. 1978. Translated by Robert Hurley. New York: Vintage, 1990.

Horkheimer, Max, and Theodor Adorno. *The Dialectic of Enlightenment*. Translated by John Cumming. New York: Herder and Herder, 1972. First published 1944.

Huxley, Aldous. *Brave New World*. 1932. New York: Perennial Classics, 1996.

_____. *Collected Essays*, New York: Harper and Brothers, 1959.

_____. *Island*. 1962, New York: Perennial Classics, 2002.

Johnson, Samuel. "Preface to Shakespeare," 1765. In *Samuel Johnson Selected Poetry and Prose*, edited by Frank Brady and W. K. Wimsatt, 299–336. Berkeley: University of California Press, 1978.

Propp, V. I. *Morphology of the Folktale*. 2nd ed. Translated by Laurence Scott. Austin, TX: University of Texas Press, 1968. First published 1928.

Sawyer, Dana. *Aldous Huxley: A Biography*. New York: Crossroad Publishing, 2002.

Sisk, David W. *Transformations of Language in Modern Dystopias*. London: Greenwood Press, 1997.

Tennyson, Alfred Lord. "The Play," in *Demeter and Other Poems*. London: Macmillan, 1889. Reprinted in *The Poetic and Dramatic Works of Alfred Lord Tennyson*, 555. Whitefish, MT: Kessinger Publishing, 2004.

Zizek, Slavoj. "The Undergrowth of Enjoyment." *New Formations* 9 (1989): 7–29. Reprinted in *The Zizek Reader*, edited by Elizabeth Wright and Edmond Wright, 11–36. Malden, MA: Blackwell Publishers, 1999.

Brave New World and Ralph Ellison's Invisible Man

JOHN COUGHLIN

My first exposure to Aldous Huxley's *Brave New World* came when I was about ten years old. My mother was teaching a catechism class to a room full of junior high students, and having been brought along for lack of a babysitter, I was sitting in the back working my way through my "Classics of Science Fiction" coloring book. Twenty worlds all bound together between a dog-eared, oversized cover, it was the favorite of my growing collection. Working from beginning to end, I had already made my way through the shifting desert landscape of the *Martian Chronicles*, across the iron deck of the *Nautilus* entwined in the glistening tentacles of a giant squid, and into the tropical jungles of *The Lost World*, thick with bubbling tar pits, enormous ferns and dagger-toothed dinosaurs. Now, finally, I found myself on the very last page of the book. It was a page I had dreaded, for it didn't feature any of the fixtures of science fiction I found so appealing — no flashing computers or stoic aliens. No, this page depicted an emaciated young man, eyes wide and terrified, hands raised before his face as if he were awaiting the blow of an axe. Around him spun what seemed to be a never-ending double helix of human embryos encased in bottles. Many years later, I can still see those eyes and remember how even at the time I thought he looked to me as if he were about to be crushed beneath some huge, unseen object.

Fast forward into the future: languishing between jobs after graduating from college, I was staying at my sister's apartment and one afternoon, bored, picked a copy of Ralph Ellison's *Invisible Man* off her bookshelf. Reading through the prologue, I found myself fascinated by the nameless narrator, surviving like a mole under the weight of a dark and unsympathetic city. As fate would have it, I didn't get the opportunity to finish the novel at that time, but I was left with the impression that here too was a man who had been crushed beneath some faceless, unstoppable force.

Just recently having completed in their entirety both *Invisible Man* and *Brave New World*, I am once again struck by how similar they are in theme. Both books are, without a doubt, political in nature, and at this level, seem

completely dissimilar — *Invisible Man* attempts to illuminate the social entrap-
ment of black Americans, while *Brave New World* cautions against an over
reliance on technology and the amorality it can potentially inspire. At a deeper
level, however, both books are also about the status of the individual in society, and it is here that there is a remarkable similarity between the two novels.
For in both, we see men fighting against societies that devalue their individuality and thereby lessen their sense of identity and self-worth. "I've always tried
to create characters who were pretty forthright in stating what they felt society should be," said Ellison in a 1963 interview (Geller 85). This statement captures the underlying theme of both novels: that an ideal society is one that is
founded upon the ability of individuals to assert themselves freely and without prejudice. Close examination of both works show that while they are wildly
different in many ways, at this one level, they are very much the same.

In order to see this similarity in theme more clearly, we must first peel back
the layer of political meaning, which isn't easy. These are both political novels
on the surface, and sixty years of critical commentary that has focused
specifically on this level has done little to make an alternative reading any eas-
ier. However, we can find support for the idea that these stories are primarily
about individualism in the comments of the writers themselves. "All novels are
about certain minorities," says Ellison, "The individual is a minority. The universal in the novel — and isn't that what we're all clamoring for these days?— is
reached only through the description of the specific man in a specific circum-
stance" (Chester 9). Huxley says something along the same lines in the forward
to a later edition of *Brave New World*: "The theme of *Brave New World* is not
the advancement of science as such; it is the advancement of science as it affects
human individuals" (Huxley 16). Both statements suggest that Ellison and Huxley are more concerned about the state of the individual than the state of society, and this is an important distinction for one of the more subtle points of
both novels is that the health of society is determined by the health of the individuals of which it is composed.

The sickness inherent in both societies becomes apparent early on. *In Invisible Man*, Ellison depicts a classed society in which a select group of people uses
the narrator for their own selfish purposes, refusing to see the inherent individual worth beyond the color of his skin. One of our first examples of this is
when Mr. Norton, the wealthy supporter of the institute the narrator attends,
describes how the students there are all building blocks in his destiny. "'I mean
that upon you depends the outcome of the years I have spent in helping your
school,' says Mr. Norton, growing teary eyed upon reflection of his charity,
'That has been my real life's work, not my banking or my researches, but my
first hand organizing of human life'" (42). By asserting that he is responsible
for "organizing" the young narrator's life, Mr. Norton is implying that he is
somehow responsible for the man's future worth to society. This is diametrically opposed to the idea Ellison is trying to develop in the book, that such

achievement (and its accompanying sense of accomplishment) rests entirely on the shoulders of the narrator. Enforcing this point during one interview, Ellison remarked that the narrator "must assert and achieve his own humanity; he cannot run with the pack and do this" (Chester 16). In order for the narrator of *Invisible Man* to achieve humanity, therefore, he must shed the misconception that his life has been organized by anyone but himself and count any achievement as solely his own.

Mr. Norton's use of the word "organization" is not without significance when comparing *Invisible Man* to *Brave New World*, for in this second novel, we see a society where organization has been taken to the extreme. In the Brave New World, the highest tiers of individuals (labeled as Alphas and Betas and led by the illustrious Mustapha Mond, an Alpha double plus) have organized the more numerous lower classes (Deltas and Epsilons) into what they consider efficient and contented sub-races, "modeled" on nothing so cold and inhuman as an iceberg: "The optimum population," said Mustapha Mond, "is modeled on the iceberg-eight ninths below the water, one ninth above" (172). The Alphas and Betas believe that they have invented the perfect workforce-one that is happy, well organized, and, above all, incapable of asserting individual will against the upper classes because of lower intellectual capabilities and preoccupation with work. When Mr. Norton talks to the narrator of *Invisible Man* about his fate, we see shades of Mustapha Mond: "If you become a good farmer, a chef, a preacher, doctor, singer, mechanic, — whatever you become, and even if you fail, you are my fate" (44). In keeping with the mission of the Tuskegee Institute, it is noteworthy that the vocations mentioned by Mr. Norton are all ones that will keep the narrator out of a position where he might challenge Mr. Norton's authority by asserting his own. Mr. Norton is, in essence, organizing the narrator into a perfect Epsilon, pigeonholed into an innocuous social position and securely submerged below the waterline.

The idea of keeping an individual preoccupied with meaningless tasks so that he might never question his own individuality is an important one, for throughout *Invisible Man* we are reminded of the line "keep the nigger running." The narrator spends most of the book doing just that, shuffling from one situation to the next almost against his will, until we wonder whether he'll ever stop and evaluate where he's at and where he's going. "The major flaw in the hero's character," says Ellison, "is his unquestioning willingness to do what is required of him by others as a way to success" (Chester 15). It is because of this willingness to fulfill others' expectations that he is never able to get a firm grasp on his own identity or sense of individuality. It is not until the end of the action, when the narrator has slipped out of society completely and found himself alone and isolated, that he is finally able to stop running and evaluate himself as an individual based on his own terms.

The citizens of *Brave New World* are constantly running, too. From birth they are conditioned via "hypnopaedia" to dread being alone, for isolation breeds introspection that in turns fosters a sense of individuality. This is expressed in a wonderfully satiric scene where Bernard takes Lenina out on their first date — he suggests that they go for a walk along the mall and talk, but she, finding such an activity completely distasteful, instead persuades him to take her to the Semi-Demi Finals of the Woman's Heavyweight Wrestling Championship.

That the fabric of the *Brave New World* is strengthened by needless labor is later born out by Mustapha Mond. "The experiment was tried, more than a century and a half ago," he says, describing why Epsilons work seven-hour days, "The whole of Ireland was put on to the four-hour day. What was the result? Unrest and a large increase in the consumption of soma; that's all" (172).

In *Brave New World*, as in *Invisible Man*, isolation from labor leads inevitably to unrest and instability. The solution? To keep the citizens running by having them perform worthless labor under the auspices that they are contributing to society.

Worthless labor is not the only way that the powers that be in *Invisible Man* and *Brave New World* exercise control over their societies. In both novels, hallucinogenic drugs are perceived as evils that dull the senses and destroy one's sense of urgency and desire for action. In *Brave New World* this comes in the form of soma, a perfect designer drug the citizens consume whenever they have the slightest psychological or physical ill. In many ways, soma represents the perfect form of mind control, as it ultimately dulls all stimuli that would move an individual to independent thought and revolution. In *Invisible Man*, the importance of drugs in suppressing one's individuality and desire for action is not as pronounced as in *Brave New World*, but we see it here and there, particularly in the book's prologue when the narrator talks about a vision he had while smoking marijuana. "I haven't smoked reefer since," he says, "not because they're illegal, but because to see around corners is enough (that is not unusual when you're invisible). But to hear around them is too much; it inhibits action. And despite Brother Jack and all that sad lost period of the Brotherhood, I believe in nothing if not action" (13). While the reefer in *Invisible Man* is decidedly less sinister than the soma in *Brave New World*, this passage nonetheless illustrates a common theme in both books— that drugs have the ability to warp reality and subdue the individual into a mode of inaction.

In reality, however, it's not really drugs the writers are rallying against, but rather what they symbolize — the ability for any artificial stimuli to distract an individual's attention from a fight for self-assertion. Ellison discusses the use of symbol where he talks about Picasso: "Symbols serve a dual function: they allow the artist to speak of complex experiences and to annihilate time with simple lines and curves; and they allow the viewer an orientation, both emotional and associative, which goes so deep that a total culture may resound in a simple rhythm, an image" (Chester 10). In this regard, drugs in both stories are a symbol for an easy out in the oftentimes-painful search for identity.

Do the heroes of *Invisible Man* and *Brave New World* find their individuality, and if so, how? In *Invisible Man*, this is hard to say, for we are confronted with a narrator who is really at the beginning of a new story. Having severed himself from society, he supposedly has become aware of his own identity. Nonetheless, we can't help but feel a little bit skeptical of this revelation — didn't we see variations of this already, first in his expulsion from school, then in his discovery of Dr. Bledsoe's treachery, and then in his entry into the Brotherhood? It's not unfair to wonder if this newfound "invisibility" is really a more enlightened state of being or just another dead end he'll eventually have to wander out of. Without having another chapter to tell us, it's impossible to say for certain, but one could conjecture that the character has found the wisdom for which he was searching: "Each time he allows someone else to define him," says Ellison, "to give him an identity or an identity which he tries to assume, he runs into difficulty. And so in the last chapter, he becomes aware of this when he starts burning all these papers to make light for himself" (Crewdson 259). Thus, the invisible man finds his sense of individuality by burning away all of his old identities and by disassociating himself from the society that created them. This final act makes the ultimate tone of the book uplifting, at least in the sense that the narrator has found what he was looking for, and in that it offers a glimmer of hope for others involved in a similar quest.

The situation in *Brave New World* has interesting parallels. First, as in *Invisible Man*, Bernard and Helmholtz are ejected from society by being shipped off at the novel's end to an island where they will live the rest of their days in exile with other "revolutionaries." There, Mustapha Mond assures them, they can pursue their individuality to their hearts' content without "infecting" other elements of society. Bernard and Helmholtz, when compared to the narrator of *Invisible Man*, however, have a much more muted reaction to this affirmation of their individuality (Bernard, when told he is to be exiled, actually becomes so hysterical that he has to be sedated in soma spray). In this sense, they have not discovered their true sense of identity but rather stumbled into it accidentally.

A closer parallel to the narrator of *Invisible Man* exists in the Huxley's character of John the Savage (who is actually *Brave New World*'s most humane individual). He possesses a sense of individuality from his introduction so his journey is less one of discovery than of reaffirmation. It is in John's ultimate fate that we see perhaps the most interesting dissimilarity between *Invisible Man* and *Brave New World*, for unlike the narrator of Ellison's novel, John cannot separate himself from society — Mustapha Mond has determined that John will remain a part of the society whether he wants to be or not.

> "He said he wanted to go on with the experiment. But I'm damned," the Savage added with sudden fury, "I'm damned if I'll go on being experimented with. Not for all the Controllers in the world. I shall go away tomorrow too."
> "But where?" the others asked in unison.

"The Savage shrugged his shoulders. "Anywhere. I don't care. So long as I can be alone" [186].

And off John goes to be alone, but his separation from society proves a short one, for the denizens of the *Brave New World* have by this time become infatuated with his exotic ways, and it is not long before they have hunted him down, forced him to confront their inane reality that he despises, and ultimately drive him to commit suicide out of an overwhelming sense of despair. Death is the only act remaining to him that he can be solely responsible for choosing. There is no escape in exile: the only way out for the true individual in such a world is death.

In his foreword to the 1946 edition of *Brave New World*, Huxley describes John's lack of choices in asserting his individuality as a flaw of the novel, and remarks that if he were to rewrite it, he would have John travel to an intermediary world between the Indian reservation whence he came and the Brave New World, where "he had an opportunity of learning something at first hand about the nature of a society composed of freely co-operating individuals devoted to the pursuit of sanity" (15). Had the book been written this way, I believe it would have been closer in spirit to *Invisible Man* in that there would have been a glimmer of hope, however small, that an individual might still assert himself and find his own identity. We are left instead with only the Brave New World and its crushing social conformism that leaves no room for individual identity.

Following this same line, there is one other interesting (albeit troubling) parallel between the two novels, and this is a comparison between the characters of Todd Clifton and Lenina. Both characters, like the narrator of *Invisible Man* and John of *Brave New World*, seem to have a moment of self-enlightenment, but it is a strange inversion of the enlightenment experienced by the primary characters. In Lenina's case, this moment comes when she visits John in the very last scene: "Her blue eyes seemed to grow larger, brighter; and suddenly two tears rolled down her cheeks" (197).

The fact that Lenina had the emotion of pathos was her greatest assertion of individual humanity and compassion, with compassion heretofore an unknown element.

Compare this with the narrator's description of Todd Clifton in *Invisible Man*: "It was Clifton, riding easily back and forth on his knees, flexing his legs without shifting his feet, his right shoulder raised at an angle and his arm pointing stiffly at the bouncing doll as he spieled from the corner of his mouth." "Who else wants little Sambo before we take it on the lambo. Speak up, ladies and gentleman, who wants little...?" [433].

In *Brave New World*, Lenina realizes the virtue of John's ways and shows for the first time in the novel true affection for someone despite her conditioning to *not* be emotionally attached to a single person. Similarly, in *Invisible*

Man, Todd Clifton sheds his aura of respectability and becomes a dealer of Sambo dolls on the sidewalk. In both cases, the characters are demonstrating their individuality by disassociating themselves with what is expected of them. In comparing their fates with those of the main characters, we can see another interesting parallel: Lenina lives where John dies; Todd dies where the narrator of *Invisible Man* lives. It almost seems like Lenina and Todd act as counterweights to what is happening to the main characters (John and the narrator, respectively). In Lenina's conversion maybe we are supposed to see a tenuous thread of hope for the individual, while in Todd's death, the inevitable fate of someone who bucks the system. Thus, perhaps the tone of the respective novels, as determined by the fate of its primary characters, is not intended as an absolute, but rather as only one possibility.

Both *Invisible Man* and *Brave New World* share common themes as works of literature. Symbolically, they are representative of an individual's fight for recognition and self-determination in a tyrannical society that devalues individual worth. Despite their many similarities, however, the novels seem to diverge in their final opinion of whether the individual has a place in our society. Perhaps this is in the nature of the novels themselves, for each was written with a slightly different intent: *Invisible Man* to inspire greater freedom for all people in an existing American system, and *Brave New World* to inspire fear and loathing towards a possible future system that we still have time to avoid. It is because of this close affinity to our own distinctly American reality that *Invisible Man* offers a ray of hope where *Brave New World* does not. The invisible man must persist, because if he does not, there is no hope for our future. "The thing that Americans have to learn over and over again," said Ellison shortly before his death, "is that they are individuals with individual vision" (Townley 391). It is upon the strengths of these individuals that our entire society is built. And unlike John, the embattled "savage" of *Brave New World*, whose desperation I recognized even as a child peering into a coloring book, the individuals in *Invisible Man* still have the power to make themselves heard and continue the grand cycle of applying their "individual vision" to the tapestry of society.

Works Cited

Chester, Allfred, and Vilma Howard. "The Art of Fiction: An Interview." In *Conversations with Ralph Ellison*, edited by Amritjit Singh and Maryemma Graham. Jackson, Mississippi: University Press of Mississippi, 1995.

Crewdson, Arlene, and Rita Thomson. "Interview With Ralph Ellison." In *Conversations with Ralph Ellison*, edited by Amritjit Singh and Maryemma Graham. Jackson, Mississippi: University Press of Mississippi, 1995.

Ellison, Ralph. *Invisible Man*. New York: Vintage Books, 1995.

Geller, Alan. "An Interview with Ralph Ellison." In *Conversations with Ralph Ellison*, edited by Amritjit Singh and Maryemma Graham. Jackson, Mississippi: University Press of Mississippi, 1995.

Graham, Maryemma, and Amritjit Singh, eds. *Conversations with Ralph Ellison*. Jackson, Mississippi: University Press of Mississippi, 1995.
Huxley, Aldous. *Brave New World and Brave New World Revisited*. New York: Harper Collins, 1957.
Townley, Roderick. "Television Makes Us See One Another." In *Conversations with Ralph Ellison*, edited by Amritjit Singh and Maryemma Graham. Jackson, Mississippi: University Press of Mississippi, 1995.

"O brave new world that has no poets in it": Shakespeare and Scientific Utopia in Brave New World

PAUL SMETHURST

The fact that Huxley's satiric vision of scientific utopia introduces Shakespeare as a symbol of high art has led some critics to accuse the author of cultural arrogance.[1] But I would argue that the positioning of Shakespeare in the Brave New World envisioned by Huxley is ambivalent, especially when read from a twenty-first-century perspective. From a conventional, liberal, humanist point of view, Shakespeare is the champion of that high art which conveys the values of a free society while speaking of the ideals of truth and beauty. Low art, on the other hand, is a distraction, performing rather than discoursing on the values of free society. Low art is therefore negatively associated with mass culture and an uncritical consumerist society. In the abstract, hypothetical and impossibly schematic world that Huxley conjures up, high art confronts low art in a culture war, which it seems bound to lose, although that defeat is surely ironic. In other words, and again from a liberal, humanist position, we are compelled to read the self-destruction of the Shakespeare-spouting Savage, the exile of the doubters and the uninterrupted stasis of the scientific utopia as unnatural and not a reasonable envisioning of the state of things in a future Western society. This conclusion to the novel is not intended as prediction of the future but as incitement to the cultured classes of intellectuals to find ways of avoiding such realization of a scientific utopia and to fight for those humanist values of individual freedom that Shakespeare somehow guarantees. The freethinking individual is being asked to prevail over blind, unthinking compliance with capitalist, totalitarian rule and to reject a future in which individuals are reduced to genetically engineered and emotionally conditioned "mass beings." A liberal society is one which privileges individual freedom and expression above social well-being and stability for all, and a liberal, humanist reading of the novel assumes a comfortable middle-class readership for whom even the promise of achieving Alpha status in a world without poverty, disease, war and crime would not be sufficient compensation for losing the right, however illusory, to think and act as individual beings.

The role of Shakespeare in this clash between middle-class individualism and scientific utopia is iconic and dramatic. If Shakespeare is to prevail, then his words must find a way through the emotional engineering and sleep training that has helped bring social stability at the cost of freethinking and private emotion. Probably as a matter of design, despite plenty of opportunities, in the latter half of the novel, Shakespeare turns out to be misunderstood or engaged with on a sentimental level at best, and a figure of ridicule at worst. But this culture war may be less one of high principles and low instincts and more a matter of class. From a middle-class perspective, Shakespeare is a bastion of those human values that speak to us of beauty, destiny, and higher thoughts and feelings, whose loss, through design or irrelevance, betokens the end of a particular kind of civilization. Clearly, Huxley did not have in mind a causal relation here — i.e., that the end of Shakespeare might precipitate the fall of the world. But there is a clear correlation between, on the one hand, individual freedom and the high culture that Shakespeare stands for with its associated privileging of individual freedom, and, on the other, low art, mass culture and mass being.

One must peer into that abyss that follows the end of Shakespeare and high culture, and connect this with the progress of science toward the kind of utopia Huxley was warning us against — or was he? Rather than taking the more usual dystopian reading of the novel, I would like instead to take a neutral position by entertaining the possibility of scientific utopia and questioning the aesthetic, structural, and political reasons why Shakespeare would have to be excluded from it. Many features of present-day society and Huxley's *Brave New World* converge. Not only are technological possibilities and global (utopian) economic aspirations bringing us closer to Huxley's vision of the future, but also coincidentally, or perhaps not, Shakespeare and high culture are being turned inside out by postmodernism. This situation demands a different approach to *Brave New World*. From today's perspective, the novel is more evenly poised than it was, and that charge of cultural arrogance that is consequent on a humanist, dystopian reading of *Brave New World* no longer holds. The argument, similar to that of the Controller in the novel, is that scientific utopia precludes Shakespeare, because he is seen as regressive, conservative, attached to metaphysics and theology, and, conversely, because the aesthetics through which he speaks are disordering, disruptive, and dialectical, and so have no place in a stable utopia at the end of history.

The exclusion of Shakespeare from scientific utopia because he is a regressive figure associated with high art is an argument already presented in the novel itself. But I would also argue that he would have to be excluded because of the textual strategies that poeticize nature, the world and human being. These strategies are not only regressive, but they may also be revolutionary by introducing an aesthetics of instability and ordered chaos that would run counter to the stability demanded in utopia. There are two main themes which inform this rereading of *Brave New World*: one is contemporary, namely the recent "firings" of the English canon of literature and the repositioning of high art in postmodern society; and the other is already there in Huxley's own prescient views on relations between literature and science expressed in his essays. This is an against-the-grain reading of *Brave New World* in which Shakespeare is not redeemed by bracketing off the Brave New World as a dystopian fantasy. Instead, we must face his demise (or read him differently) in the face of greater convergence between Huxley's Brave New World and a postmodern scientific utopia. Although "utopia" is not quite the right term to use here, the globality we inhabit has structural similarities with the kind of scientific utopia Huxley believed might be achievable. At the beginning of the twenty-first century, as societies across the globe become more connected and interdependent than at any time before, there is a common aspiration for a stable society in which technology and consumerism are foremost.[1] In which case, and if Shakespeare and scientific utopia are indeed mutually exclusive, we may eventually have to face the fact that we are entering a phase of history where Shakespeare no longer speaks to us, or at least not with humanist inflection.

Because the high art of Shakespeare is displaced in the novel by low art, a dystopian reading of Huxley's vision implying cultural elitism seems inevitable. In real life, the masses might be happy with their recreational drugs and low art but for the Alphas whom Huxley addresses, high art is surely a means to elevate themselves above the masses. But suppose now, as is fashionable in North American universities, we no longer admit that Shakespeare or that whole idea of literature and the canon is essentially good for us, and there is no intrinsic literary-critical difference between *Jurassic Park* and *Mansfield Park*. Given this shift, we might then agree with Huxley's Controller that scientific utopia has no need of Shakespeare. A world without Shakespeare is not necessarily the dystopia of banal total entertainment playing to the elite as well as to the dumbed-down masses. Indeed, for most people today, even for Alphas, Shakespeare has already become largely redundant or been reinvented for a mass audience, and this does not seem such an awful proposition as it did perhaps for Huxley's original audience.

To admit the criticism that Huxley is guilty of cultural arrogance is to see Shakespeare as representing the best of culture in contradistinction to the banal distractions offered to the Brave New Worldians at the feelies. The Savage is put into the unlikely position (Huxley admits this himself in the preface) of the voice of reason, and he becomes the defender of high art. His acquaintance with Shakespeare informs his thinking and reasoning, and Shakespeare's texts are the poetic filter through which he regards and judges the Brave New World. In other words, the Savage speaks to us of his complaint with this future world through the familiar texts and value systems of Shakespeare. As Huxley has himself admitted, the Savage is being set up on the horns of an impossible dilemma — a choice between a primitive existence tamed and enriched through familiarity with Shakespeare, or life in the perfect but saccharine happiness of a scientific utopia. The choice is monstrously hypothetical — this is satire, not a realist novel. If Huxley felt that he might improve the novel by introducing a third option for the Savage, an option in which he was offered the choice of some borderlands or exile in which he would converse with people in between the new world and the old, he was mistaken. Not only would the novel lose its structure and its dramatic force, it would also split the field of Shakespeare between the primitive ground of nature where it is now, and the complex ground of margins and exiles (the blasted heaths and storm-lashed islands) which also have such powerful agency in Shakespeare's plays.

The choice offered to Huxley's implied audience of Alphas is equally improbable and binary: either a stable society of conditioned and cushioned happiness or a passionate and engaged humanity tossed on the stormy seas of war, envy, and unrequited love: the world of *Othello* or the world of bumble-puppy, scent organs and the feelies. In his final showdown with the Controller, the discursive crux of the novel, the Savage explicitly pits *Othello* against Helmholtz's latest feelie, *Three Weeks in a Helicopter*, although the only connection between them is that both have black men as heroes. Helmholtz is a link back to Shakespeare from Brave New World, a liminal or residual memory of a time when words attached to a deeper level of meaning (of which more later). In this intertextual universe, Helmholtz and the Savage are mere players, unaware of the greater spheres of meaning understood by the Controller, whose role is authorial and authoritarian, and by Huxley's middle-class readership. The Controller is familiar with the plays of Shakespeare and all the major texts of Western history and literature. His knowledge of texts appears to give him power over the rest of society, which in itself suggests that the power circles in scientific utopia extend beyond simple class conditioning. He can quote Shakespeare at will, yet forbids others to read the texts or perform the plays. The reasons he gives the Savage are firstly progressive: *Othello* is old and beautiful, and "we don't want people to be attracted to old things. We want them to like the new ones" (*BNW* 200); secondly conservative, under the guise of pragmatism, "people couldn't understand it" and the reason they couldn't understand it is, he says: "Because our world is not the same as Othello's world … you can't make tragedies without social instability" (*BNW* 200–1).

Of course, no world was ever the same as Othello's world; it is the role of literature to imagine other worlds. The Controller's Brave New World is also an imaginative world, and in many respects, a much better world than that of Othello. The Controller's argument here is that there is no need for a literature that is concerned with common human emotions, because scientific utopia has eradicated the triggers for those emotions. This in itself does not make Shakespeare irrelevant, any more than is a literature irrelevant that is created in a world where gods and spirits are assumed to control human destiny. The people of this Brave New World are conditioned to be incurious, so there is no interest in how people were or how they might otherwise be. Scientific utopia is no place for poetry or history, because in ideal times, alternatives are unconceivable.

Nevertheless, the Savage is still repulsed by the low art that utopia produces. The Controller agrees that it is good, but argues that for the sake of stability high art must be sacrificed. The Controller inevitably wins this and all other arguments—the dialogues are Socratic and weighted in his favor. He speaks from a unique position of power informed not only by scientific and historical knowledge, but also knowledge of the kind offered by high art, not least the ability to turn an argument on its head and the dangerous ability to dazzle with words. The conversations between the Controller and the Savage are designed not only to expose the error of savage ways, but also, to undermine Shakespeare. With his Miranda-like sensibility, a primitive of noble birth, brought up in a remote place on a rich diet of literature, the Savage is a misfit and a parodic figure in scientific utopia. By using Shakespeare's texts as his window on this world, Shakespeare is implicated in this parody.

The Shakespeare–spouting Savage is an absurd and problematic figure. Through him, Huxley connects the noble savage — a creature of nature, not of civilization — with the best values of high art figured in the works of Shakespeare. He is not just an educated fool, because he is also genetically a citizen of the Brave New World: it is his nurture rather than his nature that is primitive. The Savage could therefore be viewed as a regressive human, genetically linked to the ruling classes but nurtured as a primitive. Here, the inheritance plot goes wrong because, just as scientific utopia is no place for Shakespeare, neither is it the place for the Victorian bourgeois fantasy of the poor orphan finding his rightful place in society. The Savage is a regressive Brave New Worldian who confronts the Brave New World afresh through the filter of Shakespeare's poeticized world: a world which although it never actually existed, alludes to and presages the first blooming of modernity. Shakespeare came to prominence in a time when people were beginning to challenge nature and learning to negotiate boundaries between private and public realms. The Savage's journey from the reservation through the imaginary world of Shakespeare to the scientific utopia of the Brave New World is a journey, we could say, from one end of modernity to the other: to the end of modernity as the total triumph of human over nature. Furthermore, it is these two ends, and *ends* in the teleological sense of modernity, that the novel brings into question. We may be forced to ask if Shakespeare really is still relevant at the end of modernity where we can find the full flush of scientific utopia, and if so, to whom does he speak? At the beginning of modernity, in his own time, Shakespeare may have spoken across the spectrum to the commoners and to the court; in the late eighteenth century, he was appropriated in England by a highbrow conspiracy to confirm and consolidate national power structures. Shakespeare has been a lynchpin of high culture and a national institution. But in postmodernity, as distinctions between high and low art are relaxed and national institutions are reexamined, Shakespeare is used differently. We might speak today of a spectral Shakespeare whose famous lines are extracted from their context to echo across unfamiliar times and territories. *Brave New World* not only anticipates a scientific utopia that finds no relevance for Shakespeare, but also anticipates the casual and out-of-context use of his poetry in advertising and smart one-liners. Shakespeare, in the novel, and in present-day society, evokes a lost sense of beauty and exploits a residual memory of high art whose meaning, if it ever existed, has dissipated into superficial and sentimental affect.

> Nay, but to live
> In the rank sweat of an enseamed bed,
> Stew'd in corruption, honeying and making love
> Over the nasty sty ... (*Hamlet*, Act III, Scene IV, ll: 92–95)

When the Savage first reads Shakespeare, he has little idea what these lines from *Hamlet* could possibly mean, but he recognizes a strong magic in them. These half-understood words provoke rage in the Savage who now finds a reason for hating Popé, his mother's lover. But this is surely a reason that goes beyond reason, equivalent to the beating of drums, men singing for corn and the rest of the native magic around him. This is the Savage's Shakespeare, the emotional fuel that drives him to extremes of love and hate that are Oedipal in their intensity and simplicity. Although he does not understand the words or the stories that they come from, the Savage finds that Shakespeare makes his hatred for Popé more real. In Shakespeare then, the Savage finds a window onto the world, and a means for conveying reality, as well as the words that charge that reality with emotion. This reality, such as it is, has little relevance to scientific utopia. So, when the Savage is brought into the new world, his reality prop no longer works for him. The absurdity of the Savage's position is revealed when he ineptly explores the theme of love. Shakespeare does not always treat courtly love seriously. For example, Malvolio is upbraided for trying to raise his game in *Twelfth Night* by using language beyond his station. He is turned from would-be lover to object of ridicule. In *Brave New World*, the Savage tries to woo the receptive and pneumatic Lenina by using the language of Shakespeare. He begins well enough with lines from *The Tempest:* "'Admired Lenina ... indeed the top of admiration, worth what's dearest in the world." When the Savage quotes *The Tempest* ("Oh, you so perfect ... and so peerless are created ... of every creature's best"), Lenina is already in the mood for love. But the Savage has other ideas. He wants to deserve her love, an idea that he derives from primitive society where a man might bring the skin of a lion as a token of his love. This is also an idea that he derives from Shakespeare, where love can never lead to immediate gratification, for that would simply be animal lust. In Shakespeare's plays, love is a long-drawn-out business, which does not always end well. The Savage at least expects to wait for marriage ceremonies to be complete and again quotes from *The Tempest*: "If thou dost break her virgin knot before all sanctimonious ceremonies may with full and holy rite ..." (*BNW* 174) But, no virgin, and quite sufficiently wooed, Lenina is already stripping for action. As his sexual excitement increases, the Savage shifts from words of love to demands of restraint. The Savage is shocked by Lenina's direct sexual advance and repulsed by the poetry she cites from the Feelies. But for Lenina, it is the words of the Savage and of Shakespeare that make no sense. In a world in which instant gratification is the norm, his language simply confuses and frustrates her.

The words and gestures of courtly love have no meaning in this society. There is no need here to channel sexual desire and frustration into poetry. In determining to delay the sexual act until he has proven himself worthy and then married her, the Savage regards Lenina quite inappropriately and ironically as Miranda in *The Tempest*. Putting Shakespeare's words into this modern context makes a mockery of so-called high art. It seems impossible to see the world through this travesty, and we inevitably read the situation from Lenina's perspective. The situation is the more ludicrous because the roles of Miranda and Ferdinand are reversed — the naïve here is the man, whereas the woman, though innocent of Shakespeare, is sexually very experienced. As the date scene progresses, the Savage becomes more agitated, more incapable of sexual action, and retreats into Shakespearean stupor and rage in parodies of scenes from Shakespeare. From the gentle courtly love of *The Tempest*, he moves to *Timon of Athens* to find expression for, or in subterfuge from, the sexual excitement caused by the site of Lenina stripping in front of him: "For those milk paps that through the window bars bore at men's eyes..." (*BNW* 175). The significance of seeing Lenina's breasts and perhaps some of the Savage's sexual confusion, might be the result of being the only man in the new world to have experienced viviparous relations— the only man who ever fed at his mother's breast. No one else here had this relationship with his mother or could consider breasts containing milk without revulsion. Sexual relations are entirely divorced from procreation in this scientific utopia, so the reference to milk paps is as ludicrous as the idea that men should be driven mad by the sight of a woman's naked breasts.

For sexual rage, the savage turns to *Othello* and hurls insults at poor Lenina quoted from the play. As the Savage threatens to kill her, Lenina retreats to the bathroom, and he now courts madness through the words of *King Lear*. The rage of the Savage suggests a Freudian confusion between mother and lover, and virgin and whore. Like Shakespeare, Freud, for even more obvious reasons, has no place in this scientific utopia. The Savage has constructed a romantic notion of women that demands they reject sexual advances as a sign of their purity and desirability. The scene with Lenina triggers the Savage's memories of seeing his mother and her lover having sex, and after trying unsuccessfully to use Shakespeare to poeticize a potentially traumatic moment, he shifts back to the earlier meaning in rage through which he was able to express his hatred for Popé.

Shakespeare falls on more fertile ground with Helmholtz. The poet speaks to the author of *Three Weeks in a Helicopter* and master of hypnopaedic verse composition — one emotional engineer to another perhaps. Helmholtz has already been showing regressive tendencies. He has been searching for a theme that would do justice to his skill in producing words "like X-rays" which would "go through anything" (*BNW* 62). Helmholtz connects with the Savage and, to a limited extent with Shakespeare, after he experiments with writing about solitude. These latent tendencies towards individualism are of course quite unacceptable in the new world. In his book, *Literature and Science* (1963), Huxley writes that literature's main concern is with "man's more private experiences, and with the interactions between the private worlds of sentient, self-conscious individuals and the public universe of 'objective reality,' logic social conventions, and the accumulated information currently available." (*LS* 92). But the scientific utopia envisioned in *Brave New World* specifically legislates against those private worlds to which literature speaks. Helmholtz therefore only begins to feel the effects of poetry as he moves away from the policed and preformed unconscious that is essential to this new world. The unconscious, such as it is, in a post–Freudian world, is preformed by hypnopaedic teaching which reduces to a single unified world the otherwise infinite possibilities of the imagination. There is no room for madness, re-inventing the self, or the radical playing out of alternative worlds.

According to Huxley, in their natural state, outside this utopia, men and women are "multiple amphibians inhabiting half a dozen disparate universes at the same time — chemical, psychological, verbal and nonverbal, individual, cultural and generic" (*LS* 141). Shakespeare speaks to this multiplicity of lived worlds, not to the prescribed unity of utopia. This prescribed unity is the ultimate goal of science, so the new world is only an extension of the practices of science — less a utopia than the essential ends of modernity. In *Literature and Science* Huxley describes the goal of science as "the creation of a monistic system in which — on the symbolic level and in terms of the inferred components of invisibly and intangibly fine structure — the world's enormous multiplicity is reduced to something like unity, and the endless succession of unique events of a great many different kinds gets tidied and simplified into a single rational order" (*LS* 94). This "rational order" is no place for Shakespeare, as there is no longer any disjuncture between different kinds of worlds to be negotiated. Not only are public and private elided, but also chemical, psychological, verbal, and nonverbal worlds are conflated. When Helmholtz is introduced to Shakespeare, new themes become apparent to him, and he senses a different kind of reality that might reinvolve the psyche. Such brooding tendencies are not only unhealthy, they also threaten the stability of the new world and cannot be tolerated. Helmholtz is sent to the Falkland Islands, a place he chooses for its stormy and brooding atmosphere, and so a fitting fate. Such are the margins and places of exile that the new world allows itself for the liminal poets. Individual fate is of course a major theme in Shakespeare's plays, and hubris inevitably leads to tragedy. This is a crucial difference between the worlds of Shakespeare's texts and the worlds they speak to and this new world of scientific utopia. In the Brave New World, hubris does not, cannot, operate because humanity utterly dominates nature, and there is no higher power to knock humans back into place if they overreach themselves. The freethinking individual, negotiating between his or her own physical limitations and metaphysical forms of domination, has no place here, and neither does the Shakespeare to whom he speaks.

It is important to note that there are two aspects of high art at issue here. One is represented by the figure of Shakespeare as cultural icon, and the other is implicit in the kinds of text that constitute high art, and here Shakespeare, rightly or wrongly, is used as the prime example of literature writ large. As already mentioned, the figure of Shakespeare as cultural icon has undergone some shifts since *Brave New World* was written. In the 1960s, Huxley could still refer to an unexploded canon of English literature represented by Shakespeare and Wordsworth. But in recent years, the valorization of Shakespeare has been found to be based on rather shaky ground. And Shakespeare has been accused of being an emotional engineer himself whose works inculcate a value system by bracketing poetry, madness, passion, love, and other forms of disorder within a larger unseen framework of conservative bourgeois patriarchy. There is an argument that Shakespeare became attached to the establishment and was placed at the heart of a resurgent pride in national identity. In this case, Shakespeare might be read as a conservative, in the end corralling linguistic magic into order and stability. Just as Prospero can wield his magic on a remote island but must reign in his trickery when he returns to civilization.

Part of the attraction to Helmholtz in hearing lines from *Romeo and Juliet* is the potential for exploiting the effects of the sounds of the words to connect with ideas that might be subconsciously reinforced, as in subliminal advertising. Surprisingly, Huxley regarded the advertisement, not as a low form of art, but as "the most exciting, the most arduous literary form of all ... the most pregnant in curious possibilities." He calls this "applied literature" (*Advertisement* 127–8). But the idea of using Shakespeare as an emotional engineer in this sense is not presented as a serious proposition in *Brave New World*. It is really the redundancy of Shakespeare in scientific utopia that is the issue here, and this comes down not only to the idea of literature itself and the specific themes that Shakespeare deals with, but with the aesthetic fashioning present in Shakespeare's texts. In *Literature and Science*, Huxley points out that theology and metaphysics has underpinned humans' inner world in poetry, but gradually, as modernity proceeds, the underlying hypotheses are scientific, and even feeling begins to have a scientific explanation (*LS* 144). Science disenchants and de-poeticizes nature, and yet poetry continues to operate through metaphors whose source domains are theology and metaphysics. This is particularly true in Shakespeare, but Huxley argues, slightly unconvincingly I feel, that Wordsworth began to see the world as "poetical intrinsically," and what nature means is simply itself: "Its significance is the enormous mystery of its existence and of our awareness of its existence" (*LS* 148). In a world devoid of metaphysical and theological possibility, a world like Huxley's scientific utopia, things would simply mean themselves.

Indeed, the novel equates scientific utopia with order and stability, and essential to this trope of order is the end of history and with it the end of literature and forms, which are dialectical, dialogic, and open. In scientific utopia, there is an end to progress, and humans are and remain what they have become to date. Society must be immune from the revolutionary and creative processes suggested by Shakespeare's poetry. Shakespeare must be kept out of utopia not only because he speaks of another world that Brave New Worldians could not relate to, but also because he speaks of the possibilities of other worlds, of remaking the world, of seeing the world other than it really is.

In "Shakespeare and Religion," Huxley suggests that "thought is determined by life, and life is determined by passing time" (*SR* 160). But in *Brave New World*, society subsumes life, is unaffected by passing time and thought has already been *thunk*. History is no longer an active constituent of society but only a label for the extent of those dark ages, now concluded, out of which the New Worldians have emerged as a new species of historical human being. The wondrous creatures of this Brave New World have achieved what to a Buddhist might appear as nirvana — being *in* time, without being *of* time. In this scientific utopia there is no need for that play of mighty opposites that underpins literature's plots, because these have already been played out. Destiny and fate are sealed at birth, or even before birth, not mysteriously, theologically, or metaphysically, but transparently, scientifically and according to clearly defined social bounds.

The major concern with keeping high art out of scientific utopia, makes the Brave New World a dystopia for culture vultures, but was Huxley so concerned about this? If getting rid of high art was the only price to pay for peace, happiness, and stability, surely it would be a price worth paying. Of course, scientific utopia is not only achieved by policing culture: it comes with other controls and restrictions far more radical, but Huxley does choose to position Shakespeare and high art as a central theme, and a possible reading of the novel's closure is that Shakespeare and scientific utopia are mutually exclusive, so Shakespeare must go if this kind of utopia is to be achieved and maintained. The disappearance of Shakespeare, and his subsequent reappearance as spectral ghost of a lost civilization, may be the inevitable consequence of the realization of scientific utopia. The more usual negative reading of the novel as dystopia may be influenced by a reactionary defense of high art and a repulsion toward low art and entertainment, a reading that suggests cultural arrogance that may exist in the text's unconscious, but which is not, I think, manifest. Although stability seems some way off in a post–9/11 world, the driver of global markets does seem to make for an underlying equilibrium, and very few governments dare make political decisions that will rock that boat. This is, I hasten to add, more of a hunch than a developed argument.

Works Cited

Huxley, Aldous. "Advertisement." In *On the Margin: Notes and Essay*. London: Chatto and Windus, 1923. 127–133.

_____. *Brave New World* [*BNW*]. London: HarperCollins Flamingo, 1994.

_____. "Literature and Science." In *Aldous Huxley: Complete Essays*, Vol. VI, edited by Robert S. Baker and James Sexton, 90–151. Chicago: Ivan R. Dee, 2002. First published 1963.

_____. "Shakespeare and Religion." In *Aldous Huxley: Complete Essays*, Vol. VI, edited by Robert S. Baker and James Sexton, 152–160. Chicago: Ivan R. Dee, 2002. First published 1964.

The Birth of Tragedy and the Dionysian Principle in Brave New World

KIM KIRKPATRICK

Brave New World's penultimate scene, when John kills Lenina, culminates in a Nietzschean birth of tragedy within the Brave New World society. Throughout his sojourn in the high-tech society, John the Savage bemoans the lack of art, and he finally has the opportunity to participate in a birth of tragedy of Greek proportions. His desire to sequester himself in a remote lighthouse frustrates the birth of art. Only when Lenina seeks him out, forcing him to break his isolation as she reaches out her arms to include him, is art created through "the fraternal union of Apollo and Dionysus, the climax of the Apollonian as well as the Dionysian artistic aims" (Nietzsche, *Birth* 333). In *The Birth of Tragedy*, Friedrich Nietzsche compares the Apollonian and Dionysian principles to the two sexes: just as both male and female, sperm and ovum, are needed for procreation to take place, so both the Apollonian and Dionysian need to merge for high art and tragedy to be created. Huxley brings Nietzsche's Apollonian and Dionysian principles together to create the birth of tragedy when John kills Lenina in a public Dionysian ritual complete with the Brave New World onlookers acting as tragic chorus. Here, the focus will be on Huxley's use of Dionysian and Apollonian principles embodied in John and Lenina and also in the dual dystopias of the Brave New World and the "Savage Reservation." By following the application of these principles, Lenina emerges as a far more necessary character within Huxley's novel than has been discussed previously. In fact, she is cast as the Dionysian god figure and, therefore, is the hero of the tragedy, with the expectation that she will be sacrificed at the conclusion of the drama so that the community can prosper and become artistically fertile.

Brave New World provides Huxley the opportunity to experiment with philosophies and ideas of the great thinkers of the late nineteenth and early twentieth centuries. Many he invokes by name, like Freud and Ford, William James and Cardinal Newman, but Huxley does not specifically mention Nietzsche and D. H. Lawrence, perhaps the two most important philosophical thinkers behind Huxley's conception of *Brave New World*. That Nietzsche and the Dionysian had a profound influence on Lawrence is well documented.[1] Lawrence was a close friend whose letters Huxley edited and, indeed, Huxley was present when Lawrence died in Italy in 1930. Brad Buchanan has suggested that John's reservation in New Mexico is a direct invocation and tribute to Lawrence's ranch in the same area just outside of Taos, and that Huxley based his character John upon Lawrence (87). Buchanan writes that "Lawrence would have provided an excellent model for John the Savage" and "we cannot avoid suspecting that [Huxley's] portrayal of John ... is heavily indebted to his friend" (86, 87). This leads to a reading of John as a character who tries to model himself as a Dionysian figure. Ironically, although John may wish himself to be Dionysian, his behavior and ethics reveal him to be Apollonian instead. John tells Mustapha Mond, "But I don't want comfort. I want God, I want poetry, I want real danger, I want freedom, I want goodness. I want sin" (240), but he spends his time avoiding danger, quoting Shakespeare rather than writing his own poetry, and moralizing about how to avoid sin. Rather than pursuing freedom, he seems to be limiting himself and setting boundaries for himself so that his lifestyle is ascetic. In Nietzschean terms, he is a naysayer to life and embraces a slave morality.

Nietzsche begins *The Birth of Tragedy* with an emphasis upon the Apollonian principle represented by the dream and the Dionysian represented by drunkenness. These same traits are associated with John and Lenina, respectively. Huxley recasts Nietzsche's discussion of Apollonian and Dionysian principles by contrasting the reservation against the Brave New World and John against Lenina. The Apollonian represents a "higher truth" than what is found in everyday living. It looks for a spiritual ethic, a life that is better and more meaningful than what is daily experienced. This "higher truth" is associated with the dream, "measured restraint, ... freedom from the wilder emotions, ... philosophical calm," "precision and clarity," logic, virtuosity, strict form, boundaries, individuation, words (Nietzsche, *Birth* 170–1, 220, 259, 260). The Dionysian is most accurately defined as someone in a state of drunkenness in which boundaries confining the individual are loosed so that one can experience a state of self-forgetfulness and commune freely with others. It is associated with song, freedom, passion, death, and rebirth (Nietzsche, *Birth* 172–3 and Rapp 320–1). The Apollonian and Dionysian must meet before art can be created: the Apollonian and Dionysian "appear coupled with each other, and through this coupling eventually generate the art-product, equally Dionysian and Apollonian, of Attic tragedy" (Nietzsche, *Birth* 167–8). This is the very concept Lawrence worked on in his 1915 novel *The Rainbow*. The rainbow is a Lawrentian symbol representing the dual presence of the Dionysian and Apollonian principles. Each color within the rainbow is complete and individual yet their collected presence speaks to unity. In this novel, Lawrence's women represent the Apollonian principle and the men the Dionysian. Three couples are brought together to demonstrate varying successes and one failure at creating relationships mirroring a combined Nietzschean Apollonian and Dionysian principle. In his essay "The Marriage of Opposites in *The Rainbow*," Mark Kinkead-Weekes applies this rainbow symbol to the novel's relationships when Tom and Lydia meet and have a successful marriage. Conversely, the relationship of Ursula and Skrebensky never achieves rainbow status. According to Kinkead-Weekes, the archetypal man and woman are brought together in Tom and Lydia; they are "polar opposite[s]": "One is a world of being, the other is a world of knowing and acting upon ... one is a unity with all nature, the other is a process of separation and distinction. One is a life of the flesh, the other a life of thought and utterance" (24). Tom and Lydia's marriage becomes a creative conflict in which "they are able to abandon themselves to each other, but never to merge or absorb ... the opposite forces pass right through each other, and the result is an arch like a rainbow" (26). Huxley imitates Lawrence when he brings Lenina and John together, allowing them to meet and produce art in performing a reenactment of a Dionysian ritual, complete with chorus and maenads. Their meeting results in tragedy reminiscent of Sophocles and Shakespeare. In Lawrentian terms, a rainbow has been created. Lenina is the *Brave New World* character who best embodies the Dionysian principles. She is dismissed too easily by critics as an inconsequential character. Both David Higdon and Deanna Madden discuss Huxley's misogynistic treatment of her, and, although Madden shows the rebelliousness of Lenina's character, Higdon identifies how Huxley degrades women as a class, by identifying Linda and Lenina as Betas whereas the major male characters are Alphas[2]; how he objectifies them as sexual objects; and how he shows that they hinder men's spiritual advancement. But Lenina is the Nietzschean "yea-sayer to life" who provides the Dionysian ethic in the birth of tragedy. She is the character wanting to experience multiple relationships and to travel to nature preserves like the Indian reservation and the Arctic, yet she is not afraid of death and believes in a rebirth as bodies are converted to phosphorus for the good of the community. Throughout the novel, Lenina is associated with the traditional Dionysian traits and symbols of wine, animal flesh, song, and nature. Of all the characters in *Brave New World*, she is the one most reliant upon soma. Whereas Dionysus is the god of wine and drunkenness, soma is the alcohol of this high tech world, without the uncomfortable side effects of a hangover. According to the *The American Heritage Dictionary of the English Language*, soma is "an intoxicating or hallucinogenic beverage, used as an offering to the Hindu gods and consumed by participants in Vedic ritual sacrifices." Huxley's soma, then, represents Dionysian wine, which enables users to lose their individuality so that they may more easily commune with one another and reach a godlike state of euphoria. John rejects the primary Dionysian symbol wine when he objects to Linda's use of mescal. He notes that in the Brave New World, rather than alcohol, the inhabitants rely on soma to forget and cope, and he condemns its use because it is so mind-enslaving that it takes away users' indi-

viduality. John's refusal to habitually use soma and his condemnation of others' use represents an anti–Dionysian tendency and negates his quest to bring
a better life to others. Both the soma and wine accomplish the same end: allowing the consumer to step back from individuality and facilitate a pleasant communal unity. But Soma is also a Hindu god and is associated with the bull and
the underworld, not unlike Dionysius. Lenina is frequently identified as "meat"
to be consumed by others during sex. Specifically, she is described as mutton
(Huxley 24–6). Although this degrades Lenina within most readings of the
novel, this Dionysian approach recognizes that the god was closely associated
with meat, usually of a bull or goat, to be consumed by the maenads in a sexual frenzy. The god as meat identifies him as a god-sacrifice to be consumed
and used by his worshippers as part of his sacrificial death and rebirth cycle.
Dionysius must die, his blood must spill upon the earth, his flesh must be consumed in order that crops, livestock, and worshippers remain fertile and pro-
create. Whereas Dionysus is represented by the choric dithyramb, Lenina relies
upon snatches of songs, like "orgy-porgy," to invoke the unity of her communal background. As Dionysius is a nature god, so Lenina habitually wears the
natural color green, even though, as Higdon points out, this is the color of
Gammas and she should be conditioned to abhor it (80).

John, on the other hand, embodies Apollonian principles, as he is concerned with discovering in the Brave New World a structured world of beauty.
Instead, his hopes are just illusory dreams. He is intent on seeing the world as
better than it is and believes in his status as individual and in "measured
restraint" to rise above those who seem to revel in their drunken state like
Lenina (Nietzsche, *Birth* 170). He is focused upon poetry and, whereas Lenina
responds to situations with songs that have taken on folklore status, John
responds with formulaic Shakespeare. Nietzsche's Apollonian ethic is defined
by Schopenhauer's *principium individuations*, the individual with a focus on
the word and structured art, particularly plastic art like sculpture, but in *Brave
New World* we can connect John's reliance upon using Shakespeare's measured
lines to express himself with his inability to deviate from a prewritten script:
he is unable to ad lib, as it were. John is interested in finding "the beauty of art
[which] triumph[s] over life" (Rapp 320). But both the Dionysian world represented by Lenina and the Apollonian world represented by John are sterile,
unfriendly, and anti-art. For there to be a birth of tragedy in the Nietzschean
manner, the Apollonian and Dionysian principles must be brought together.

Huxley juxtaposes the Brave New World against the "Savage Reservation"
with the conclusion that they are both artistically sterile. The novel opens with
emphasis upon the cleanliness and dehumanizing sterility of the advanced technological society devoid of natural procreation. As June Deery writes, "The
talk may be of fertility, but the society as a whole is sterile" (268). Lenina and
Bernard's introduction to the reservation, however, emphasizes the dirt and
decay of a grossly unclean environment of aging and decrepit bodies. What-

ever is produced here has little chance of health when the smell of death lingers in the air (Huxley XXX). Lenina and Bernard arrive just in time for the religious summer festival, which may offer genuine spirituality and meaning. This is underscored by Lenina's forgetting her soma and realizing that she must experience the festival *au natural*, as it were, without the calming mask of the drugs. But the Indian ritual offers no high art, because it is so structured and orchestrated that no room is left for emotional spontaneity, nor is everyone allowed to participate in the ritual. The rituals reflect the attention to form associated with Nietzsche's Apollonian. Likewise, high art cannot be created in the Brave New World where frustrated artists like Helmholtz bemoan the lack of words, or form, in which to express their thoughts and feelings. Here, the theater is home to the feelies, which indulge emotion for emotion's sake but without attaining Dionysian passion. On the one hand, the reservation is too formalized and individualized and an artist is stifled by this environment so that crafts are produced, true to form, but without artistic merit. On the other hand, the Brave New World society is too communal and artists cannot understand their own passions and create art out of them. Nietzsche describes these types of sterile art when he gives his opinion of Euripides' plays: "Thou hast forsaken Dionysus, Apollo hath also forsaken thee; ... thy very heroes have but counterfeit, masked passions, and utter but counterfeit, masked words" (*Birth* 234). Just as John sees no artistic or spiritual value in the feelies, Bernard and Lenina find none in the summer festival. Dionysian aspects have become so structured within the Indian ritual that John can only focus on the number of times Palowhtiwa, the ritual's Dionysian sacrifice, has danced around the snakes and the amount of blood he has spilled. John does not consider the meaning behind the performance because he focuses on the minutiae and hears only "counterfeit words." Likewise, the feelies provide a basic emotional response, but they provide no intellectual or philosophical content; they produce "counterfeit, masked passions." A synthesis needs to be created before art can be born. Huxley proposes two ways in which art may be produced: 1) when Helmholtz and Bernard, coming from the community-oriented Brave New World, are sent to an island where it is suggested they will explore more individualized circumstances and less comfortable environments which could provide a vocabulary for art, and 2) when the individual John finally communes with Lenina's Dionysian elements, losing his individuality, resulting in art.

Three episodes in Aldous Huxley's *Brave New World* (1932) demonstrate John's desire to participate in the creation of art via Dionysian rituals. The first is on the reservation when he opines how he was passed over as the sacrifice for the summer festival. Later when he tries to incite the Deltas to rebel against their soma rations, he incites a frenzy, which would have led to his being beaten up and dismembered if security had not intervened. Finally, at the lighthouse, John, in a dreamlike state resembling drunkenness or euphoria, whips Lenina to death, allowing her blood to pour upon the earth in a scene echoing the reservation's summer ritual. Huxley adds an ironic twist in that John has grown up wanting to be the god-sacrifice in the Dionysian ritual on the reservation, but he finally participates in the divine by killing the god-sacrifice in the form of Lenina. Both on the reservation and in the Brave New World, he never identifies himself as a maenad. He casts himself always as the figure whose blood is spilled and not the initiate caught up in ecstatic frenzy who kills and dismembers the god.

In a Dionysian ritual, the god or the god-sacrifice communes with the worshippers, the maenads, then is torn apart by them so that his blood is spilled upon the ground and/or his flesh is consumed by the maenads, cementing his communal relationship with them and allowing each worshipper to have a little piece of the god. The god-sacrifice, then, is the means by which the maenads draw closer to the god. The sacrificial blood falling upon the earth figuratively stands for the fertile sperm impregnating the earth mother, resulting in a full harvest. Even though the sacrifice is indeed sacrificed and at least figuratively dies, he becomes the hero in the ritual as he brings divinity to all and ensures the continuing life of the community and the fertility of the earth. The god-sacrifice is wanted and needed by the community. John wishes to become that hero and prepares for the Indian ritual by imitating Jesus's death, standing "against a rock in the middle of the day, in summer, with my arms out, like Jesus on the cross" (137) and by spilling his own blood upon the earth (136). These two activities, however, are done outside of the community. He is alone and his potential companions, the reservation Indian boys, do not participate. Although, individually, John is able to discover "Time and Death and God" by letting his blood and standing in the sun, he is unable to draw closer to his community. John wants to be the god-sacrifice "for the sake of the pueblo—to make the rain come and the corn grow. And to please Pookong and Jesus. And then to show that I can bear pain without crying out. Yes, ... to show that I'm a man" (117). For John, the ultimate goal is not to know god, serve god, or worship god, but to merge with others in a communal activity, to benefit others by giving of himself, thereby making others acknowledge his worth and accept him as a man, like one of them. As an outcast from his reservation society, John grasps at the opportunity to join his mother's civilized society, which Linda has described as highly communal. Depressed that he is "alone, always alone," John longs for that "Other Place" where "nobody was ever alone" (137). He views this technological world as his opportunity to merge with others, lose his marginal status, and discover artistic meaning in his life.

John's second attempt to force the Apollonian and Dionysian together is when he sees an opportunity for himself to become a Dionysian figure, offering himself on behalf of others so that they can experience a fuller, better life. After Linda's death, he seizes the opportunity to provide clarity to the Deltas as he tries to open their eyes to the mind-controlling characteristics of the drug soma. He transforms the soma distribution into potential Dionysian death and rebirth when he identifies, seeing the possibility of a new life, "the possibility of transforming even the nightmare into something fine and noble. 'O brave new world!' It was a challenge, a command" (210). Nevertheless, his ultimate purpose is to aggrandize himself. No matter how much he tries to convince himself that he wants to help others, he ends up placing the focus upon himself, as when he says, "I come to bring you freedom" and later when he says, " I'll teach you; I'll *make* you be free whether you want to or not" (211, 213). He even stoops to abusing those he claims he wants to help because they do not respond as he would like, so he "throw[s] insults at those he had come to save" (212). Rather than allowing the Apollonian and Dionysian to meet, he is trying to force them together, not recognizing that "the marriage of opposites involves a kind of death of the self" (Kinkead-Weekes 26). Focusing upon his role as the individual savior, John is allowing his own Apollonian traits to dominate the community of Deltas. He sees himself as the central figure, not the Deltas he has chosen to deliver. He destructively descends upon them, inciting them to a frenzy which will soon turn upon him and destroy him: "'They'll kill him. They'll ...' A great shout suddenly went up from the mob; a wave of movement drove it menacingly towards the Savage ... Howling, the Deltas charged with a redoubled fury" (213). His self-destructive sacrifice is interrupted by security, which quickly sedates both the frenzied Deltas and the god-seeking John. Although Bernard registers the intervention of the police as a means of salvation, the security forces frustrate John's plan of becoming the hero and dying on behalf of others. Yet once again, his opportunity to merge with the divine has been whisked away.

The book concludes with a reenactment of a maenad orgy in which the Dionysian followers participate in the ritual loss of the self in communal sex, resulting in the dismemberment of the god. John as Apollonian principle and Lenina as a Dionysian come together in this ritualistic death scene, producing tragedy and art. In this case, John instigates the ritual by approaching and whipping Lenina, who has arrived via helicopter to John's lighthouse. Huxley has crafted this scene carefully in imitation of the birth of ancient Greek tragedy. According to Meyer Reinhold, tragedy originated with the "Dithyramb, choral lyric in honor of Dionysus, god of wine, performed in circular dancing-place (*orchestra*) by chorus of men dressed in goatskins (hence the term *tragoedia*— goat-song). They represented satyrs, companions of Dionysus. A story about Dionysus was improvised by the leader of the chorus" (60). The chorus is associated with the maenads, Dionysus worshippers who have come to witness and kill the sacrificial god. Huxley incorporates many of these elements in his orgy, specifically a chorus performing a circular dance led by a maenad who improvises the traditional story of the death of Dionysus.

A chorus of onlookers descends upon John and the lighthouse. They surround John and prophesy his actions with their "loud reiterated refrain" of "We — want — the whip! We — want — the whip!" (257). As worshippers of the

god of wine, they appear drunk and unaware of what they are doing although
they revel in the community they are forming: "They were all crying together;
and, intoxicated by the noise, the unanimity, the sense of rhythmical atonement, they might, it seemed, have gone on for hours—almost indefinitely"
(256). They begin "to mime the frenzy of his gestures, striking at one another
as the Savage struck at his own rebellious flesh, or at that plump incarnation
of turpitude writhing in the heather at his feet." "Then suddenly somebody
started singing 'Orgy-porgy' and, in a moment, they had all caught up the
refrain and, singing, had begun to dance. Orgy-porgy, round and round and
round, beating one another in six-eight time" (258). As maenads, they imitate
the actions they see as they begin to strike each other, finally choreographing
their struggles into communal song and dance around Lenina and John. Huxley uses words like "frenzy," "intoxicated," "orgy," all associated with Dionysian
ritual.

Lenina, dressed in green as befitting a nature god and representing Dionysus, descends from above in a manner suggesting that she is offering comfort
or extending grace to John and the chorus. With her arms extended, she
approaches John as though to embrace him, even though he is holding a whip
and threatening violence. The last time she had seen John like this, she hid in
the bathroom in fear. Displaying godlike calm, she shows no fear now. In reaching out to him, she is identifying him as an individual and is ready to acknowledge his Apollonian traits. This contradicts her earlier behavior when she went
to his apartment and tried to force herself upon him, thereby negating his individuality and personal desires. Here, with open arms, she accepts him and
accepts her own fate as well. John reacts as though he were in an Apollonian
dream. With the crowd around him, he loses his individuation, responds as a
part of the communal unit, and listens to the advice of the chorus. He begins
to act, not as a Dionysian god, but as a maenad. Significantly, he cannot understand Lenina's words, meaning that words are no longer important to him, and
that he can no longer hear an individual's words as he is attuned only to the
communal chorus. John loses his understanding of himself as an individual so
that he confuses whipping himself with whipping Lenina. Just as the maenads
would consume the god-sacrifice, thereby becoming part god, that is, "at one
with the god" (Rapp 326), so John has merged with the god-sacrifice and is
unable to differentiate between himself and Lenina. Finally, John has achieved
the state of the Dionysian that he has so long desired "with the collapse of the
individual, with the breaking of boundaries. The Dionysian state was a losing
of one's self, a self-forgetfulness" (Rapp 320). John joins the crowd reacting as
maenads caught up in the frenzy of a Dionysian ritual as the god is torn apart
and consumed.

Through her death, John and Lenina meet like a rainbow and usher art
into the Brave New World. Although this has misogynistic overtones if it is
read as the female being subjugated by the male in order for art to be produced,

by staying focused on the Nietzschean principles of the Apollonian and Dionysian, we see that Lenina has embraced the Dionysian approach to life and the tragedy she creates is necessarily married to rebirth. Every year, Dionysus died to ensure life and fertility, and every year he returned. This repetition suggests too the repletion of a drama being performed over and over. The chorus of onlookers return the next evening, after Lenina's death, expecting a repetition of the tragedy in the tradition of Sophocles or Shakespeare. The Brave New World chorus recognizes that art has been created and can now be reborn over and over. The possibility of resurrection is what tragedy achieves and its repetition assures it (Rapp 327). Linda is the yea-sayer, as "The tragic artist is no pessimist: he is precisely the one who says Yes to everything questionable, even to the terrible — he is Dionysian" (Nietzsche, *Portable* 484). She was successful in her role as the god-sacrifice; the chorus was successful in returning to perform again; John, who has all along desired art and to participate in the Dionysian divine, has not survived the birth of tragedy and threatens the continuance of art. Upon awakening, he does not recognize his situation as a Dionysian ritual similar to the summer festival from the reservation. Neither does he interpret it as a cycle of rebirth, as all of the Brave New World understand death, or of creation, or of art. As Edward Mooney interprets Nietzsche's philosophy, the artist who cannot live with the eternal repetition of the Dionysian tragedy, is not capable of "infus[ing] his life with meaning" (41). Mooney continues, "It is up to the performer, through imagination and commitment, to make his steps a celebration of life" (42). John makes no commitment to art and, therefore, makes no commitment to life. John's reaction is to kill himself, the opposite of Nietzsche's yea to life. Although he participates in the birth of tragedy, as an artist he cannot allow himself to participate in the process of inexhaustible reaffirmation and re-creation of art. Only the chorus is left to continue the rebirth of art.

Notes

1. See Pollnitz (111–13) and Merivale (194–219) on Lawrence's use of Nietzsche and the Dionysian principle. Furthermore, see Pollnitz (127–8) about how Lawrence saw himself as a Dionysus figure and Buchanan (86–87) about how Huxley used Lawrence as the basis for John the Savage.
2. As Higdon points out, Huxley, while identifying Linda as a Beta, never does indicate to which class Lenina belongs (80–1).

Works Cited

Buchanan, Brad. "Oedipus in Dystopia: Freud and Lawrence in Aldous Huxley's *Brave New World*." *Journal of Modern Literature* 25 (2002): 75–89.
Deery, June. "Technology and Gender in Aldous Huxley's Alternative (?) Worlds." *Extrapolation: A Journal of Science Fiction and Fantasy* 33, no.3 (1992): 258–73.
Hamilton, Edith. *The Greek Way.* New York: Discus, 1973.

Higdon, David Leon. "The Provocations of Lenina in Huxley's *Brave New World*." *International Fiction Review* 29 (2002): 78–83.

Huxley, Aldous. *Brave New World*. New York: Perennial Classics, 1998.

Kinkead-Weekes, Mark. "The Marriage of Opposites in *The Rainbow*." In *D.H. Lawrence: Centenary Essays*, edited by Mara Kalnins, 21–39. Bristol, England: Bristol Classical, 1986.

Lawrence, D.H. *The Rainbow*. London: Penguin, 1989.

Madden, Deanna. "Women in Dystopia: Misogyny in *Brave New World*, 1984, and *A Clockwork Orange*." In *Misogyny in Literature: An Essay Collection*, edited by Katherine Anne Ackley, 289–313. New York: Garland, 1992.

Merivale, Patricia. *Pan the Goat-God*. Cambridge. Mass.: Harvard University Press, 1969.

Mooney, Edward. "Nietzsche and the Dance." *Philosophy Today* 14 (1970): 38–43.

Nietzsche, Friedrich. *The Birth of Tragedy*. In *The Philosophy of Nietzsche*. New York: Modern Library, 1900.

_____. *The Portable Nietzsche*. Edited and translated by Walter Kaufmann. New York: Penguin, 1976.

Pollnitz, Christopher. "'Raptus Virginis': The Dark God in the Poetry of D.H. Lawrence." In *D.H. Lawrence: Centenary Essays*, edited by Mara Kalnins, 111–138. Bristol, England: Bristol Classical, 1986.

Porter, James. *The Invention of Dionysus*. Stanford, CA: Stanford University Press, 2000.

Rapp, Richard. "Nietzsche's Concept of Dionysus." *Philosophy Today* 18 (1974): 319–329.

Reinhold, Meyer. *Essentials of Greek and Roman Classics*. New York: Barron's, 1952.

"Soma." *The American Heritage Dictionary of the English Language*. 4th ed. Boston: Houghton Mifflin, 2000.

To Reflect, to Sit Down: The Hinzutretende and Huxleyan Characters in Horkheimer's and Adorno's Philosophy

ANGELA HOLZER

In his lectures on the doctrine of history and freedom, *Zur Lehre von der Geschichte und von der Freiheit,*[1] Theodor W. Adorno mentions Aldous Huxley at the outset, but not again after that. The lectures, published first in 2001[2] and again in 2006 in paperback, can partly be seen as an elaboration and preparation of central ideas and arguments of the *Negative Dialektik* (1966). The manuscript of the first lecture held at the *J. W. Goethe-Universität* in Frankfurt on November 10, 1964, is no longer extant; however, Adorno's notes as well as the manuscript of one of his listeners, Hilmar Tillack, have been published.

At the beginning of the semester Adorno sketched the task of a philosophy of history after Kant and Hegel by pointing to the deficiencies of their idealist conceptions. In the first lecture, he immediately contradicted the central thesis of Hegel, namely that history is the "progress in the consciousness of freedom" (Hegel 32).[3] In order to prepare his later, and more elaborate, discussion of Hegel's dialectics and of his own concept of negativity, Adorno claimed: "…[T]his much can be said: we cannot state an immediate progress toward freedom" (11).[4] This progress, he continues, is "objectively impossible" due to the density of the "net of society" (11), and due to the increasing concentration of the economy and administration degrading humans by turning them into mere "functions." The remaining freedom has the "character of an epiphenomenon"; even in the sphere of consumption the human individual has lost all personal liberty and has become an "appendix to the machinery." In the social hierarchy freedom has been lost as well; even the commanders in political and economic affairs have become functions rather than thinkers, lacking any real authority to make decisions. "Freedom becomes pathetic, pitiful, shrinks to the possibility to maintain one's own life" (12).

In this context of the absence of substantial freedom, not only in the social

117

and economic, but also in the private realm, Adorno mentions Huxley — or more precisely, one of his characters from *Brave New World*. "Where there seems to be an optimum of freedom, people don't even reach it. To sit down, to reflect, to make decisions: with these activities one would fall behind, one would become a weirdo like the loner in Huxley's *Brave New World*" (12).

Presumably, Adorno refers to Bernard Marx; John the Savage reads Shakespeare, but he is too strange to the *Brave New World* to really become a weirdo in it. Helmholtz Watson and maybe even the young Mustapha Mond, however, are also close to fitting the description. Every Alpha (the superior caste), potentially, could develop into a weirdo, a loner, and would then have to be eliminated: "The greater a man's talents, the greater his power to lead astray.... Unorthodoxy threatens more than the life of a mere individual; it strikes at Society itself" (*BNW* 148).

The simile in Adorno's lecture makes use of a novelistic character in order to state a factual development in history with regard to personal freedom. Given that this is not the only instance of a similar emblematic character transfer in Adorno's work, this essay will inquire into the status of this intertextual transport by addressing Huxley's and Adorno's views on the individual in history. The focus on the notion of the reflective individual seems to allow, for Adorno, an illustrative magnification of historical developments. I assume that this rather casual simile in the lecture gains additional importance through a comparison with other passages of Adorno's and/or Horkheimer's texts that introduce a similar character and thereby turn it into a type.

The reflective individual as socially aberrant type in Huxley's dystopia not only recurs in Adorno's lectures on the doctrine of history and freedom, but reappears either as "outsider" (*Dialektik der Aufklärung* 159) or, in the preface to the *Negative Dialektik*, as "*Gedankenarchitekt*": "The architect of thought lives behind that very moon which the technicians confiscate" (13). This figure not only marks the reflection about culture and society, but also accompanies the diachronic development of this reflection. Being the emblem of a non-functionalized humanity threatened with extinction, this symbolic type additionally seems to carry a remainder of hope in modern, "deformed," standardized and technology-driven life — but this type of thinker, especially in Adorno's critique of Huxley's novel in *Prisms*, "Huxley and Utopia," is also a problematic, disparagingly described configuration of a non-dialectical relationship between history and individual, between culture and material basis. However, in Huxley's novel as well as in Adorno's reference to it, the socially aberrant outsider is the only figure that deserves to be called "individual" by reaching the consciousness of independent thinking within himself. "What the two men [Bernhard Marx and Helmholtz Watson] shared was the knowledge that they were individuals" (*BNW* 60). The one physically defective, the other aware of his mental excess, these two members of the Alpha class are a danger to social stability and will be excluded from this society by the end of the novel. The consciousness of their deformation in comparison to other social beings in their class lies at the root of their individuality. From Adorno's point of view, this individuality must be considered false because it is directed against a false totality. The "rescuing moment," the moment of freedom, lies in the non-causality of their actions—or better, in the incapacity to act. One must therefore consider these concrete novelistic characters as illustrations of necessarily impotent individuality and locate them in the vicinity and as concretization of Adorno's notion of the *Hinzutretende*—but also as characters that fail with regard to concrete action and a dialectical consciousness in Huxley's "reactionary" prolongation of contemporary life (Adorno, "Huxley und die Utopie" 116). The loss of individuality and personal liberty paired with the greater social and demagogic insistence on them are topics that have not lost anything of their urgency in a "post-industrial" world that combines Orwellian techniques of surveillance with Huxleyan uninhibited insistence on consumption, pleasure, and "wellness."

Huxley in Horkheimer's and Adorno's Writings

Adorno's attitude has indeed been compared to Huxley's, who considered America, the land of Ford, as a prototype for *Brave New World*—it can be illustrated with a quote from Adorno's letters to his parents, in which he announces mailing a present for Christmas (November 11, 1943): "Huxley's book—from the year 1928 [actually 1932] is a great prolongation of American conditions and will certainly be enjoyed by Oscar [Adorno's father]" (*Letters to his Parents* 227). The editors of the letters agree that *Brave New World* must be referred to rather than *Point Counter Point*, which is Huxley's novel from 1928. Why does he consider *Brave New World* that he scathingly criticized in a talk he wrote for the Institute of Social Research in Los Angeles the year before, enjoyable for his aging and thoroughly European father? Would the book sardonically reinforce European prejudices? Or would it be enjoyable for different reasons?

This ambivalent view of Huxley and America displays a more refined position toward the "American conditions." From another point of view, Peter Uwe Hohendahl argued against a facile attitude that depicted Adorno as a European elitist uncritical of or even having a position "that would identify 'bad' mass culture exclusively with America and 'good' high culture with Europe," although "evidence for this negative view can be found in Adorno's letters as well as in *Minima Moralia*, where the New World is seemingly portrayed in terms that remind the reader of Huxley's *Brave New World*" (77).[5]

Hohendahl supplied a number of more differentiated moments in which Adorno and Horkheimer "were not as far removed from contemporary Amer-

ican thought as has typically been assumed...," especially the shift in the American left wing from a socialist to a liberal position that had left its marks (77).
"When Horkheimer and Adorno returned to Germany after the war, they shared
an explicitly anti-communist bias with American intellectuals like Sidney Hook
and Irving Kristol" (78).

The influence of Huxley, especially his most famous novel, on Horkheimer
and Adorno has been considered immense, but it is quite difficult to gauge. In
his discussion of Adorno's literary studies, Jan Philipp Reemtsma chides Adorno
for not taking into account Sterne and Melville in his discussion of the novel
as form, but he himself nowhere mentions Huxley.[6]

David Garrett Izzo assumes that "Horkheimer and Adorno agree with
Huxley more than Orwell; in fact, their essays, particularly the well-known
'Culture Industry' were influenced by Huxley's *Brave New World,* and his
essays."[7] Aldous Huxley, however, is not mentioned in *Dialectic of Enlightenment.* Izzo suggested a number of themes that occur both in Huxley and
Horkheimer/Adorno. Among these, he writes, are pop art, mass production,
the ideology of the consumer, and art as opposition to identity. Other themes
in these philosophical fragments similar to Huxley's might be detectable in the
idea of amusement as prolongation of labor and in the loss of individuality:
"In the culture industry the individual is an illusion not merely because of the
standardization of the means of production. He is tolerated only so long as his
complete identification with the generality is unquestioned. Pseudo individuality is rife" (154, trans. Cumming).[8]

In *Culture Industry*, the character of the weirdo, the loner, the outsider,
appears for the first time. This character as motif might be inspired by Huxley, despite the fact that economic aspects are emphasized by Adorno. "The one
who is hungry and cold, especially if he had had good prospects, is marked. He
is an outsider, and, apart from capital crime, it is the gravest guilt to be an outsider."[9] Bernard Marx shines through in this description. Having had good
prospects, his society destined him to be guilty of aberration. Moreover, the
use of English in the German original might be seen as an indexical moment
pointing to the by then famous novel from 1932 with which Adorno might have
become familiar in 1937.

In 1994, Robert Baker undertook an assessment of the connection between
Huxley and Horkheimer and Adorno by resorting to the figure of the Marquis
de Sade. "Adorno, as far as I can judge, was unfamiliar with Huxley's other writings, where the basis for Huxley's critique of contemporary culture was developed and refined, and where he would have discovered Huxley proceeding
along lines of inquiry at times strikingly similar to those of *Dialectic of Enlightenment.* The point where these lines intersected was in the figure of the Marquis de Sade as symbol of the European Enlightenment, both in relation to its
rationalist origins and its final stage as technocratic project."[10]

Baker's observation that de Sade occurred in similar contexts in the cosmos of both writers is interesting. However, Baker's assumption that Adorno was unfamiliar with Huxley's other writings is incorrect.[11] Adorno was aware of Huxley's work, all the more since he spent time in England. In a letter to Walter Benjamin written in Oxford on October 15, 1936, Adorno mentioned *Eyeless in Gaza,* a "sensation ... a book in which Huxley apparently tries to connect to surrealist tendencies ..." (198). On April 15, 1937, he reports reading "Huxley."[12] A number of remarks about Huxley, especially about *Brave New World,* from 1944 and 1945, display Adorno's deep familiarity with and the perceived pertinence of this particular novel during the work at the *Dialektik-Projekt.* Writing to Max Horkheimer on December 2, 1944, from Los Angeles, he credits Huxley with having foretold the productive instrumentalization of human hierarchy in terms of consumption (374). In a letter to Horkheimer on January 25, 1945, from Los Angeles, he again credits Huxley with having predicted the mechanisms of "death conditioning. "It is truly frightening that everything seems calculable, that even all cruelties, which this society has still in stock, can be calculated in advance" (39). In this same letter, Adorno also refers to Shakespeare, and to his own opinion on the subject and his reflexive character: "In the world that exists today, only the individual in his/her extreme can represent the concern of society against society" (40). It is this type of the extreme and abject individual, the "weirdo" and "outsider" that appears in Adorno's philosophy — a linguistic mark representing social concerns in a dialectic of individual and society, as well as the inability to overcome the state of pure opposition.

Individual and Freedom

While the theoretical role of the individual increased greatly since the Enlightenment, the individual ability to act in social, economic, and political contexts has decreased because of the failure to confront increasing responsibility.[13] Since the circumstances of practical life never ushered in the autonomy promised philosophically, this failure leads, according to Adorno, to a feeling of guilt. Having already discussed the increasing lack of individual freedom even in higher social hierarchies in the late industrial society and having importantly emphasized that increasing democratization will *not* change this "loss of consciousness of freedom" (2006, 13),[14] Adorno again turns to this "problematic"[15] at the end of the lectures when dealing with the notion of "freedom." Noting that a positive description of freedom is extraordinarily difficult, because the notion lends itself to abuse,[16] he claims that what one considers first [*zunächst*] and reasonably [*vernünftigerweise*] as "freedom" is the "freedom of the individual/single human being" (Freiheit des einzelnen Menschen 241).

In order to do justice to the role of the individual in Adorno's lectures, this role has to be considered objectively, with regard to the individual's function in the dialectics of the general [*des Allgemeinen*] and the particular [*des*

Besonderen] as well as subjectively, with regard to the individual's inner constitution, or rather, deformation. The relationship between the general and the specific, i.e., history and individuality, is one of the major focal points of Adorno's philosophical inquiry at large and in these lectures.[17]

It is crucial to consider Adorno's definition of individuality as both referring to each individual existence and its immediate experience as well as to a moment in the dialectic that should not, however, be taken abstractly. Individuality designates both immediate existence as opposed to a historical generality and the moment of connection to the general course of history via a historical dialectic. The individual as individual appears most clearly in the individual's opposition to society, constituted by, but not identical to it. Therefore, one could consider Adorno's repeated allusion to Huxley's character, created by, but diverging from *Brave New World* in a variety of contexts to circumscribe the individuality of the individual, at once determined by the general and different from it.

In comparison to Huxley's reflection on the individual and freedom, as well as on freedom and history, it seems important to stress two moments in Adorno's elaborations. First, in keeping with his positing the historicity and historical specificity of ideas while adhering to his (anti)methodology of model analyses, which one would however assume to treat more marginal themes, objects, and notions,[18] Adorno is very much interested in delineating the history of the idea of individual freedom. This concept, he claims, has already been infected with the virus of deformation in its philosophical foundations that were laid by Kant. Kant's doctrine of freedom is paradoxical and corresponds to its status in reality. Kant's doctrine "cannot ... accept freedom without force" and therefore anticipates the "liquidation of its own freedom" (*Negative Dialektik* 229) in bourgeois consciousness.

Adorno stated from an epistemological point of view, like Huxley, that "thinking is identifying" (*Denken heißt identifizieren*) (*Negative Dialektik* 15) in order to develop his critique of philosophical thought from within ("("the contradiction of freedom and thinking can neither be resolved by thinking or for thinking, but requires its self-reflection") (*Negative Dialektik* 230). In *Ends and Means* (1937), Huxley had taken this epistemological principle as a foundation for his reflections and "practical recipes" (11): "The human mind has an invincible tendency to reduce the diverse to the identical" (13).

Huxley, contrary to Adorno and Horkheimer whose work was intended against scientific specialization at that point, considered this "tendency ... towards identification and generalization" (14) not a problem in the disciplines of "organized sciences" (14), and moreover suggested that "we shall never deal effectively with our human problems until we follow the example of natural scientists and temper our longing for rational simplification by the recognition in things and events of a certain residue of irrationality, diversity and specificity" (16). Apparently, Huxley considered theoretical developments in physics (collapse of wave function) as a corrective of logical positivism. The call for the acknowledgement of an irreducible residue hints, very generally, in the manner of Adorno's elaborate theory of negativity and especially of the *Hinzutretende*.

Returning to Adorno, like all thinking in general, the philosophical constitution of the notion of freedom is subject to and associated with repression and "degraded to undeducible force" (*Negative Dialektik* 229). Historically, the class that insisted on the universality of freedom at the same time also aborted the concept and its realization. The still-existing emphasis on the factual existence of freedom, however, is part of its repressive instrumentalization. This is the second moment relating the concept of freedom to its importance in the relationship between society and individual. It still might be imperative to bear in mind the coalition between the social overemphasis on the existence of freedom and factual repression (*Negative Dialektik* 229). This is precisely the status quo in Huxley's utopia that is illuminated and magnified by the depression of Bernard Marx and the rebellion of Helmholtz Watson. It finds exemplary expression in the private dialogue between Bernard and Lenina, a completely complacent, well-functioning female, during their trip to the sea that will be echoed later, on a social scale, in the action of the John the Savage trying to bring freedom to the soma-seeking Deltas. "Don't you wish you were free, Lenina?" I don't know what you mean. I am free. Free to have the most wonderful time" (81).

Hinzutreten: To Join, to Step Toward

It is not only freedom, but also the individual that is difficult to define and seems deformed already at the outset. Following the Freudian notion of repression, Adorno discusses the difficulties to theoretically constitute a self-identical subject that could be the carrier of consciousness and of freedom — not to speak of an empirical subject that has to be considered in this context and is crucially important for his *Hinzutretende*. The discussion of freedom leads to the discussion of the free will. On February 2, 1964, Adorno introduced the *Hinzutretende* in his twenty-fourth lecture, a lecture dealing with freedom. Crucial to the philosophical and historical reflection is the acknowledgement of the force with which the "*I*" as category has been constituted, "the unfreedom of the principle of the freedom of the "*I*" (305). Reminding one of the argumentation in the *Dialectic of Enlightenment* with the addition of the principle of repression (in the Freudian sense), Adorno reiterates the idea that the "*I*" interiorly imitates the force that it experiences from the outside. The consciousness of freedom of the subject is "something like blindness" (305, *Verblendungszusammenhang*), i.e., the incapacity of the self-maintaining subject to see through and recognize the determination of the mechanisms of self-maintenance. The notion of freedom does not only crystallize as the naïve positing of the instance that dominates nature, the "*I*," but also as the positive counter image to the experience of social repression. In this context, the above-mentioned dialogue between Bernard Marx and Lenina could be viewed as an illustration of petit-bourgeois consciousness that exists through the imagination, the wish phantasm (*Wunschphantasie*) of interior freedom. "According to social repression that the *I* is subject to, it develops the idea that it would be better to be different, that it would be better to be free; and assuming within this context of blindness a substituting function, being subject to exterior repression, it believes to be free at least interiorly" (*ZLGF* 306). Bernard's consciousness represents this "certainly old, archaic" (306) mechanism. His longing for freedom is the imagination of a false, oppositional, undialectical freedom unable to change a deformed society. The philosophical tradition that sees in the subject a sphere of absolute origins, of the freedom of the subject, finds its counterpart in the doctrine of unfreedom. Both construct the subject according to this mechanism of blindness. The autonomy of the subject, which is not identical with itself, depends on the "institution of the world und the constitution of the world" (308) that grants or denies autonomy. The hypostasized construction of a subject dependent on itself is erroneous. Autonomy is fictive if the concrete world is neglected and it becomes "such a thin and abstract principle that by using it nothing at all can be said about the real and factual behavior of humans" (308). At this point, the emphasis on the reflection of real, empirical individuals, which can neither be theoretically reduced nor abstracted, occurs. This emphasis on *Wirklichkeit* and concreteness in regard to the idea of the individual as well as its relation to the world leads to a discussion of Kant's *experimenta crucis* introducing a real example as evidence. They, however, are criticized by Adorno as being built on the premises they are to prove and as improbable in regard to the real. Adorno then introduces the term that is "rather arbitrarily invented and therefore suitable to me" (317): *Hinzutretende*. The intention of this notion is to delineate the failure of idealist philosophy that posited the identity of consciousness and will. Real subjects do not, according to Adorno, make decisions along the chain of causality (which is at the root of Kant's definition of the will since it is basically conceived of as identical with reason). "I call this moment which we are dealing with the moment of the *Hinzutretende*: the decisions of the subject do not unfold along a causal chain, rather, when speaking of acts of will, something like a jerk occurs" (317). Adorno even calls this jerk *impulse*, "bodily impulse, somatic impulse" (317)—something that is decidedly not the intervention of consciousness.

Paradoxically, in order to emphasize this critique of Kant's rationalism, and elaborate the difference between consciousness and will, thinking and acting, i.e., the divergence of the spheres of pure reasoning and of action, Adorno refers to another literary figure that exemplifies this break between interior and exterior—Hamlet. Hamlet serves as a "model" (*ZLGF* 320) for a historical and philosophical fact. It is not the difference between madness and reason that is the problem of Hamlet. According to Adorno, it is rather the realization of the rupture in the spheres of reason and action. Literature thus gains a specific status not only for Adorno's philosophy, but also for the establishment of knowledge as such. Serving as a vessel for philosophical and historical realizations, it is an irreducible category of experience on its own. Far from being a mere mirror of history and philosophy, the use of literary examples by Adorno here attests to the acknowledgement of the status of literature as an autonomous category in the constitution of modern reflexivity.

If this philosophical rupture is expressed in Hamlet as exemplary character, indecision and inhibition are the outward result and defining features of the figure. Bernard Marx is Hamlet's relative with regard to these psychological symptoms. Marx is also torn between different possibilities of moral action. Duty, loyalty, and egotism exert pressure on him in chapter XVI of *Brave New World*, where he experiences different impulses that result in "an agony of humiliated indecision" (195). As torn individuals, the characters that Adorno employs in these philosophical texts typify the melancholic temperament of the intellectual, indexing a mode of reflexivity in modern life that does not gloss over the agonistic, unmediated abysses it is confronted with. Moreover, in the weirdo, the outsider, or the architect of thought behind the moon, economic and intellectual impotence are closely related to an unfree liberty. The status of the artist in the culture industry is considered as false freedom in which divergence from the norm is punished by exclusion, following mechanisms quite similar to the ones active in *Brave New World*, but exemplified with reference to de Tocqueville's analysis of American politics: "'The ruler no longer says: You must think as I do or die. He says: You are free not to think as I do; your life, your property, everything shall remain yours, but from this day on you are a stranger among us'." Not to conform means to become powerless, economically and by consequence, intellectually. Rendered meaningless, the weirdo ["outsider" in Cummings translation] can easily be found guilty of inadequacy.

['Der Herrscher sagt dort nicht mehr: du sollst denken wie ich oder sterben. Er sagt: es steht dir frei, nicht zu denken wie ich, dein Leben, deine Güter, alles soll dir bleiben, aber von diesem Tage an bist du ein Fremdling unter uns.' Was nicht konformiert, wird mit einer ökonomischen Ohnmacht geschlagen, die sich in der geistigen des Eigenbrötlers fortsetzt. Vom Betrieb ausgeschaltet, wird er leicht der Unzulänglichkeit überführt.] [Dialektik der Aufklärung 141].

Whereas Hamlet marks the beginning of a modern subjectivity accepting the rupture between interior and exterior, Bernard Marx entails a corrective to Kant's bourgeois notion of consciousness and the will, thus as a corrective to the philosophy of a subject that is considered identical with itself. The references to outsiders, weirdoes, *Eigenbrötler*, inspired by characters from *Brave New World*, mark the consequences of the historical enlightenment that resulted in subjecting the individual to the technical apparatus and thus mark reflective individuality both as anachronistic and as a sliver of hope for a human future. They serve as indexes of Adorno's urge to provide concrete models, in this case, for the concreteness of modern individuality constituted through the rift between thought and action ("*Bruch von ... Gedanken und Tat*" 321) — and the parallel emptying out of reality that renders the "relationship of the individual to this reality problematic. And where the individual should begin to act, the *horror vacui* takes hold of him" (*ZLGF 323*).

In addition, they are witnesses to the irreducible importance of the literary. In his discussion of Shakespeare, Adorno points to the "approximately contemporary" (322) philosophy of Descartes that also gives voice to the opposition of interior and outer *res*. It could be added that with Descartes, the importance of literature as irreducible medium of knowledge also gains traction. Although the clarity of the "notion" wins over the "metaphor" in discursive history, which itself is the sign of a crisis of insecurity, it is precisely Descartes to emphasize literary form versus notional clarity, himself probing different literary styles in his *Discours, Meditationes, Le Monde*, and *Recherche*.[19]

The paradox that the transport of these literary characters into Adorno's philosophy brings consists in the reference to a fictive and abstract universe, be it a utopian or a royal one, and to a typified character in order to model the concrete, in order to model irreducible concrete individuality constituted through the erratic *Hinzutretende*.

The General and the Particular

This comes back to the larger question that was addressed at the outset, namely to the dialectic between the individual and history in Huxley's as well as Adorno's conceptions of philosophical history. The differences in these conceptions are structural. Certainly, both thinkers speculated on a way out of the contemporary present that they considered catastrophic. Shortly before the Second World War, Huxley quite directly called his *Ends and Means* a "cookery book of reform" in fact, working toward the possibility of a "better" state of the world. The protagonist of this improvement is the "realist idealist," who is non-attached to sensations, lust, power, possessions, wealth, fame, social position, and exclusive love. "The ideal man is the non-attached man" (4). Based on a tradition of prophets, ascetics, and founders of religion, the Huxleyan ideal world consists of ideal individuals that are not conscious of their concrete individuality but rather lose their attachment in a charitable totality by way of acknowledging that there are no separate individuals. Huxley is, like Adorno, basically skeptical of the concept of identity, to which all diversity is reduced — especially by the sciences. But from Huxley's point of view, it is also modern science that led the way to a "religious" understanding of reality, in that it discovered that "separate, individual existents are illusions of common sense. Scientific investigation reveals (and these findings, as we shall see later on, are confirmed by the direct intuition of the trained mystic and contemplative) that concrete reality consists of the interdependent parts of a totality and that independent existents are merely abstractions from that reality" (294–95). He is also aware of the limits of this concept: "That we can never completely ignore the animal in us or its biological needs is obvious. Our separateness is not wholly an illusion" (346).

Huxley is also, on a very basic level, critical of Hegel, claiming that "his mistake was to imagine that nature was wholly rational and therefore deducible *a priori*. It would be convenient if this were the case; but unfortunately it isn't" (*Ends and Means* 292). Huxley tries to posit a certain irrationality against Hegel, but his position remains contradictory: do scientists serve as models for this insight or are they the ones who reduce diversity? What is the relationship between the individual and the general, if we are not separate but the separateness is not "wholly" an illusion? Although there are similar themes perceptible in both thinkers, Huxley's appeal to quasi-missionary practices, the belief that the insight into the mutual dependence of all life, and the religiously inspired vision of ideal, charitable, cooperative society place him in a different context from Adorno. The ideal individual, in Huxley's early book, is a non-dialectic being, basically detached from the materiality of the world that it seeks to change.

Huxley's book appeared in 1937. Adorno's *Minima Moralia*, quite different by making use of the aphoristic style, was written from 1944 to 1947; it addresses, albeit less "practically," similar, non-disciplinary, fundamental questions, and deals with "the doctrine of the right life" (7). Having rid themselves of a certain naiveté that the Huxleyan program exudes, they also skeptically view the possibility of "reflections that originate in and presuppose the subject" (8). The "old subject" has been liquidated by the "overpowering objectivity" of history. The aphorisms, however, consider as essential that which is vanishing, the subject. Adorno here regards Hegel as contradicting his own insight and as executor of a historical move in theory that led to the annihilation of the particular, the individual, in order to glorify totality. The dialectical "reconciliation of the general and the special" constructed by Hegel has yet to be realized (11). Adorno's vision remains attached to this idea of "reconciliation." But, as he writes about twenty years later in *Negative Dialectic*: "it can be only achieved negatively" (16). "Dialectic unfolds the difference of the particular from the general that was dictated by the general ... Dialectic serves reconciliation" (16). "Reconciliation would free the non-identical ... would open the diversity of the different, about which dialectic would no longer have dominion." (16).

In this state, neither would there exist an unmediated sublation of the individual in society, the particular in the general, nor the individual as hypostasized, absolute and independent. The lectures, however, written long after *Minima Moralia* and shortly before *Negative Dialectic*, seem to mark the attempt to save the idea of objectivity in history, with and against Hegel: they do so in order to save the individual. To understand the "particularity of the general, i.e. of progressing reason" means to understand more about the dialectic of the general and the special as the structure of history (21). It is thus not the general as such, but the general as particular that has to be grasped, i.e., the development of the Hegelian spirit as rationality — an argument not crucially different from *Dialectic of Enlightenment*. The reassessment of the general, however, of the Hegelian idea of objectivity in history is a new moment. Albeit the development of reason as the general correlates to an increasing fatality that can only be experienced as negativity, Adorno reappraises the "objective tendency," the *Weltgeist* that might not be *Weltgeist* but "its opposite" (43) as a principle of history.

This tendency cannot be denied; it is crucial, however, to understand that objectivity makes use of the individuals; it exists in them and through them, penetrating the individual but remaining impenetrable. Unlike in Hegel's system, this structure leads to the insight that history can be understood as senseless and incomprehensible.

> This contradiction ... says nothing other than, if I am to say it metaphysically, that it is the limitation to look after their own interests and nothing but their own interests, which the way of the world imposes upon humans, that it is this force that turns against man and succeeds as blind and inescapable fate above their heads. And this structure, I believe will if at all, be able to reach, to result in what I would like to lead you to: namely a conception of the philosophy of history that at once allows to grasp history, — but to grasp, that is go beyond its pure existence, to understand it as something pointless, meaningless, senseless [42].

Huxley's character encapsulated this experience of the individual in the dialectic of history, confronted with the consciousness of individuality and the heteronomy of this consciousness. It exists in a world that lacks freedom, since "freedom is also an area of subjective experience, i.e. not only to take after the measurements that have been objectively prescribed" (12). Therefore, the character could serve, in a variety of adaptations, as a type in Adorno's and Horkheimer's philosophy. While this character type bears traces of the modern subject as exemplified by Hamlet, it also, as a type, posits the possibility of identification with a concrete, albeit literary, character. This character, however, is also tainted by the criticism that Adorno levels against the novel as a whole. Whereas Adorno identifies Marx as a "skeptically empathic caricature of a Jew" (*Prismen* 109), and discusses this problematic identification, it is the unmediated and unreflected opposition that characterizes Marx's behavior in *Brave New World*, his position that marks him as an intellectual unable to understand the social and material foundations of his own rebellion. He becomes thus a participant in Huxley's "isolated world of values of interiority and deepness" (*Prismen* 115) that only provides stiff alternatives. Marx ends up as an impotent figure due to his lack of reflection. "Reason for the untrue [of

Brave New World] is the separation that has become reified as stiff alternative" (115).

If Huxley failed on a number of levels according to Adorno, it is this figure that has become useful as a type in a number of contexts in his critical philosophy; it is the reflective subjectivity that runs both the risk of adhering to a false intellectuality against the material conditions—reason in an affirmative sense—and that, as reflective individuality, bears the possibility to overcome the line of separation. It is thus an expression of reason having become particular-one that must overcome this particularity without falling back to being an "isolated interest of totality." This is, according to Adorno's doctrine of history and liberty, a crucial problem of history that has not been, and might never be, solved:

> *Und wie allerdings dieses Problem zu lösen sei: wie also auf der einen Seite die Vernunft sich befreien kann von der Partikularität des sturen Einzelinteresses, auf der anderen Seite aber dann nicht wieder zu einem genauso sturen Einzelinteresse der Totalität wird,— das ist nicht nur ein Problem, an dem die Philosophie bis heute gescheitert ist, sondern auch ein Problem, an dem die Einrichtung der Menschheit bis heute gescheitert ist"* [ZLGF, 68].
>
> [How this problem can be solved: how on the one hand reason can liberate itself from the particularity of stolid isolated interest, but on the other hand evades becoming a just as stolid isolated interest of totality — this is not only a problem which could not be solved by philosophy until today, but also a problem which has led to the failure of an establishment of humanity.]

Notes

1. From now on: *ZLGF,* Frankfurt: Suhrkamp, 2006.
2. *Nachgelassene Schriften IV, 13* (2001) and *ZLGF* 1785 (2006).
3. G. W. F. Hegel, *Vorlesungen über die Philosophie der Geschichte,* 1986, 32. "Die Weltgeschichte ist der Fortschritt im Bewußtsein der Freiheit — ein Fortschritt, den wir in seiner Notwendigkeit zu erkennen haben."
4. Th W. Adorno, *Zur Lehre von der Geschichte und von der Freiheit,* 2006, 11."Das kann gesagt werden: ein unmittelbarer Fortschritt zur Freiheit ist nicht zu behaupten."
5. Peter Uwe Hohendal, "The Displaced Intellectual? Adorno's American Years Revisited." *New German Critique* 56 (1992): 77–78.
6. Peter Uwe Hohendal, "The Displaced Intellectual? Adorno's American Years Revisited." *New German Critique* 56 (1992): 77–78.
7. Jan Philipp Reemtsma, "Der Traum von der Ich-Ferne. Adornos literarische Aufsätze." In *Dialektik der Freiheit,* edited by Axel Honneth (Frankfurt: Suhrkamp, 2003), 328.
8. David Garrett Izzo, *The Perennial Philosophy as Literary Theory— with Examples From Modern Literature* (dissertation,Temple University, 2005), 248.
9. Theodor W. Adorno and Max Horkheimer, *Dialektik der Aufklärung* (Frankfurt: Fischer, 2000), 163. First published 1944. "In der Kulturindustrie ist das Individuum illusionär nicht bloß wegen der Standardisierung ihrer Produktionsweise. Es wird nur so weit geduldet, wie seine rückhaltlose Identität mit dem Allgemeinen außer Frage steht."
10. Theodor W. Adorno and Max Horkheimer, *Dialektik der Aufklärung* (Frankfurt: Fischer, 2000), 163. First published 1944. "In der Kulturindustrie ist das Individuum illusionär nicht bloß wegen der Standardisierung ihrer Produktionsweise. Es wird nur so weit geduldet, wie seine rückhaltlose Identität mit dem Allgemeinen außer Frage steht."

11. Ibid., 159. *"Wer hungert und friert, gar wenn er einmal gute Aussichten hatte, ist geze-ichnet. Er ist ein Outsider, und, von Kapitalverbrechen zuweilen abgesehen, ist es die schwerste Schuld, Outsider zu sein."*

12. Robert Baker, "The Nightmare of the Frankfort School: The Marquis de Sade and the Problem of Modernity in Aldous Huxley's Dystopian Narrative," in *Now More Than Ever: Proceedings of the Aldous Huxley Centenary Symposium Muenster 1994*, edited by Bernfried Nugel (Frankfurt, Berlin, New York: Peter Lang), 246.

13. There are a number of mentions of Huxley in Adorno's letters. On October 15, 1936, e.g., shortly after having arrived at Oxford, he writes to Walter Benjamin: "But the sensa-tion is Huxley's new book, *Eyeless in Gaza*, where he apparently forcefully tries to make a connection to surrealist tendencies." Back in Frankfurt on April 15, 1937, he reports to Ben-jamin that he is reading Huxley. Although it is unclear which text he read, it is likely that it was not *Brave New World*, which was published five years earlier. See *Theodor W. Adorno, Walter Benjamin. Briefwechsel 1928–1940*, edited by Henri Lonitz (Frankfurt: Suhrkamp, 1994), 198 and 229. On other occasions, he deals with Huxley's *Brave New World*.

14. Baker's article supplies a good deal of information, but it seems inadequate with regard to his analysis of Adorno's and Horkheimer's work (calling it "poetically oblique and method-ologically obscure" (248), and considering Adorno's discussion of Kant reaching "extrava-gant heights" (250). Baker considers *Dialectic of Enlightenment* as "an important intertext that sheds light on Huxley's use of Sade, and that connects Huxley's critique of science and the instrumental ethic of positivism to the current theoretical debate on modernity and mod-ernism" (248). His assumption that Huxley's Sade figures, or the associations of some figures with Sade, ultimately serve as a critique of scientific reason and that the "prefiguration" of Adorno and Horkheimer's use of the same character remains insufficiently proven. What does the notion "prefiguration" entail and how can it be made useful from a culturally inter-pretative point of view? Horkheimer mentions Sade years before *Dialectic of Enlightenment* appeared (see footnote 7). The mere fact that ultimately both resorted to Sade as a cultural *chiffre* highlighting similar aspects of his presumed character does not, as such, illuminate much. Although Baker discussed the book on Sade by Gorer saying that it "anticipates many of the issues explored by Huxley ... as well as Adorno's and Horkheimer's *Dialectic of Enlight-enment*" (Baker 251), he did not mention a piece of information that is crucial to this obser-vation, namely that the title of Horkheimer's and Adorno's influential book and its thematic complex occurred first in a passage written by Horkheimer after reading "the book on Sade by Gorer." He does not point out the importance of Sade for Horkheimer and Adorno, namely his status as a symbol of decay, i.e. of the dissolution of religion, metaphysics and morality [see Rolf Wiggershaus, *Die Frankfurter Schule* (München: DTV, 1988): 368]. Baker moreover missed the chance to criticize and point to the problems of the use of Sade by analyzing the semiotic logic in the resurfacing of this figure, its "iconographical role" and "emblematic sta-tus" (Baker 250) in modern and postmodern debates.

15. Je mehr Freiheit das Subjekt, und die Gemeinschaft der Subjekte, sich zuschreibt, desto größer seine Verantwortung, und vor ihr versagt es in einem bürgerlichen Leben, dessen Praxis nie dem Subjekt die ungeschmälerte Autonomie gewährte, die es ihm theo-retisch zuschob. Darum muß es sich schuldig fühlen" [The more freedom the subject, and the community of subjects, ascribes to ifself, the greater the responsibility, in front of which the subject fails in bourgeois life, since this life's practice and experience have never granted to the subject the unlimited autonomy which it theoretically gave him.] (*Negative Dialek-tik*, 218).

16. Die fortschreitende Demokratisierung der politischen Formen wird am Verlust des Freiheitsbewußtseins, am Desinteressement, an der Schwäche zur Freiheit nichts ändern, weil der ökonomisch-soziale Inhalt auch der freiesten politischen Formen einem solchen Freiheitsbewußtsein gegenübersteht." (*ZLGF* 13).

17. Problematik des Begriffes Freiheit," *ZLGF*, 241.

18. Ibid., 241. See also *Negative Dialektik*, 229. Wird Freiheit positiv, als Gegebenes oder Unvermeidliches inmitten von Gegebenem gesetzt, so wird sie unmittelbar zum Unfreien." [If freedom is posited positively, as given or unavoidable in the midst of the given, it imme-

diately becomes unfree.] Adorno also insisted on the fact that freedom can only be grasped in relationship to the "concrete form of unfreedom "(229).

19. Denn wenn wir hier uns in einem weiten Maß mit dem Verhältnis von Allgemeinem und Besonderem, von historischem Zug und Individualität befassen, dann hat natürlich dabei die Individualität gegenüber jenem übergreifenden Trend, jenem übergreifenden Zug eben immer etwas von jener Unmittelbarkeit der einzelmenschlichen Erfahrung, von der ich Ihnen gesprochen habe ... daß die Unmittelbarkeit der Individualität, das heißt: des sich am Leben erhaltenden Einzelwesens, ebenso ein Moment in der Dialektik ist wie die übergreifende Allgemeinheit; nur eben ein Element, und genausowenig abstrakt zu hypostasieren wie auf der anderen Seite die Allgemeinheit" (*Negative Dialektic,* 33).

20. Philosophie hat, nach dem geschichtlichen Stande, ihr wahres Interesse dort, wo Hegel, einig mit der Tradition, sein Desinteressement bekundete: beim Begriffslosen, Einzelnen und Besonderen; bei dem, was seit Platon als vergänglich und unerheblich abgefertigt wurde und worauf Hegel das Etikett der faulen Existenz klebte" (*Negative Dialektic,* 18).

21. Ralf Konersmann, *Der Schleier des Timanthes* (Frankfurt: Fischer, 1994), 27.

Works Cited

Adorno, Theodor W. "Aldous Huxley und die Utopie" In *Kulturkritik und Gesellschaft I,* 97–122. Frankfurt: Suhrkamp, 1977.
_____. *Briefe an die Eltern.* Edited by Henri Lonitz and Christoph Gödde. Frankfurt: Suhrkamp, 2003.
_____. *Minima Moralia. Reflexionen aus dem beschädigten Leben.* Frankfurt: Suhrkamp, 2001. First published 1951.
_____. *Negative Dialektic.* Frankfurt: Suhrkamp, 1966.
_____. *Zur Lehre von der Geschichte und von der Freiheit.* In *Nachgelassene Schriften IV, 13.* Frankfurt: Suhrkamp, 2001.
_____. *Zur Lehre von der Geschichte und von der Freiheit.* Frankfurt: Suhrkamp, 2006.
_____, and Walter Benjamin. *Briefwechsel 1928–1940.* Edited by Henri Lonitz. Frankfurt: Suhrkamp, 1994.
_____, and Max Horkheimer. *Briefwechsel 1927–1969.* Bd 4/ I-III. Edited by Christoph Gödde and Henri Lonitz) Frankfurt: Suhrkamp, 2003–2005.
_____. *Dialektik der Aufklärung.* Frankfurt: Fischer, 2000. First published 1944.
Baker, Robert. "The Nightmare of the Frankfurt School: The Marquis de Sade and the Problem of Modernity in Aldous Huxley's Dystopian Narrative." In *Now More Than Ever: Proceedings of the Aldous Huxley Centenary Symposium, Münster 1994,* edited by Bernfried Nugel. 245–60. Frankfurt, Berlin, New York: Peter Lang, 1995.
Hegel, G. W. F. *Vorlesungen über die Philosophie der Geschichte.* Frankfurt: Suhrkamp, 1986.
Hohendahl, Peter Uwe. "The Displaced Intellectual? Adorno's American Years Revisited." *New German Critique* 56 (1992): 76–100.
Huxley, Aldous. *Brave New World.* Perennial Classics. Harper Collins, 1998. First published 1932.
_____. *Ends and Means. An Enquiry into the Nature of Ideals and into the Methods Employed for their Realization.* London: Chatto & Windus, 1937.
Izzo, David Garrett. *The Perennial Philosophy as Literary Theory — with Examples From Modern Literature.* Dissertation.Temple University, 2005.
Konersmann, Ralf. *Der Schleier des Timanthes.* Frankfurt: Fischer, 1994.
Reemtsma, Jan Philipp. "Der Traum von der Ich-Ferne. Adornos literarische Aufsätze. In *Dialektik der Freiheit,* edited by Axel Honneth. Frankfurt: Suhrkamp, 2003.
Wiggershaus, Rolf. *Die Frankfurter Schule.* München: DTV, 1988.

Brave New World
as Prototypical
Musicalized Fiction

THEO GARNEAU

Even if Aldous Huxley hadn't coined the term "the musicalization of fiction" in *Point Counter Point*, his novel of 1928, and even if he hadn't drawn there a list of writerly techniques he imagined could bring the effect of narrative fiction closer to expressing the inducible truths he heard in Beethoven or Bach's polyphony, the sheer aurality and musicality of *Brave New World* would demand ultimately that the novel be considered as an experiment aimed at enlarging the bounds of textual signification. *Brave New World*, in spite of its often-explored dystopian polemics (consumerist propaganda, subconscious brainwashing, eugenics, and so on), is a literary experiment that asks first and foremost to be heard *as music*.

Authorial intention will help us here. We know that an aurally acute Huxley was passionately interested in music and voice, and we know that he long wrestled with the problem of transmuting music's meaning into words. His biographers have pointed to his "famous voice: beautifully modulated, silvery, precise" (Murray 6). Yehudi Menuhin once said that "he had made himself into an instrument of music ... his voice was the gentlest melody" (Murray 7). As a young man he played piano, against certain odds. His lifelong friend Naomi Mitchison remembers him playing music from Braille, and more importantly she recalls "his long hands on the piano and his half-blind face reaching forward into the music. I only listened," she continues, "but he was immersed" (Murray 34).

Huxley's ongoing immersion in music would lead him to write numerous searching essays on sound and music, to rhetorize upon the social stakes of the commercial manipulation of music, to use musical terms as literary titles, to include references to music-making in virtually all of his works, large and small, and to communicate his avid interest in the semantic and epistemological problems musical meaning posed to writers who wished to express it. In various letters written just before the publication of *Brave New World*, he shares with friends his preoccupation with the interstices between music and text. In 1930, for instance, he writes to Paul Valéry, "I myself have much meditated on philosophy-music, especially that of Beethoven. The Mass in D, the Quartet in A Minor, the Sonata Opus 222, are profound philosophic works, subtle and by all the evidence true. But in what does this truth consist? One does not know how to put it" (*Letters* 323). In a letter to Scudder Klyce, also of 1930, he writes, "[t]he most perfect statements and human solutions of the great metaphysical problems are all artistic, especially, it seems to me, musical.... Though of course what they 'say' cannot be rendered in words—just as the final mystery, the continuous Whole, cannot be rendered in words.... It is good that attempts should constantly be made to get the unutterable on to paper, even though the attempts are in the last resort vain" (*Letters* 324–5).

And, surely, Huxley writes his most important passage on the notion of intertwining musical meaning with fictive text just four years before he publishes *Brave New World*. I'm referring to the famous "musicalization of fiction" passage from *Point Counter Point*, a novel Jerome Meckier calls "a tribute in words to the musical compositions of Bach and Beethoven" (4). The passage has spawned a critical genre in literary studies, and it is here in its near entirety because the thoroughness with which Huxley describes an imagined orchestral/textual palette bears directly on a musical reading of *Brave New World*, chronologically among the first Huxley texts one should read to find out how, exactly, a novelist might get the sound of Beethoven into a fictional narrative.

> The musicalization of fiction. Not in the symbolist way, by subordinating sense to sound. (*Pleuvent les bleus baisers des astres taciturnes.* Mere glossolalia.) But on a large scale, in the construction. Meditate on Beethoven. The changes of moods, the abrupt transitions. (Majesty alternating with a joke, for example, in the first movement of the B flat major Quartet. Comedy suddenly hinting at prodigious and tragic solemnities in the scherzo of the C sharp minor Quartet.) More interesting still, the modulations, not merely from one key to another, but from mood to mood. A theme is stated, then developed, pushed out of shape, imperceptibly deformed, until, though still recognizably the same, it has become quite different. In sets of variations the process is carried a step further. Those incredible Diabelli variations, for example. The whole range of thought and feeling, yet all in organic relation to a ridiculous little waltz tune. *Get this into a novel. How?* The abrupt transitions are easy enough. All you need is a sufficiency of characters and parallel, contrapuntal plots.... You alternate the themes. More interesting, the modulations and variations are also more difficult. A novelist modulates by reduplicating situations and characters. He shows several people falling in love, or dying, or praying in different ways—dissimilars solving the same problem. Or, *vice versa,* similar people confronted with dissimilar problems. In this way you can modulate through all the aspects of your theme, you can write variations in any number of different moods. Another way: The novelist can assume the god-like creative privilege and simply elect to consider the events of the story in their various aspects—emotional, scientific, economic, religious, metaphysical, etc. He will modulate from one to the other—as, from the esthetic to the physico-chemical aspect of things, from the religious to the physiological or financial. But perhaps this is a too tyrannical imposition of the author's will. Some people would think so. But need the author be so retiring? I think we're a bit too squeamish about these personal appearances nowadays [306].

Applying the techniques Huxley lists in this passage to the narrative strategies of *Brave New World* suggests an entirely different way of reading and hearing the text. And given the close historical proximity of the creation of this passage to the writing of *Brave New World*, I suggest that reading the text with these notions in mind should be, in fact, of primary concern. Further, if Huxley's anti-utopian novel of 1932 is an attempt at a musicalization of fiction, I offer that attentive and imaginative reading should also foreground the book's countless, pervasive aural tropes, should analyze these aural signifiers in terms of their imagined musical influence on larger aural structures. For Huxley does not "subordinate sense to sound" as might the poetry he maligns above. I propose, rather, that as an extension of his own idiosyncratic attention to ambient sonority and his historical "immersion" in music, he subtly *creates* not "mere glossolalia," but real musical/social sense with the linguistic signification of sound here. This is to say that he steadfastly and not so subtly underscores the withering anti-musical ideology of the Fordians with his microscopic depiction of the sound and music of the society, at the same time calling us to listen closely to the musical portrait he is constructing.[1] (Note here in passing the important "intermedial" efforts of the many who posit the historical regression of hearing in ratios of the senses and call for its renewed primacy in narrative textual signification: various poetic movements, "sensory world" historian Lucien LeFebvre and his followers, media theorists Marshall McLuhan and Walter Ong, "musicalization of fiction" researchers Werner Wolf, Steven Sher, etc.)

In any case, the list of musical formulations that Huxley's protagonist Philip Quarles imagines above makes heard in a new and striking way many of the passages in *Brave New World*: the changes of moods, majesty alternating with a joke, the abrupt transitions, the statement and development of a theme, the sets of variations, the parallel/contrapuntal plots, the alternation of themes by reduplicating situations and characters, the modulation from the aesthetic to the physico-chemical aspect of things. In fact, these formulations *all* find a place in the text and thus strongly suggest that Huxley was thinking of this novel as a grand piece of music in literary fiction.

Musicalization of Fiction in Brave New World

In the following pages I will consider a few of Huxley's many applications of musicalized fiction in *Brave New World*.

As the narrative begins with a student tour of the London Hatchery and Conditioning Centre, we notice that Huxley is careful to compose a suitably sterile "soundtrack" to accompany the central reproductive enterprise of this "civilization," an oligarchy whose cynical (though rhythmic and rhyming with "T") motto, "Community, Identity, Stability," belies the fact that these words, like the music here, are bereft of higher meaning (6). Everything is *hush, hush.* Like a bemused Henry Adams, we too barely hear the tyrannical triumph of the well-oiled ideological machine. The year is 632 Ford, and notions of History, Literature, Art, and serious music have been *whisked* away by a happy, hedonistic, addle-headed, whistle-while-you-work allegiance to the supposed values of Henry Ford, patron saint of utilitarian repetition at the cost of calculated human reification.

Huxley orchestrates with the pianissimo sound of Fordian efficiency. As narrator, he opens and relaxes our inner ear by scoring all the many sounds *piano, piano.* As students observe the Bokanovsky process at work, the narrator notes that the machines "faintly purred" (4). Faintly *stirred*, faintly *purred*: repetitive, assonant, onomatopoeic, anthropomorphic, suggestive of stainless-steel soul, the assembly line as feline. We hear, too, the efficient, repetitive, percussive "[w]hizz and then, click!" of the lift hatches from the Organ Store (8). But while machines purr on, humans peter out. As our group descends into the dark basement Embryo Store, the director tires of talking and asks his assistant to continue. Quietly, yet with a rhythmic and oral miming of standardized proletarian repetition, we hear twelve consecutive sentences, variations on a theme, beginning with a similarly accented past participle: "Mr. Foster duly *told* them: *Told* them of the growing embryo ... *Made* them taste the rich blood surrogate ... *Explained* why it had to be stimulated ... *Showed* them the jets..." (emphasis added, 11). While "passing Metre 320," a mechanic adjusts the "blood-surrogate pump of a passing bottle," and, if we listen carefully, we hear (in microtones) "the hum of the electric motor deepen ... by *fractions of a tone* as he turns the nuts. *Down, down....*" (emphasis added, 12). Impressed by savings gained through such virtuostic efficiency, the students counter-intuitively "murmur" the word "enormous" (14); the director himself "murmurs" as he rhythmically, repetitively gives the voluptuous technician Lenina "two or three little pats" (15), then a final pat (16); "pat" chosen for its hushed yet percussive, onomatopoeic quality.

This assiduous and pervasive dynamic scoring is central on the level of detail to Huxley's overarching structural plan, a temporal/textual plan which he will repeat many times throughout the book; for, in the next scene, and to considerable effect, he will demonically turn up the volume, *subito.*

As we reach the Neo-Pavlovian Conditioning Rooms, the Delta children are receiving programming which will cause them to flee books for life: we hear toddlers approach books placed before them: these "*little squeals* of excitement, *gurgles and twitterings* of pleasure" will soon give way (emphasis added, 19), however, to aural depictions of terror, to the "abrupt transition" of a musicalization of fiction, as the director activates the conditioning device which achieves its means through sound.

The aural imagery in this passage is perhaps horrifying, surely structural. The verb "shriek," the adverb "maddeningly" modifying "sounded," the "sharp spasmodic yelps," the narrator's parenthetical admission that "the noise was deafening," the often repeated and sibilant "s" throughout: these aural imaginings audibly give substance and form to a process of dehumanization; equally, and in tandem with the carefully attenuated quiet passage which precedes them, they give substance and form to the musicalization of fiction. (Among many other Beethovenian moments, for example, the narrative construction above bears an uncanny resemblance to the *Gewitter, Sturm* sequence in the Sixth Symphony.) And like a demented conductor torturing a human orchestra, Huxley bends the "tone" of the babies' screams as electricity is added to the mix; bodies twitch and stiffen, and one imagines, for perhaps he knew of Plato's and Quintilianus's writings on music and strings, that he is sadistically playing on the Attic notion of soul as musically vibrating cord.

Having achieved his desired anti-music horror, a structural fortissimo, Huxley carefully describes a polyphonic attenuation which, like a symphonic decrescendo, lessens by degrees and disappears: "The *explosions ceased*, the *bells stopped ringing...*" (emphasis added, 21).

Books and loud noises will, then, be indissolubly linked in the minds of the Deltas. The whirring and purring and murmuring Neo-Pavlovians will repeat this aural conditioning some two hundred times to make sure (21).

Sonic Repetition as Central Trope

We can see, then, the above scene as constituting a large set piece implementing a carefully designed dynamic scheme, which begins quietly, rises to a shrieking howl and then decrescendos to a close. A dynamic contour like this is only one of many variations in Huxley's "musicalization of fiction," one of many modulations or "reduplicating situations" he employs in *Brave New World*. Yet, there are other aural situations with this same form.

In chapter II, for instance, in a small parenthetical piece illustrating early attempts at hypnopaedia, the director tells his listeners of a boy, asleep hearing a voice speak from a box near him (25). The volume rises as the boy rhythmically, though without comprehension, intones a hypnopaedic phrase. He then bursts into tears and "howls" (25). As the passage decrescendos, the director orally (thus aurally) explains to his listeners that the howl "discouraged the earliest investigators" (25), and the text soon regains its quiet with one of the narrator's more witty constructions, at the same time oxymoronic and aural: "'Silence, silence' whispered a loudspeaker as they stepped out on the fourteenth floor" (26). The chapter and the director's tour continue in pointed near-silence with extensive dynamic markings: "silence, silence" is repeated (26). A carefully crafted rising volume, however, will structure the closing of the chapter as the director, becoming excited while recounting the gains made in hypnopaedia, awakens the sleeping children by banging on a table and almost shouting (28).

Another small set piece, a contrapuntal plot, a modulation, using techniques of aural repetition and composed to a microscopically gradual dynamic progression, is the marriage of John's mother Linda in chapter VIII. It begins as they "walked in *silence*, and in *silence*, behind them came the brothers and sisters and cousins and all the troop..." (emphasis added 136). They will next "*murmur* a few words"; then, old Mitsima will say, "in a *loud* voice, 'They are married.'" In the ensuing decrescendo, John will run away, pay "no attention to [his mother's] calling" and finish "in *silence* and a long way off" (emphasis added, 137).

In another more global aspect of his "orchestration," Huxley crafts into his plot several pieces of explicit musical performance that follow various aurally imagistic and repetitive schemas on a vastly larger scale. In chapter V, he scores the synthetic aural ethos of Fordianism at the Ford's Day Celebration, copiously and technically describing the music itself, the repetitive chanting of the participants, and the synthetic musical instruments. This is where we hear sixteen "sexophones" and the ultimate, powerful, and suggestive "Thunder in A flat major" (76).

In chapter VII, in the celebration at the reservation, he gives equal attention to depicting the counterintuitive though musically expressive "soft repeated thunder" and the "thunderous silence of the drums." The narrator notes here of Lenina that "there was nothing left in the world [for her] but that one deep pulse of sound" (113). Yet, in fugal counterpoint to Lenina's whispering "orgy-porgy" to herself, we simultaneously hear the "shrill" voices of the women, "the deep savage affirmation of ... manhood" in the voices of the men, a "subterranean flute," and constant drumming (113). In chapter XI, Huxley describes another large and public musical gathering: this time, Lenina and John go to the musical/pornographic "ALL-SUPER-SINGING, SYNTHETIC-TALKING ... STEREOSCOPIC FEELY" (170).

The Highly Symphonic and Polyphonic "Hive of Industry"

This scene that opens chapter X is equally aural and dedicated to underlining through musical and sonorous imagery the endlessly repeating and ideological actual reality of the Brave New World. Seizing "actual reality" is the writer's "greatest difficulty," Huxley notes in *Music at Night* (291), and in this case, his "seized reality" is highly sonorous. In a critical detail from this scene, the hands of "four thousand electric clocks in ... four thousand rooms" mark the time as the workers do their purely repetitive tasks. One interpretation of the omnipresence and repetition of the number four and the sound "for," or "Ford," in *Brave New World* is musical[2]; doubly suggestive since the four thousand clocks mark the *time*. Four-four, "common time," is a rhythmic convention in Western popular music in particular. Max Weber, the only founding father of the field of sociology to write extensively on music in society, lamented the increasing "rationalization" of Western music, a seemingly "natural" process that since the twelfth century has been increasingly constraining music into ever more narrowly defined ways of sounding (examples: tonality itself, musical notation, the equal-tempered keyboard, standardized pitch). In the sense that four-four time constitutes what Weber called a "pattern of feeling" not consciously noticed by many listeners (Shepard), the pervasive music of "common time" thus becomes rhetorical and ideological. The predictable and repeating rhythmic pattern of four-four time offers, therefore, a subtle musical analog to the method of the hypnopaedic program: an exercise in extensive and repeated aural brainwashing, establishing what Theodor Adorno calls the "basic culture-industrial principle: the affirmation of life as it is" (37). Of course, the reified "bees" in the Fordian hive are happy with life as it is: "Buzz, buzz!" writes the narrator: "The hive was humming, busily, joyfully. Blithe was the singing of the young girls ... the Predestinators whistled as they worked" (149).

Chapter IX as Sonata-Allegro

A close reading of chapter IX suggests that Huxley is applying the technique of *da capo* recapitulation, the idea of a *return,* of circular action "imperceptibly deformed," as a musicalization of fiction in a symphonic movement which both shapes and gives sound to the entire chapter.[3]

As if to signal a Nabokovian textual game, the playful and deeply repetitive chapter begins with a subject and a reflexive pronoun: "Lenina felt *herself* entitled," as the sentence continues, Huxley employs paired nouns: "after this day of *queerness* and *horror,*" paired adjectives: "to a *complete* and *absolute* holiday" (emphasis added, 142). In grammatically repetitive structures, the narration paces the musicalized chapter with the repetitive and rhythmic click of the verbal clock: "They climbed into the machine and started off" (emphasis added, 143). This grammatical, temporal, and sometimes oral *idée fixe* continues as might a metronome.

Huxley, as we have seen, repeats letters, syllables, phrases, images, homonymic sounds, rhymes—whatever semiotic material he finds. Perhaps the most interesting object of frenzied repetition is the newly coined noun "zipper," a symbolic motif which has become here an onomatopoeic and Wagnerian leitmotif returning—with variation—to sound many times throughout the text and until the last pages.[4]

There is an aural and abrupt transition to the repetitive next paragraph, a paragraph which not only repeats syntactical structures, but which repeats purely sonorous images (145). Similar grammatical repetition continues unabated for the rest of the short chapter.

The Savage finally stumbles upon Lenina herself, somatose on a bed. As he kneels beside her bed, he quotes two stanzas of a repetitive, rhythmic Shakespeare (the oral tradition), and he emphatically invokes the sound of the voice (146). He is interrupted by yet another sonorous modulation (again the abrupt transitions of a musicalized fiction): "A fly buzzed round her." (The verb "buzz," precisely for its lack of elegance, is also a leitmotif in *Brave New World*. It signifies the sound of all that is mechanistic, repulsive and predatory;[5] it signals the presence of foreshadowing flies. It signals the swarms of locust-like helicopters that buzz from the beginning of chapter III and transport those who drive the Savage to suicide in the last.) Here, however, in chapter IX, the buzzing of flies in juxtaposition with a semi-erotic verse of Shakespeare epitomizes Huxley's Beethovenian notion of "majesty alternating with a joke," while modulating to another auditory sign which furthers the plot; but not before the Savage is given this echoing thought by the narrator: "How beautiful she was! How beautiful!" (146). The approaching and aurally signifying helicopter is bringing Bernard back to the reservation in a return of the subject that, in this essay which argues for a sustained intermediality of fiction and music, marks the recapitulation and return of Bernard, who personifies here the opening theme in sonata-allegro form.

Chapter III as Choral Fugue

With its experimental narrative structure, its gradual descent into what one might term textual cacophony, chapter III is surely the most overtly polyphonic, the most explicitly "musicalized" chapter of *Brave New World*, yet it opens as might any chapter in any traditionally fictive text. Beginning with a brief though pointedly aural description of naked children at erotic play, the first paragraph does conclude, however, with a line that is aurally significant: "The air was drowsy with the murmur of bees and helicopters" (29). This imagistic, poetic mixing of anthropomorphized natural and mechanical symbols, the wry juxtaposition of two aural forces which are absurdly paired, prepares the reader for the gradual unfolding of what with little need for argument can be seen as a chapter-length fugue, concretizing what Huxley termed in *Point Counter Point* the "musicalization of fiction ... on a large scale, in the construction" (306).[5]

We hear many voices in this chapter, speaking voices that enter the texture as in a fugue, sequentially, one at a time, and are then carefully grouped into discrete, competing choruses. (This fugal technique also finds an analog in Beethoven's practice of fragmenting his main themes in symphonic movements.) As the passages become progressively shorter, the ever-changing voices—generally without being identified by the narrator—will appear to sing simultaneously, in purely polyphonic fashion. At the height of this fugue, sentences are often left incomplete and finish with ellipses, a technique which encourages the notion of a musical intertwining in the reader's ear. The effect is prodigious, baroque. Further, by systematically decreasing the length of time each speaker or chorus speaks as the chapter progresses, Huxley creates the illusion of an increasing tempo, an illusion of voices speaking rapidly and sounding simultaneously (51–52).

Throughout, however, the chapter contains other aural signifiers on the level of musical detail that further enrich the clearly choral soundscape Huxley is working to sustain. Huxley, who more than appreciated the music of Bach, surely knew that the voice of Christ or the paragon of faith in Bach's Masses and cantatas is often given to the bass, so his choice of register for a Fordian world controller, "Our Fordship," is clearly significant.

We also note in this chapter-long fugue the Fordian instrumental accompaniment of the "Synthetic Music machine [which] was warbling out a super-cornet solo" (36). And, while the sound quality of the voices of the other participants in the "choir" is not described, we can imagine those of the male students (which will be identical since they are most likely clones) to be somewhere in a tenor register between the deep bass of Mond and the higher alto and soprano voices of the "eighty superb … specimens." We can imagine the hypnopaedic "voices" to be constant, identical, soft, eerie — the textual equivalent of *tremulando* strings. Interestingly, as a sometimes-soundless thinker, it is Bernard Marx who brings an emotional and anti–Fordian *quiet* to the music. The dissident, soulful, and supremely jealous pseudo-intellectual is horrified by the blithe comments Henry Foster and the assistant predestinator make about having Lenina sexually, and thus he *thinks*: "Ford, how I hate them!" (53). Since Huxley dedicated an essay to the role of silence in music, since he wrote that "silence is an integral part of all good music" (MN 19), we can take Bernard's thoughtful and rebellious silence in the chapter to be of significance in the "scoring" of this attempt at a musicalization of fiction.

"Meditate on Beethoven. The changes of moods, the abrupt transitions." Huxley's notion of incorporating Beethoven's "changes of moods" and "abrupt transitions" gets a frenetic workout in chapter III. Furthermore, these abrupt transitions are very often conversational, thus aural. At this point, a nearly complete, systematic, and parodic repetition of repetitious interruptions will begin and ultimately take over the chapter.

It is also important to consider the narrator's poetic and symbolic "whisk" passage in the context of Beethovenian interruptions and "abrupt transitions" in chapter III. In this brief paragraph the narrator rhapsodizes while calculating the cost of "Our Ford's" dogma, "History is bunk … History is bunk" (34). His onomatopoeic "whisk" acts on several levels as a performative in a musicalization of fiction. First, the imagistic "whisking" away of cultural heritage obeys the chapter's compositional praxis of rapid modulation from one situation to another. Second, the verb "whisk" — "to move (something) about, away, back, etc. with a light sweeping motion" (*Oxford Dictionary*) — suggests an interruption of a status quo or discourse. Third, the "lightness" of the whisk posits a blithe disregard for cultural heritage. Pointedly here, Huxley works in emphatic order as he whisks, positioning the musical artifacts, the Passions (of Bach), the Requiem (of Mozart), the Symphony (etymologically "voices in concert"), as the last three cultural treasures to be "whisked." In this context, the notion of a "whisk" becomes a mimetic metaphor for ideological degeneration. Most important, the word aurally constitutes a percussive, sibilant, and mimetic musical sound, and, because of its one syllable, becomes a repeating rhythmic motif in the passage; further, the expulsory assonance of "whisk" serves to concretize the moment and the energy of the "abrupt transitions."

Another significant detail: that the narrator notes at the beginning of the passage that Mond "waved his hand ... with an invisible feather wisk" as might a symphony conductor with a baton points to Huxley's persistent though subtle crafting of musical imagery into a fictive and purely verbal text.

A last point: while History is swept away in this passage, the "whisk" remains. Huxley's ellipsis after the last "whisk" leaves our inner ear with the sound of the word, yet also suggests the corrosive sweeping away is continuing and we do not hear it, for the solo voice has once again abruptly changed: immediately after this last whisk, we read, "Going to the Feelies this evening Henry?" (34). The sublime majesty of a defunct symphony alternates with a joke, and the forced Fordian poly-cacophony continues.

Chapter III begins with the theme of naked children at erotic play and ends with naked children at erotic play. As "his fordship" speaks his penultimate words of the chapter (a very long sentence of 123 words which, when juxtaposed with the previous brief sentences, has the musical affect of slowing the tempo), he is loudly interrupted — in mid sentence — by the director who scolds the children for interrupting the Controller: "Go away, little girl," shouted the D.H.C. angrily. "Go away, little boy! Can't you see that his fordship's busy? Go and do your erotic play somewhere else" (56).

Chapter III begins with an aural image, with the quiet "murmur of bees and helicopters," and it finishes with an aural image, *pianissimo,* as "[s]lowly, majestically, with a faint humming of machinery, the Conveyors moved forward" (56). This highly fugal and experimental chapter thus constitutes another large, circular, sonic form complete with extensive dynamic markings, tempo changes, and Beethovenian techniques Huxley enumerates in his earlier *Point Counter Point.*

Conclusion

The purpose here was not to analyze how Huxley's myriad musical/aural forces act as rhetorical forces in Fordian London, nor to provide a systematic overview of Huxley's application of music to narrative fiction. It has not been the intention to advance any theory of dialectic between reader and text which may make manifest affective or sensory states of mind resembling those states of mind inspired by listening to music. (Remember Huxley's words to Scudder Klyce in 1930: "It is good that attempts should constantly be made to get the unutterable on to paper, even though the attempts are in the last resort vain.") Rather, one can argue that *Brave New World* is pervasively informed by the linguistic signification of aural referents, and that this text, to an extent previously unremarked, is expressly shaped by structures and moods common to musical experience, as Huxley hears them and conceptualizes them.

This essay began by stating that "the sheer aurality and musicality of *Brave New World* would demand ultimately that the novel be considered as an experiment aimed at enlarging the bounds of textual signification." A tall claim, yet it has certain merit. This essay considers but a few sonic forms and aural tropes from the text's eighteen chapters. It is no exaggeration, however, to claim that nearly every scene in *Brave New World* comments with form upon sound, strains to make itself heard in detail, thus strains to convey in "seized reality" the cacophonous sound ethos of the brave new world. The dynamic indications are constant and crafted; the formal techniques Huxley lists in *Point Counter Point* shape many other scenes, transitions, and juxtapositions throughout.

Reading with an ear to the text's music will reveal other sonic repetition, aural interruption, and extensive, attenuating dynamic indications beneath plot action. Attentive reading will reveal a discourse on synthetic music; ubiquitous, telling instances of synthetic, metonymic and human voice; personified loudspeakers; an "ideological apparatus" as music industry; an "arch-songster-of-Canterbury"; Fordian song lyrics; a persistent ticking clock; a ferocious antipathy to silence; a rich intertextuality of sonorous and explicitly musical images between Zamyatin's *We*, Wells's *Time Machine*, Shakespeare, and others. The title *Brave New World* itself refers to the aural tradition and it is spoken within the text. Shakespeare, in verses from a poem with other references to music, tellingly refers to music within *Brave New World*:

> Let the bird of loudest lay
> On the sole Arabian tree
> Herald sad and trumpet be ... (186)

Huxley develops the leitmotif of symbolic thunder — synthetic, natural, musically pitched, and anthropomorphized. He offers striking aural images; this one, for instance, which crescendos: "The noise of fourteen thousand aeroplanes advancing in open order" (47). He proffers scathing social commentary in an image of anti-musical voice as John realizes the cloned "multitude" who accost him after the death of his mother have only two voices among them:

> "Who are you pushing? Where do you think you're going?"
> High, low, from a multitude of separate throats, only two voices squeaked or growled [214]

"We — want — the whip."

They were all crying together; and intoxicated by the noise, the unanimity, the sense of rhythmical atonement, they might, it seemed, have gone on for hours ... [264].

In his last chapter Huxley gives readers another musical moment which points to a topic at the heart of all musical discourse: the arguably prelinguistic human impulse to sing. As John, who is out of London and once again in nature, slowly heals from the death of his mother and his purging of civilization, as he becomes increasingly content whittling white ash for a bow and arrows from "a whole copse full of beautifully straight hazel saplings" (254), he realizes "with a start" that he is "singing — *singing!*" (italics Huxley's, 254). Surely this impulse — the human breath at the root of music — fascinated the musical Huxley. The inchoate energy of unformed song, carefully crafted through technique, talent, education, reason, taste, and most importantly, inspiration, is the genesis of all the great music that Huxley loved. It is only in a society that has purposefully stifled human potential for growth and freedom — personal, political, aesthetic, and spiritual — that a person will be, as John is, ashamed for having given birth to song. In this climactic moment, the natural and miraculous impulse to sing becomes the central defining characteristic of the doomed protagonist of *Brave New World*. John, with his wooden bow and string, becomes another Orpheus, torn to shreds by other Maenads.

Notes

1. Though not ostensibly the subject of this paper, one sees that the plausible distinction between "musical" and "aural" signification is somewhat suspect. Beginning with the expressionist, dodecaphonic experiments of Schoenberg and Berg in the twenties and continuing in the later schools of the indeterminate (Cage), minimalist (Glass), and *musique concrète* (Stockhausen), radical changes in musical practice have shaken the once stable Western notion of what music even is. For example, in his lecture "Four Criteria of Electronic Music," composer Karlheinz Stockhausen gives the tenor of his musical interrogation of ambient aurality as he tells of becoming interested in "sounds and noises," and asks his audience, "what is the difference between a piano sound and a vowel aaah and the sound of the wind — shhh or whsss" (89). As we imagine and hear the soundscape of *Brave New World*, we may also profit from the observations of ethnomusicologists who claim, as does Kathleen Marie Higgins, that "the basis on which Western musical aesthetics is formulated serve as an inadequate basis for dealing with 'music in as broad a sense as it can be understood'" (90). In her article "Musical Idiosyncrasy and Perspectival Listening," she writes of native peoples of Papua, New Guinea, whose "music" is formed by "a layered, nonsynchronous overlap among multiple voices, including the 'voices' of the rainforest soundscape" (92). Perception of environmental sounds as constituting a part of a living music usefully problematizes the traditional opposition between the musical and the merely aural. This tenet of ethnomusicologists also harmonizes with sociologist Tia DeNora, who likewise seeks to deconstruct limiting notions of what the notion of "music" means. Importantly, she concludes her text *After Adorno: Rethinking Music Sociology* by noting that "[m]usic sociology will have achieved its ultimate aim, in other words, when — in all realms of social life — we come to attend to the sounds that are all around us, to know these as our accomplices (and opponents) in the doing, being, and feeling that is social life" (158–9). Further, since at least the first century,

when Iamblichus wrote of Pythagoras's remarking upon the musical notes of a smithy as he hammered on metal (52), we have known that vibrating bodies give resonance to definable, traditionally "musical" notes. The neighbor's lawn mower, the gas-powered leaf blower, the truck which beeps as it backs up, the telephone's ring and dial tone: these all produce "musical" if often disagreeable notes. It is important to remember, then, that while hearing Huxley's soundtrack we remember his "whirring" and "purring" machinery produces definable pitch. The "buzz" of his flies, the motors of the helicopters and planes, the sirens, alarm bells and the howls of the children are all discernable, pitched, and "singing" notes.

2. In chapter III, in "the four thousand rooms of the Centre the four thousand electric clocks simultaneously struck four" (33).

3. "A theme is stated, then developed, pushed out of shape, imperceptibly deformed, until, though still recognizably the same, it has become quite different. In sets of variations the process is carried a step further. Those incredible Diabelli variations, for example."

4. "Zipper was registered in the U.S. as a trademark in April 1925 (with use of the term claimed since June 1923), but in the sense 'boots made of rubber and fabric.' It is no longer a proprietary term in any of its uses. Quot. 1925, which appeared in the first Supplement to the O.E.D. (1933), and in the Dictionary of Americanisms ..." (Oxford English Dictionary online)

5. The passage depicting the reporter from *The Hourly Radio* in Chapter XVIII offers buzzing amidst a set piece of highly sonorous musicalized fiction: "[He] pressed a switch on the left side of the hat — and from within came a faint waspy buzzing; [he] turned a knob on the right — and the buzzing was interrupted by a stethoscopic wheeze and cackle, by hiccoughs and sudden squeaks, 'Hullo,' he said to the microphone, 'hullo, hullo ...' A bell suddenly rang inside his hat" (257).

6. It is also interesting to note that the fugues of J. S. Bach were undergoing a rebirth in Europe in 1927, precisely when Huxley was writing *Point Counter Point*. The eminent Bach specialist Gerhard Herz writes that "[t]he appearance of *The Art of the Fugue* in the concert halls of Europe finally occurred in 1927. In that year, in which Wolfgang Graeser republished the work — scoring its first four fugues for string quartet — the true performance history of *The Art of the Fugue* had its inception" (4).

Works Cited

Adorno, Theodor. *Introduction to the Sociology of Music*. New York: Seabury, 1976.

DeNora, Tia. *After Adorno: Rethinking Music Sociology*. Cambridge: Cambridge University Press, 2003.

Herz, Gerhard. "J. S. Bach: Die Kunst Der Fuge." Liner notes. Juilliard String Quartet. Sony Classical, S2K45937, 1987.

Higgins, Kathleen Marie. "Musical Idiosyncrasy and Perspectival Listening." In *Music and Meaning*, edited by Jenefer Robinson, 83–104. Ithaca: Cornell University Press, 1997.

Huxley, Aldous. *Brave New World*. New York: Harper, 1969.

_____.*Letters of Aldous Huxley*. Edited by Grover Smith. New York: Harper, 1969.

_____. *Music At Night: And Other Essays, Including "Vulgarity in Literature."* London: Chatto and Windus, 1960.

_____.*Point Counter Point*. New York: Avon, 1928.

Iamblichus: On the Pythagorean Life. Translated by Gillian Clark. Liverpool: Liverpool University Press, 1989.

Murray, Nicholas. *Aldous Huxley: A Biography*. New York: St. Martin's, 2002.

Shepherd, John. "Sociology of Music." Grove Music Online. Edited by L. Macy. http://www.grovemusic.com (accessed 5 May 2006).

Stockhausen, Karlheinz. *Stockhausen on Music*. Compiled by Robin Maconie. London: Marion Boyars, 1991.

Deconstructing the Savage Reservation in Brave New World

KATHERINE TOY MILLER

Living in Taos, New Mexico, where Native American cultures and traditions are much respected and admired, I was provoked to question how Aldous Huxley arrived at his unflattering depiction of the "Savage Reservation" and the characters in it. "I had no trouble finding my way around the English part of *Brave New World*," Huxley said in a *Paris Review* interview in 1960, "but I had to do an enormous amount of reading up on New Mexico, because I'd never been there. I read all sorts of Smithsonian reports on the place and then did the best I could to imagine it. I didn't actually go there until six years later, in 1937, when we visited Frieda Lawrence [D. H. Lawrence's wife]" (Interview).

Huxley's friendship with Lawrence, nine years his senior, was arguably one of the two great friendships in his formative years (Bedford 536). Lawrence — and Frieda, a German baroness six years older than Lawrence and the model for most of his significant female characters — had a large impact on Huxley's writing: three of Huxley's eleven novels have characters based on them (*Point Counter Point, Brave New World,* and *The Genius and the Goddess*); a fourth was influenced by Frieda's stories of her first husband (*Eyeless in Gaza*). "Of course I base my characters partly on the people I know — one can't escape it," Huxley explained (Interview).

Why in *Brave New World* Huxley chose to juxtapose his own social and political concerns — which he had been developing and writing about for years — with the cultural and geographical concerns and personal conflicts Lawrence struggled with may be the result of how intertwined Lawrence's (and Frieda's) lives were with Huxley's prior to and at the time of his composing it.

According to biographer Dana Sawyer, Huxley was often autobiographical in his novels (31), and *Brave New World* is in many ways an autobiographical novel, chronicling Huxley's experiences, ideas, and reading. Huxley said, "To write fiction, one needs a whole series of inspirations about people in an actual environment, and then a whole lot of hard work on the basis of those inspirations" (Interview). What follows is a chronology of Huxley's involvement with the Lawrences leading to the production of *Brave New World*.

Huxley first met the Lawrences in 1915 at Garsington, Philip and Ottoline Morrell's manor house in Oxfordshire, a gathering place for important artists and intellectuals. Huxley told Ottoline he was "very much impressed" by Lawrence (Squires and Talbot 136). Shortly after, Huxley came to tea at the Lawrences' Hampstead Heath flat. Huxley recalled that Lawrence talked not of World War I, which was then raging, but of a utopian community, "that colony of escape, of which up to the last he never ceased to dream" (*The Letters of D. H. L. xxviii–xxix*), the sort of community Huxley banishes Bernard and Helmholtz to— and forbids John to go to— at the end of *Brave New World* (227, 229, 242–243).

During the winter of 1923–24 Huxley met up with the Lawrences again while the Lawrences were visiting London (Bedford 178n). The Lawrences had left England in 1919 after being isolated in the English countryside during World War I and, in pursuit of Lawrence's goal of writing a novel about every developed continent, had traveled throughout Europe and to Ceylon, Australia, America, and Mexico. In 1925 the Huxleys journeyed around the world — similar to the Lawrences— visiting India, Burma, Malaya, Japan, China, and also America. But Lawrence's more lengthy experiences in America, particularly in New Mexico where he had hoped to be inspired by the Native Americans to find a new direction for western culture, had a much deeper and lasting impact on his worldview than Huxley's brief experience in America had on him. When asked if his later relocation from England to America affected his writing, Huxley responded, "I don't know. I don't think so. I never strongly felt that the place where I lived had great importance to me" (Interview).

Despite this, Huxley Americanized his revision of *Brave New World* according to Huxley scholar Jerome Meckier's detailed analysis of the original typescript.

> Initially, Huxley appears to have imagined *Brave New World* as a pro-Lawrencian tract…. [A] noble savage from Lawrence's beloved American Southwest, spouting a preference for God, freedom, and poetry, was to pose a formidable challenge to the ascendancy of technology and material comfort in the brave new world's deceptively blissful society. By the time Huxley penned the Savage's suicide, however, Lawrence's influence, waning steadily since his death, had faded almost completely…. Huxley resolved not to let New Mexico furnish a Lawrencian alternative to the Wellsian future … [and] made both madhouses fundamentally American [online].

The chronology shows, however, that Lawrence's influence on Huxley did not wane; rather Huxley's attitude shifted: he felt both sympathy and enthusiasm for Lawrence and recalled both Lawrence's frightening savagery and "terrible sadness" (*The Letters of D. H. L. xxxii–xxxiii*).

Huxley described Lawrence as "different and superior in kind, not degree… [a] being, somehow, of another order, more sensitive, more highly conscious, more capable of feeling than even the most gifted of common men"

(*The Letters of D. H. L.* xxx) which could explain why Lawrence — and Lawrence's writing — could have a profound influence on him. Also, Huxley needed a passionate man like Lawrence to draw on for his characters. "Isn't it remarkable how everyone who knew Lawrence felt compelled to write about him? Why, he's had more books written about him than any writer since Byron!" Huxley said (Interview). As we see in *Brave New World*, Huxley was more of a writer of ideas than of character or plot. "I don't think of myself as a congenital novelist — no. For example, I have great difficulty in inventing plots.... I'm not very good at creating people.... I don't happen to have the right kind of temperament (Interview). "He can express what he thinks superbly but not what he feels," Frieda wrote of Huxley (*Frieda Lawrence* 392). No one ever said that of Lawrence, and none of Lawrence's characters appear to be based on the Huxleys. "They seem to me like people from a dead planet," Lawrence wrote in one of the letters Huxley edited (*The Letters of D. H. L.* 680).

In 1925 Lawrence, after nearly dying in Mexico from a combination of typhoid and malaria compounded by his tuberculosis, recovered at his ranch in the mountains outside of Taos and left America for the last time, settling in Italy. He had read some essays Huxley had written on Italian travel, liked them, and suggested they meet. In 1926, while they were both near Florence, they did. After that, Huxley recalled, they were together often: in Florence, Forte dei Marmi, Diablerets, Bandol, Paris, Chexbres, in Forte again, and in Vence where Lawrence died (*The Letters of D. H. L.* xxix–xxx).

Between 1925–1928 most of Lawrence's writing on Mexico and New Mexico was published. In early 1928 while at Diablerets with the Huxleys, Lawrence corrected the proofs of a collection of some of these stories and talked about New Mexico, particularly of Black-Eyed Susan, his cow, and her "bovine philosophy" of which Huxley never tired of listening (*The Letters of D. H. L.* xxxi). Huxley worked on *Point Counter Point* in which Lawrence and Frieda are represented by Mark and Mary Rampion. Huxley followed their story "quite closely in many particulars," he agreed: "[B]ut only a small part of Lawrence is in that character" (Interview). Initiating themes he later explored in *Brave New World*, Huxley wrote, "After a few hours in Mark Rampion's company he really believed in noble savagery" (quoted in Bedford 203). Rampion "condemns 'Americanization' as the deification of 'Machinery and Alfred Mond or Henry Ford ... in the name of society, progress, and human happiness'" (quoted in Meckier).

Huxley became increasingly intolerant of Frieda as Lawrence became increasingly debilitated by tuberculosis, blaming his poor health on her. In July 1929, Lawrence stayed near the Huxleys at Forte dei Marmi (Squires and Talbot 357) while Frieda visited her three children in London. When Frieda wouldn't try to persuade Lawrence to see a doctor, the Huxleys said "she's a fool and a criminal" (*Letters of Aldous Huxley* 314). By February 1930 Lawrence was in the Ad Astra sanatorium in Vence. The Huxleys rushed to see him and spent his last week with him. "We were there, in Vence, when he died.... He actually died in my first wife's arms," Huxley recalled (Interview). This was March 2. Huxley attended to the funeral details on Frieda's behalf (Crotch 31) and loaned her seven thousand francs to cover expenses (*Letters of Aldous Huxley* 335).

After Frieda accepted his offer of editing Lawrence's letters without compensation or royalties, Huxley contacted a publisher on March 8 with his proposal (*Letters of Aldous Huxley* 331). For several months Huxley hunted up Lawrence letters between Bandol, Sanary, London, and Paris (Bedford 235) and was occupied with the project until the book was published in 1932. "In the three years after *Point Counter Point* [1928–1931] Aldous did not attempt any major work," biographer Sybille Bedford noted (240).

In October 1930, Huxley went to Nottingham to see Lawrence's relatives and to the Northern Midlands to lecture and for some articles on the mining villages. This experience influenced his ideas about creating a better-run society perhaps more than his travels around the world because it brought his concerns home to England. The Brave New World begins at this time: after the Nine Years' War (World War I) and the great economic collapse (the Great Depression) (48).

The article Huxley wrote from his visit, "Abroad in England," reflects the rigid class and cultural differences that form the basis of the society in *Brave New World*. He noted that D. H. Lawrence used to tell him, "You can't exaggerate the strength and importance of class" ("Abroad" 16). In February Huxley returned to the coal mining region, entering his first mine ("Aldous Huxley") and touring the factories of Joseph Lucas and Sir Alfred Mond. He wrote about these in "Sight-Seeing in Alien Englands." The masses of workers he saw likely inspired the mass-produced workers in *Brave New World* (Meckier) which he began in April 1931: "I am writing a novel about the future — on the horror of the Wellsian Utopia and a revolt against it. Very difficult. I have hardly enough imagination to deal with such a subject. But it is none the less interesting work" (*Letters of Aldous Huxley* 348).

Other *Brave New World* themes appear in Huxley's introduction to Lawrence's letters which he made notes for in September after completing the novel in August (*Letters of Aldous Huxley* 355). The director of hatcheries and conditioning says the secret of happiness and virtue is to like "what you've got to do. All conditioning aims at that: making people like their unescapable social destiny" (16). Huxley said Lawrence was "unescapably an artist" and though at times Lawrence wanted to escape his destiny, there was no escape from his fate (*The Letters of D. H. L.* ix).

According to Huxley, for Lawrence "there were two great and criminal distractions. First, work, which he regarded as a mere stupefacient, like opium." Lawrence was also appalled that people could "forget all the delights and difficulties of immediate living" (*The Letters of D. H. L.* xix–xx). In *Brave New World* people prefer their mindless work to free time (224), and there is no "immediate living" in this planned environment.

Even more than the Huxleys—who always owned a car, usually an expensive one—the Lawrences lived simply. "No servants, no luxuries, no possessions," Frieda wrote. "As a very young man [Lawrence] realized that they waste too much time and clutter you up" (*Frieda Lawrence* 438). Lawrence could efficiently sew, darn, embroider, cook, chop wood, lay a fire, scrub a floor, and milk a cow, as Huxley knew (*The Letters of D. H. L.* xxxi). From their walks in the country, Huxley also knew one of Lawrence's greatest passions was nature and found it to be a significant force in Lawrence's novels (*The Letters of D. H. L.* xxx). As Frieda said, "In the machine Lawrence saw the deadly enemy of man, man was no longer the god in the machine but the machine had become God" (*Frieda Lawrence* 438–439). Though Huxley himself is not usually passionate about either nature or mechanization, in *Brave New World* he engineers a world where the love of nature is deliberately replaced by consumerism and modern inventions (23) as reflected in his propaganda slogan for conspicuous consumption: "Ending is better than mending. The more stitches, the less riches" (49).

What Huxley calls "the most serious defect in the story"—that the Savage "is offered only two alternatives, an insane life in Utopia, or the life of a primitive in an Indian village" (*Brave New World* viii)—reflects one of the final concerns of Lawrence's letters. Lawrence was tortured by the choice of living in primitive New Mexico/Mexico or industrialized England/Europe. Projecting his personal fears and angers onto each place he considered, Lawrence announced, "So, for the present at least, I give it up. It's no good. Mankind is too unkind" (*The Letters of D. H. L.* 570). Huxley recounted that the choice between "insanity" and "lunacy" was one "I found amusing and regarded as quite possibly true" at the time (*Brave New World* viii).

The letters Huxley collected mention *The Plumed Serpent* (637), *The Woman Who Rode Away* (614), *Mornings in Mexico* (625) which includes "The Hopi Snake Dance" and other essays on Mexico and New Mexico (610), "Indians and an Englishman" (566), and *Reflections on the Death of a Porcupine* (646), another collection of essays. Huxley used parts of these almost directly. As he said, "I read individual books that I like and take things from and am stimulated by... (Interview).

According to Huxley *The Plumed Serpent* reveals Lawrence's ambivalence about relying solely on instincts rather than intellect. The two failed societies in *Brave New World*—the rational, scientific world of England and the natural, ritualistic world of the reservation—illustrate Huxley's conclusion: "The point is that you *must have both*"—"the blood and the flesh" and the "conscious mind" (quoted in Bedford 211).

A significant source for the "Savage Reservation" is Lawrence's "The Woman Who Rode Away." Seemingly an acknowledgment of Frieda's willing sacrifice for Lawrence's vision of a revitalized world, the ending is set in a cave that Lawrence and Frieda visited with their Taos patroness Mabel Dodge Luhan

(*Not I* 151). Huxley uses this story to set up the situation of Linda who was likely inspired by Frieda. Lawrence's woman, "aroused from her stupor of subjected amazement" (45), decides to ride away from her husband in search of an ancient Indian tribe and allows herself to be caught and sacrificed by them; at the reservation Linda walks away from the director and becomes lost (97).

Lawrence describes his woman as "thirty-three [the age Frieda was when she met Lawrence], a large, blue-eyed, dazed woman, beginning to grow stout" (45), details frequently used to describe Frieda. Like Frieda, Linda in her youth "had yellow hair" and was, like Frieda, "pneumatic [sexual], particularly pneumatic" (96). Later Linda was a "very stout blonde squaw" and had "under the brown sack-shaped tunic those enormous breasts, the bulge of the stomach, the hips" (119), a description matching photos of Frieda taken when the Lawrences lived in New Mexico and Mexico.

When Lenina and Bernard arrive at Malpais, "an almost naked Indian was very slowly climbing down the ladder ... with the tremulous caution of extreme old age. His face was profoundly wrinkled and black, like a mask of obsidian" (110). The woman in Lawrence's story has brought before her on a litter "an old, old cacique.... His face was like a piece of obsidian" (58).

At the reservation, "a dead dog was lying on a rubbish heap" (112). Lawrence's woman sees in the Mexican marketplace "a dead dog lying between the meat stalls and the vegetable array, stretched out as if for ever, nobody troubling to throw it away" (45). This same detail appears in the Lawrence letters Huxley edited: in Mexico Lawrence visited a little covered market where "between the meat and the vegetables, a dead dog lay stretched as if asleep" which no one bothered to throw out (*The Letters of D. H. L.* 581).

Lawrence's woman is regularly given an herbal potion which causes her to vomit after which she feels "a great soothing languor steal over her" (53). The Indian Popé often brings Linda mescal which Linda says "ought to be called soma, only it made you feel ill afterwards" (125). For both women, the drinks (and later for Linda soma) contribute to their will-less resistance to their deaths.

Huxley apparently chose another unsavory detail from "Indians and an Englishman." Lawrence, unsympathetic to the challenges of desert living, complained, "The Apaches have a cult of water-hatred; they never wash flesh or rag. So never in my life have I smelt such an unbearable sulpher-human [*sic*] smell as comes from them when they cluster: a smell that takes the breath from the nostrils" (8). This is the only time Lawrence mentions that the Indians smell, but Huxley seems to have seized upon it. Lenina says of their guide when they first arrive at Malpais, "he smells" (108). As she and Bernard hike up to Malpais "the Indian smelt stronger and stronger" (108). When they enter an Indian home it smells of "smoke and cooked grease and long-worn, long-unwashed clothes" (112).

Among the Lawrence letters Huxley edited one included an essay headed "Just back from the Snake Dance" which Lawrence soon revised to "The Hopi

Snake Dance." Both record Lawrence's trip to the Hopi reservation in Arizona. Many of the same details appear in *Brave New World*. Lawrence's first version mocks the Indian ritual and those who come to witness it: "Hotevilla is a scrap of a place with a plaza no bigger than a fair-sized back-yard: and the chief house on the square a ruin. But into this plaza finally three thousand onlookers piled" (*The Letters of D. H. L.* 607). Similarly Huxley writes, "They stepped across the threshold and found themselves on a wide terrace. Below them, shut in by the tall houses, was the village square, crowded with Indians" (112).

For his image of the kivas—"two circular platforms of masonry and trampled clay—the roofs, it was evident, of underground chambers" (112–113)—Huxley probably borrowed from Lawrence's "Dance of the Sprouting Corn"—"the men and women crowd on the roofs of the two low round towers, the kivas" (36). Lawrence's description of the Koshare or sacred clowns "daubed with black and white earth ... some are white with black spots, like a leopard, and some have broad black lines or zigzags on their smeared bodies, and all their faces are blackened with triangle or lines till they look like weird masks" (35) Huxley likely transformed into "a ghastly troop of monsters. Hideously masked or painted out of all semblance of humanity..." (113).

Lawrence's essay is about a snake-handling ritual like the one at Huxley's reservation. In both, snakes are brought forth, images of eagles are present, corn meal is scattered, and there is a ceremony involving young men and older priests. But Huxley appears to be ascribing the tradition of the Catholic *penitentes* to the Native Americans when he has the priest beat one young man either unconscious or to death with a whip (115). Throughout the rest of the novel, John performs *penitente*-style self-flagellation which Lawrence mentions briefly in two short stories, "The Wilful Woman" and "The Princess," and was practiced by the *penitentes* in a *morada* adjacent to where the Lawrences first lived in Taos.

A final odd detail that Huxley apparently picked up from Lawrence's essay "The Death of a Porcupine" is that porcupines should be listed with other life-threatening creatures of the Southwest (103, 105), but a porcupine is a vegetarian rodent about two feet in length. Lawrence records shooting one because it was eating the bark of pine trees.

Partway into writing *Brave New World*, Huxley had a "literary catastrophe" and had to revise the novel (*Letters of Aldous Huxley* 348–349). According to Meckier, "he was creating a modern British dystopia instead of a universally frightening one." The earliest draft may have started on the reservation with Linda (then called Nina connecting her with John and Bernard's love interest, Lenina; also Niña is the nickname of the Frieda-inspired main female character in *The Plumed Serpent*) left behind by Bernard, John's father in this version. "One suspects that Bernard and his son John originally were to be reunited for insurrectionary purposes," Meckier surmised, but "Huxley demoted Bernard [Marx] from virile protagonist to farcical antihero, a process that coincided with the Savage's decline from Lawrencian standard-bearer to futile alternative. Huxley transformed Marx into a smallish man with a large inferiority complex; he transferred Bernard's original physique and potential for rebellion to Helmholtz Watson" (online). This could reflect Huxley's ambiguous feelings toward Lawrence which he discussed midway through the composition of *Brave New World*: "I enormously admire Lawrence's books and I greatly loved him personally—but in reading him I often suffer from a kind of claustrophobia…. What a relief to get out of a whale-like book like *Lady Chatterley*" (*Letters of Aldous Huxley* 349 [trans. from French]).

Helmholtz Watson, "a lecturer at the College of Emotional Engineering (Department of Writing) … [and] a working Emotional Engineer" (writer) (67) resembles Huxley. According to Sawyer, by 1924 Huxley "wished to write a novel that would truly matter artistically, which for Huxley meant pointing in a moral direction, but he was having trouble doing so" (53). Helmholtz tells Bernard that he sometimes gets "a feeling that I've got something important to say and the power to say it—only I don't know what it is, and I can't make any use of the power. If there was some different way of writing … Or else something else to write about…" (69).

Bernard Marx resembles Lawrence in some respects. Lawrence was thin and unhealthy from congenital problems with his lungs while Bernard is small because of alcohol placed in his bottle. Bernard is from "the Psychology Bureau" (34) while Huxley, in his essay "The Puritan," stated that Lawrence concerned himself with "psychological reforms" (*Music at Night* 181). Helmholtz likes Bernard for one reason Huxley liked Lawrence: "What the two men shared was the knowledge that they were individuals" (67).

The most important parallel between Bernard and Lawrence is that Bernard wants to go to the reservation in New Mexico (44), setting up the major plot line. There was no one else Huxley knew who would want to go to New Mexico besides the Lawrences, and the idea would not have likely occurred to him if he had not known them. "In his last years [Lawrence] wanted to go back to New Mexico. He had been very happy there on the ranch in Taos. But he wasn't strong enough to make the trip," Huxley said (Interview).

At the reservation, Bernard realizes he has left on his Eau de Cologne tap. He first thinks it will cost him a fortune—Lawrence was notoriously cheap—and next calls Helmholtz for help. When Lawrence heard a pirated edition of *Lady Chatterley's Lover* was being sold in Paris, he asked Aldous and Maria, who were living in Paris, to look into it which they did (*Letters of Aldous Huxley* 304) just as Helmholtz promises "to go around at once, at once, and turn off the tap, yes, at once" (103).

Helmholtz also likes Bernard despite his flaws, as Huxley liked Lawrence. "I was very fond of Lawrence as a man…. I was a little disturbed by him. You know, he *was* rather disturbing," Huxley commented (Interview). But Lawrence was famous for his brutal honesty and his brutal anger rather than for being deceitful and self-pitying like Bernard. It is possible that these unpleasant aspects of Bernard are based upon John Middleton Murry, a mutual friend of Lawrence's and Huxley's. "There is something of Murry in several of my characters," Huxley acknowledged (Interview).

Like Lawrence and Murry, Bernard is an Alpha Plus (*Brave New World* 44). "Murry's was an acute and subtle mind," Huxley wrote. Asked what attracted Lawrence to Murry, then repelled him, Huxley answered that Murry was a hypocrite — generating a great passion for something or someone while he was capable of feeling very little (*Letters of Aldous Huxley* 929–930). When Helmholtz tells Bernard that the director is sending Bernard to Iceland, we learn that Bernard had wanted to be subjected to "some great trial, some pain, some persecution; he had even longed for affliction.... The Director's threats had actually elated him, made him feel larger than life.... Now that it looked as though the threats were really to be fulfilled, Bernard was appalled. Of that imagined stoicism, that theoretical courage, not a trace was left. He raged against himself — what a fool! — against the Director — how unfair not to give him that other chance, that other chance which, he now had no doubt at all, he had always intended to take" (103–104).

When John causes the fight over soma at the hospital, Bernard collapses to the floor in fear, then tries to sneak away, afraid to be caught along with John and only reluctantly admitting they are friends (214–216). Similarly, Frieda wrote to a mutual friend that Murry had "pretended like the sneak that he is to be your friend" and that "[t]here is a very great cowardice in Jack [Murry]" (*Frieda Lawrence* 204).

John could be based on the younger, more idealistic Lawrence (and values Lawrence shared with Huxley) while Bernard has lost the Lawrentian optimism and courage and seems more like Murry. Regarding Lawrence's letters, Huxley observed, "The early ones are particularly interesting and delightful — such high spirits; which he lost as he grew older and iller" (*Letters of Aldous Huxley* 346).

Murry and Frieda had a brief affair after Lawrence's death in the villa where he died (Lucas 255) which may have inspired Huxley's original plan of Bernard fathering John, connecting both to Linda — one as lover and one as son. Lawrence — as a possible model for the earlier Bernard and John — was seen as both the lover and son of Frieda. When Lawrence died, Frieda's grown daughter Barby, who was very close to Lawrence and helped take care of him, said, sobbing, "My poor mother, her child is dead" (quoted in Squires and Talbot 364). Huxley wrote that Lawrence felt towards Frieda "as a man might feel towards his own liver": though it might give him trouble, it was necessary for his survival (*Letters of Aldous Huxley* 831). Bernard notes that John is "distressed" because his mother "remains permanently on holiday" and that in spite of her "senility and the extreme repulsiveness of her appearance, the Savage frequently goes to see her and appears to be much attracted to her" (160–161).

Like Bernard and John, Lawrence was shy about sexual matters. Bernard is offended when he overhears Henry Foster and the assistant predestinator talking about Lenina "like meat, like so much meat" (53). He also is uncomfortable when Lenina mentions in public going to the reservation together (57) and when he must participate in the Solidarity Service (78–86). When Lenina strips for John, he beats her (193–196). What stops him is a phone call about his mother dying (197), a rather Freudian interruption. Lawrence was known as the sexually risqué author of his time, but Huxley recalled Lawrence saying "'Chastity to me is better than any contact could be in this mind-spoiled world,' or some such phrase. He was profoundly shocked by the pornographic and the smoking-room story, which he regarded as a mentalization of sex" (Huxley et al 35).

One of John's obsessions is marriage—first he wants to marry Kiakimé (135) then he wants to know if Bernard and Lenina are married (139) then he wants to marry Lenina (190). Lawrence, too, believed in wedlock. Frieda said that in his letters to her he expressed "his attitude, almost religious, to marriage" (*Frieda Lawrence* 358).

Like Lawrence and Huxley, Bernard and John are loners. "'Alone, always alone,'" John says. "'So am I,'" Bernard answers. They agree that "if one's different, one's bound to be lonely" (137). Bernard "doesn't like Obstacle Golf" and "spends most of his time by himself—*alone*" (45). "I loathe the 'playboy' attitude to life," Lawrence wrote. "And I detest 'having a good time'" (*The Letters of D. H. L.* 568). Like John and Bernard, Lawrence never found a group he felt part of and lived most often in isolated circumstances. "Lawrence's psychological isolation resulted ... in his seeking physical isolation from the body of mankind" (*The Letters of D. H. L.* xxvii), Huxley stated.

Lawrence also disliked public curiosity. Huxley noted, "I have seldom met anyone who was less of a public man than Lawrence, more essentially a man of the private life.... He always regarded public curiosity about his affairs as 'damned impertinence' (that was how he put it to me)" (*Letters of Aldous Huxley* 340). It is John's extreme dislike of being a public curiosity that nearly drives him mad. John begs the crowd arriving at the lighthouse, "'Why don't you leave me alone?'" (56).

Bernard—and especially John—are given to violent outbursts like Lawrence, who frequently beat Frieda, and whom Huxley described as "difficult to get on with, passionate, queer, and violent" (*Letters of Aldous Huxley* 288). After beating Lenina in his room (194–195), at the hospital John "in his furious misery" shakes Linda by the shoulders until she chokes and looks at him "with an unspeakable terror ... and, it seemed to him, reproach" (205), knocks one of the children over (207), then, "exasperated by their bestial stupidity into throwing insults at those he had come to save," starts a fight in the lobby over soma (212–213). "Mostly other people were a torture," Frieda recalled. "When [we] were with others who seemed interested in what [Lawrence] had to say he would talk and give himself away, while [I] could feel how they mostly jeered at him; at the best they got a superficial kick out of what he told them so vehemently" (quoted in Holland 288). Then John beats Lenina again at the lighthouse while the crowd watches (257). Of Lawrence's rages Huxley wrote that Lawrence profoundly disliked "[e]motional indecency" and felt anger was "less indecent" than resignation or complaint (*The Letters of D. H. L.* xxxii).

Like John, Lawrence was associated with Christ. Frieda describes him picking mulberries in his bathing suit: "The mulberries were so juicy and red and they ran down his body so that he looked like one of those very realistic Christs we had seen on our walk across the Alps years ago" (*Not I*, 114–115). In Mexico, a Mexican muttered "Christo" while looking at the tall, thin, red-bearded Lawrence shopping at an open market with his devotee, Dorothy Brett (also Huxley's friend and portrayed in his novel *Crome Yellow* [Bedford 71]) (Foster 188). Brett painted Lawrence as Christ on the cross being observed by Lawrence as Pan (Lawrence, D. H., back cover image). In Lawrence's *The Man Who Died* (published in 1929 as *The Escaped Cock*), Christ's survival of his crucifixion parallels Lawrence's survival of his near-death experience in Mexico.

In his conversation with Mustapha Mond, John insists "But I don't want comfort. I want God, I want poetry, I want real danger, I want freedom, I want goodness, I want sin" (240). In "Pan in America" Lawrence explained, "A conquered world is no good to man. He sits stupefied with boredom upon his conquest. We need the universe to live again so that we can live with it. A conquered universe, a dead Pan, leaves us nothing to live with" (42).

Two scenes from John's life in England could be partially drawn from Huxley's and Lawrence's lives: Linda's death and John's death. Huxley's mother died of cancer when he was nine. He wrote about it in *Antic Hay*: "He hadn't known that she was going to die, but when he entered her room, when he saw her lying so weakly in the bed, he had suddenly begun to cry, uncontrollably" (quoted in Dunaway 6). At the funeral, Aldous was "shaking with sobs" (Bedford 25). According to Meckier, "Huxley wrote Linda's death scene by hand on 11 pages" while the rest of the manuscript is typed (online). Perhaps it was too emotionally difficult to write any other way.

The scene also has details reminiscent of Lawrence's death. On the last day of his life, Lawrence called out for morphia to relieve his pain. Frieda's daughter Barby got a doctor who gave him a shot which quieted him. Fearing he would need another shot, Huxley and Barby left the house in search of another doctor. Unable to find one, they returned. Lawrence had already died (*Letters of Aldous Huxley* 330; *Not I* 295–296). In *Brave New World*, after John shakes Linda, she stops breathing and turns blue. John runs up the ward shouting. The head nurse, surrounded by children, tells him not to shout. He "dragged her after him. 'Quick! Something's happened. I've killed her,'" he says. "By the time they were back at the end of the ward Linda was dead. The Savage stood for a moment in frozen silence, then fell on his knees beside the bed and, covering his face with his hands, sobbed uncontrollably" (205–206). At about the same age that John is, Lawrence, assisted by his sister Ada, actually did kill his mother, who was dying of cancer, with an overdose of morphine (Byrne 100).

John's anger at civilization and its temptations, his guilt about his attraction to Lenina, his guilt over Linda's death, his guilt from enjoying his solitary life, and his guilt over "a long-drawn frenzy of sensuality" (258)—in short, his impossibly high ideals—cause his suicide which, as critics have pointed out, parallels the suicide of Huxley's older brother Trev by hanging. "It is just the highest and best in Trev—his ideals—which have driven him to his death.... Trev was not strong, but he had the courage to face life with ideals—and his ideals were too much for him," Huxley explained (*Letters of Aldous Huxley* 61–62). One possible cause of Trev's suicide was that he had gotten a girl of a lower class pregnant (Dunaway 12–13) which may have fueled Huxley's concern with birth control in *Brave New World*.

Physically, John, who had "straw-coloured hair," pale blue eyes, and "white skin, bronzed," (116) resembles Trev who had blond hair and a "firm, athletic body" from hiking (Dunaway 12). "A nice-looking boy," Lenina thinks, "and a really beautiful body" (117). John also resembles Frieda's son, Monty (her oldest child), another handsome, well-built blond. When he was seventeen, Frieda wrote, "The boy is quite beautiful, suddenly a youth, nearly six foot already" (quoted in Jackson 58). And John's relationship with Linda is similar to Monty's relationship with Frieda. Though there is no evidence Huxley met Monty, as an adult the Huxleys knew Frieda's younger daughter Barby well.

Like Linda and John who are outcasts on the reservation, Frieda was an outcast in England during the Boer War because of her German connections: "When [I] spoke German to [my] boy in a tram or train, he would pull [my] skirts and whisper: 'Don't speak German, people are looking at us'" (*Frieda Lawrence* 87–88). Frieda and Lawrence were also outcasts in England during World War I: "Very few people wanted to be friendly to us in those days. I was a Hun and Lawrence not wanted" (*Not I* 91).

In 1915 when Huxley first met the Lawrences they were staying in London so Frieda could see her children. Her former husband limited her contact with them. When Frieda met Monty outside his school and cried upon seeing him, "he looked at me full of manly love and support.... I always felt his love strong and whole," she recalled (*Frieda Lawrence* 111–112). Linda says nearly the same thing: "And yet John *was* a great comfort to me. I don't know what I should have done without him" (122). Frieda, like Linda, frequently sobbed during times of stress. Frieda continued, "Then I wept when we sat together so near and I had to ask him for his hanky and he gave it to me, a big grubby school hanky" (*Frieda Lawrence* 111). When Linda first meets Bernard and Lenina and recalls London, "great tears oozed slowly out from behind her tight-shut eyelids." Unfortunately Linda lacks a handkerchief and blows her nose on her fingers (120).

Monty was verbally gifted, scholarly, and literary — like his father (a well-known etymologist) and John. He was also disciplined and traditional and conservative in his values like John. Lawrence described him "'as a specimen of the perfect young Englishman'" (quoted in Byrne 308–309), a description that would fit John — though raised among "savages" — as well. In 1926 while the Lawrences were in London, Frieda "made Monty [age twenty-six — near John's age] a part of their social life, introducing him to their London circle" (Byrne 323). A short time later, after the Huxleys visited the Lawrence's villa outside of Florence, Frieda wrote to Monty, "Don't be too spartan, but keep a steady core in yourself" (*Frieda Lawrence* 226), advice that might be given to John who is too spartan and struggles to keep a steady core in himself.

As adults, Barby and Monty referred to their mother as "Frieda" as John calls his mother "Linda." Monty said, "Frieda was, as ever, a cake eater and haver.... She wanted everything and didn't see why she shouldn't get it. No difficulty about it at all.... [She] absolutely reject[ed] any kind of mental discipline" (quoted in Byrne 385). Linda, too, is completely undisciplined and, unlike John, makes no attempt to conform to the rules of the society she finds herself in.

When Frieda was first with Lawrence a heel came off one shoe, so she threw both shoes into the Isar River. "'Things are there for me and not I for them, so when they are a nuisance I throw them away,'" she told him (*Not I* 38–39). Linda complains that at the reservation she is supposed to mend the woolen clothing: "Nobody ever taught me to do anything like that. It wasn't my business. Besides, it never used to be right to mend clothes. Throw them away when they've got holes in them and buy new" (121).

When John and Linda reach London, their reception is similar to the one Lawrence and Frieda usually received: everyone wanted to see John — "all upper-caste London was wild to see this delicious creature" (153) — and Lawrence. No one wanted to see Linda — or Frieda — and for the same reasons — they were fat and neither seemed as unique as John or Lawrence: "So the best people were quite determined *not* to see Linda" (153). Frieda recalled that around the time they met Huxley at Garsington "we were asked to lunch by a few lion huntresses and the human being in me felt only insulted" (*Not I* 77).

During the months the Lawrences and Huxleys spent in Les Diablerets in 1928, Frieda, "her body large and loose, cooked or lay on her bed reading books," missing her lover, Angelo Ravagli (a married Italian army officer who later became her third husband), while Maria Huxley typed *Lady Chatterley's Lover* (Squires and Talbot 340–341). Frieda could not type, and Lawrence never expected her to do work she did not want to do (*Not I* 86). Similarly in *Brave New World*, "Sometimes, for several days, Linda didn't get up at all. She lay in bed and was sad" (127). When John objects because Linda's life is being shortened by soma, the doctor responds, "You can't allow people to go popping off into eternity if they've got any serious work to do. But as she hasn't got any serious work..." (155).

After Linda's death, John recalls, "How beautiful her singing had been!" (201). Lawrence and Frieda sang constantly: "He taught me many songs, we sang by the hour in the evenings; he liked my strong voice," Frieda wrote (*Not I*, 71–72).

An account of Frieda on the day after Lawrence's death shows the Huxleys' experience with Frieda's housekeeping: "Frieda had contrived to get the kitchen into a hell of an unwholesome mess. Little Maria [Huxley], though nearly a wreck, spent the morning scrubbing it out" (quoted in Bedford 226). When Bernard and Lenina enter Linda's house, they notice that "in bowls on the floor were the remains of a meal, perhaps several meals" (118).

While Huxley was busy collecting Lawrence letters and probably dealing much with Frieda he wrote, "I like her in a way; but being with her makes me believe that Buddha was right when he numbered stupidity among the deadly sins" (*Letters of Aldous Huxley* 335). Huxley made Helmholtz and Bernard Alpha Pluses, but Linda was only a Beta-Minus according to the director (96) though she identifies herself as a Beta (120). Huxley calls Linda "a monster of flaccid and distorted senility" (202) and places her on the "Galloping Senility ward" (198).

For a year after Lawrence's death while his estate was being settled, Frieda roamed Europe visiting Monty and friends, including the Huxleys (Squires and Talbot 366). During this time Frieda's other main source of stability, her mother, also died. Huxley wrote to their mutual friend Dorothy Brett, "Don't expect to get any definite answer about anything out of Frieda. Definite answers don't grow in her brain. She's been rather ill and down, poor F, lately" (*Letters of Aldous Huxley* 347). Shortly after that, he began *Brave New World* in which John remembers that whatever he asked about "Linda never seemed to know" (130).

Like Linda, Frieda became a social outcast because of her sexual behavior — by leaving her husband for Lawrence. During her first marriage Frieda had affairs with several men. She also had affairs while she was with Lawrence which Huxley was aware of (*Letters of Aldous Huxley* 831). While Huxley wrote, "A strange and terrifying monster of middle-agedness, Linda advanced into the room, coquettishly smiling her broken and discoloured smile, and rolling as she walked, with what was meant to be a voluptuous undulation, her enormous haunches" (150), Frieda said of her relationship with Ravagli "'that an old bird like me is still capable of real passion and can inspire it too, seems a miracle'" (quoted in Crotch 27).

Like Frieda, Linda believes that no one should belong to just one person (121). It was the basis for Frieda's relationship with Lawrence. When she and Lawrence first lived together she wrote in a letter, "I have quite forgotten that I am *not* married to L" (*Frieda Lawrence* 171). When John is upset after he watches the marriage ceremony of Kiakimé, Linda, characteristic of Frieda, responds: "All I can say is, it does seem a lot of fuss to make about so little" (135). When Frieda and Lawrence married after two years of living together, Frieda wrote, "I didn't care whether I was married or not, it didn't seem to make any difference, but I think Lawrence was glad that we were respectable married people" (*Not I* 77).

Unlike Linda, Frieda was not violent. Huxley misrepresents her when he writes "Frieda used to throw plates at Lawrence, and Lawrence threw them back at her" (*Letters of Aldous Huxley* 831). "So much crockery I must have smashed through the years!!" Frieda remarked. "I did it only once! When L. told me women had no souls and couldn't love!" (*Frieda Lawrence* 390). But when attacked, she would defend herself verbally. Possibly the women who beat Linda and "'say those men are *their* men'" (126) were inspired by the two women in Taos who Frieda fought with over Lawrence: Mabel Dodge Luhan and Dorothy Brett, especially since Huxley had listened to Lawrence talk of Mabel's and Brett's escapades (Squires and Talbot 341).

Frieda continued to be an influence on Huxley's writing and life even after Lawrence's death and the publication of *Brave New World*. In 1936 Huxley published *Eyeless in Gaza* in which he "introduced the element of philology ... based upon descriptions given by Frieda Lawrence of her first husband [Ernest Weekley] who was a philologist," he said (*Letters of Aldous Huxley* 409). When the Huxleys spent the summer of 1937 with Frieda at her ranch outside of Taos, Huxley observed, "Frieda is well, cheerful, and a great deal calmer than she used to be" (*Letters of Aldous Huxley* 425, 422*)*. The Huxleys visited Frieda a few more times at the ranch; Frieda and Ravagli visited them in Hollywood. In 1943 Frieda received a letter from Maria who said "that coming to the ranch had changed her life" and led her to their rural home in Llano, California (*Frieda Lawrence*, 287–288).

In 1955 when Maria Huxley died, Huxley told Frieda that "'I thought very often of that spring night in Vence twenty-five years ago [when Lawrence died], while I was sitting beside Maria's bed [awaiting her death]'" (*Letters of Aldous Huxley* 733). He visited Frieda shortly after while writing the dramatic version of *The Genius and The Goddess*, his novel based on Frieda's famous ability to revive Lawrence which he wrote while Maria was ill. His opinion of Frieda had changed considerably: "Thanks to Frieda, Lawrence remained alive for at least five years after he ought, by all the rules of medicine, to have been in the grave" (*Letters of Aldous Huxley* 831).

Works Cited

"Aldous Huxley." Myers Literary Guide. Centre for Northern Studies. <http://online. north-umbria.ac.uk/faculties/art/humanities/cns/m-huxley.html>
Bedford, Sybille. *Aldous Huxley: a Biography*. New York: Harper/Knopf, 1973.
Byrne, Janet. *A Genius for Living: The Life of Frieda Lawrence*. HarperCollins: New York, 1995.
Crotch, Martha Gordon. *Memories of Frieda Lawrence*. Edinburgh: The Tragara Press, 1975.

Dunaway, David King. *Huxley in Hollywood.* New York: Harper & Row, 1989.

Foster, Joseph. *D. H. Lawrence in Taos.* Albuquerque: University of New Mexico Press, 1972.

Holland, James Ellery. "The Memoirs of Frieda Lawrence." Dissertation. University. of Texas at Austin, 1976.

Huxley, Aldous. "Abroad in England." *Nash's Pall Mall Magazine,* May 1931: 16-19, 84.

_____. *Brave New World.* Perennial Classics ed. New York: HarperCollins, 1998.

_____. Interview. The Art of Fiction no. 24. Writers at Work: *The Paris Review* Interviews. *The Paris Review.* Issue. 23, Spring 1960. Online.

_____. *Letters of Aldous Huxley.* Edited by. Grover Smith. New York: Harper & Row, 1969.

_____. *Music at Night.* Phoenix Library ed. London: Chatto and Windus, 1932.

_____, editor. *The Letters of D. H. Lawrence.* London: Heinemann, 1932.

_____, et al. *A Conversation on D. H. Lawrence.* Los Angeles: Friends of the U. C. L. A. Library, 1974.

Jackson, Rosie. *Frieda Lawrence.* San Francisco: Pandora, 1994.

Lawrence, D. H. *D. H. Lawrence and New Mexico.* Edited by. Keith Sagar. Paris: Alyscamps Press, 1995.

Lawrence, Frieda. *Frieda Lawrence: The Memoirs and Correspondence.* New York: Alfred A. Knopf, 1964.

_____. *Not I, But the Wind.* New York: The Viking Press, 1934.

Lucas, Robert. *Frieda Lawrence: the Story of Frieda von Richthofen and D. H. Lawrence.* New York: The Viking Press, 1972.

Meckier, Jerome. "Aldous Huxley's Americanization of the *Brave New World* Typescript." LookSmart, . <http://www.findarticles.com/p/articles/mi_m0403/is_ 4_48/ai_108194336/ print (accessed 24 October 2007).>

Myers, Alan. "Aldous Huxley." Myers Literary Guide: The North-East. http://www.seaham. i12.com/myers/m-huxley.html (accessed 24 October 2007).

Sawyer, Dana. *Aldous Huxley: A Biography.* New York: The Crossroads Publishing Company, 2002.

Squires, Michael and Lynn K. Talbot. *Living at the Edge: A Biography of D. H. Lawrence and Frieda von Richthofen.* Madison: University of Wisconsin Press, 2002.

The Eternal Now of
Brave New World:
Huxley, Joseph Campbell,
and The Perennial Philosophy

ROBERT COMBS

Aldous Huxley's best known novel, *Brave New World*, and George Orwell's *1984* have become "irreplaceable parts of (our) culture" (Calder 59): these titles have become indispensable catchphrases in cautionary discussions of the future. And for many, that future is now. Building on his knowledge of Nazi Germany and Stalinism, Orwell dared to suggest in 1948 that in wartime Britain, too, he had seen indications of totalitarianism. Huxley tended to think, already in 1932, that popular culture, especially in America, provided abundant evidence that people were willing to be complicit in their own enslavement without needing to be threatened. Which is worse, Orwell's systematic terrorism or Huxley's mindless consumerism? It is hard to say. Both authors indulge in exaggerated, grotesque visions of the future in order to criticize tendencies of the present. Both authors write melodramas of catastrophe, stories of unavailing heroism, not only to shock their readers into awareness, but also, perhaps, to suggest that solutions to the problems they examine may not actually be available, now or ever. Terror and soporifics are themselves solutions, after all. Perhaps the modern world needs something more imaginative than solutions.

Orwell's thinking gravitated predictably toward socialism, while Huxley's, to the surprise and consternation of many, moved into mysticism and experiments with hallucinogens. Jenni Calder remarks that while Orwell's dystopia tends to vitiate the experience of the commoner, Huxley's precludes any sort of exceptional, *un*common experience (43). According to such a comparison, Orwell is the realist, Huxley the romantic. In other words, Huxley is calling for individual psychological alternatives to mass behavior rather than speculating about collective political options. The crisis explored in *Brave New World* is that it is very difficult, if not impossible, to experience the self in a world driven by consumerism and its attendant narcissism. Huxley does not look to the future for some solution, but to the experience of the self in an ongoing present. The full implications of Huxley's diagnosis of the soul-sickness of modern life were not realized until 1944, with the publication of *The Perennial Philosophy*. Clearly, that work, rather than being a departure from Huxley's usual thing, satirical attacks on contemporary lifestyles, is key to bringing his vast journalistic and fictional output into focus. Bringing philosophies of Asia to bear on Western problems, *The Perennial Philosophy* makes the same kind of sense that T. S. Eliot's *Four Quartets* (1943) did after *The Waste Land* (1922).

German Romantics and American Transcendentalists, a century before, had drawn inspiration from the East in order to reconfigure the Western experience of the self. And many intellectuals in the twentieth century, not only C. G. Jung, have taken a decidedly psychological interest in the wisdom literature of Asia. Philosophically oriented psychologists tend to look to the East in order to understand better the incompleteness, not the wrongness, of Western philosophical, religious, and scientific traditions. They are interested in wholeness. Such ideas, of course, have entered twentieth-century popular culture through the self-help industry with a vengeance, in ways that need an Aldous Huxley to counterattack — the Huxley of *Antic Hay* (1922), *After Many a Summer Dies the Swan* (1939), as well as *Brave New World*. Our world was never braver. But it is impossible to read *The Perennial Philosophy* along with *Brave New World* at the beginning of the twenty-first century and not be impressed by certain clarifications. If, as Huxley says in *The Perennial Philosophy*, "a society is good to the extent that it renders contemplation possible for its members; and that the existence of at least a minority of contemplatives is necessary for the well-being of any society" (294), then Huxley's dark satire of consumer culture seems inescapably to be part of our eternal now. And it would apply to the marketing of quasi-Eastern self-help programs as well as to movies, television, cyberspace, cults, academia, and the evening news.

The popular scholar Joseph Campbell, with his enthusiasm for the power of myth to bring clarity to modern life and, simultaneously, his worldly, caustic wit, an antidote to solemnity, seems the perfect muse to invoke in bringing *Brave New World* and *The Perennial Philosophy* into a single focus. There are, of course, connections. Campbell remembers the early Huxley, George Bernard Shaw, and H. G. Wells as heroes for his generation, championing rationalism in the period after World War I, when Campbell thought the world was through with religion. "But then, in the midst of all that optimism about reason, democracy, socialism, and the like, there appeared a work that was disturbing: Oswald Spengler's *The Decline of the West*." For Campbell, historians like Spengler and Leo Frobenius and writers like James Joyce, T. S. Eliot, and W. B. Yeats, all implied that "something was beginning to disintegrate at the heart of our Occidental civilization itself" (*Myths to Live By* 83–4). Campbell credits Huxley in *The Perennial Philosophy* with pointing the way to broader, more global, ways of understanding our brave new world. The role of the modern artist, according to Campbell, is to retain the positive values that are in his or her heritage, and, at the same time, "move into a global period of life where we don't isolate ourselves and say everybody else is worshipping devils" (*The Hero's Journey* 36).

What is missing in *Brave New World*, from a Campbell perspective, is an experience of self that could endure the transition from culture-bound mythologies of the past to a new world without horizons or with constantly changing ones. Huxley's novel portrays a falsely heroic utopian orientation toward the future, which is really no future, but a repetition of the past, the culture merely insisting on replicating itself. *The Perennial Philosophy* supplies that experience of self, where the state or some other collective is not the highest good and where the contemplative experience of the divine mystery in all things is. The theme of *Brave New World* is stated by Huxley in his preface: "The advancement of science as it affects human individuals" (*Brave New World* xii). Still, Campbell would insist that it is not science *per se* that has alienated mankind, but the attendant loss of connection to the perennial self that it is one of the functions of myth to maintain. As he memorably says, "I don't see any conflict between science and religion. Religion has to accept the science of the day and penetrate it — to the mystery. The conflict is between the science of 2000 B.C. and the science of 2000 A.D." (*The Hero's Journey* 163). Campbell is convinced that Judaism, Christianity, and Islam have interpreted their myths literally in an attempt to maintain their exclusiveness and have thus isolated themselves from the worldwide perennial philosophy, of which they are rightly a part. Modern people are, therefore, stuck with the choice of maintaining literal supernatural beliefs, which modern, scientifically oriented culture cannot make sense of or choosing dogmatic atheism, which denies the legitimacy of the psychological function of myth. Campbell's solution to this impasse is simply to interpret myths metaphorically, emphasizing the commonality of the world's religions and mythologies. Campbell does not deny the cultural differences inherent in the various religious/mythological traditions, but his "accent" is on what they have in common.

Brave New World displays an environment that utterly contains its characters in opaque literalness. "Community, Identity, Stability," a parody of the motto of the French Revolution, describes their frozen psychic condition. They cannot participate in any metaphors at all, much less any which Campbell would characterize as mythically "transparent to transcendence" (*The Hero's Journey* 40). What they take to be the objective facts of their lives are post-revolutionary, post-historical, post-individual "solutions" to all the problems of life. Babies are born in bottles. Individuals are physically and psychologically conditioned to be happy in their predetermined social classes. All activities such as sports have been tied in with economic processes, so that factors like transportation to playing fields and the use of expensive sports equipment really determine their behavior. Sexual promiscuity is not only encouraged, it is required in order to drain away tension, while the mood-enhancing drug soma, which is in abundant supply, chemically soothes, consoles, and relaxes everyone. Emotional experiences transcendent in themselves, like falling in love or having particular friendships, are forbidden. All family structures and their feeling-toned relationships have been abolished. Old age and death are carefully monitored; if they are witnessed at all, they are judged unthreatening and uninteresting.

Characters in the novel bear traces in their names of past times when innovation or revolution seemed imminent, before history was reconfigured in absolute terms by a calendar centered on the birth and death of capitalist genius Henry Ford, who famously remarked, "History is bunk" (Sawyer 80). But now names like "Bernard Marx," "Helmholtz Watson," "Lenina Crowne," "Jim Bokanovsky," "Herbert Bakunin," "Benito Hoover," and "Mustapha Mond" are simply a mishmash of cultural debris. They convey no meaning, even ironically, to anyone. Two characters, Bernard Marx and Helmholtz Watson, do trouble the waters of *Brave New World*, but only briefly. Bernard Marx, physically slight, experiences feelings of masculine inferiority and sexual jealousy. His opposite, Helmholtz Watson, is exceptionally brilliant and attractive. Consequently, he feels unchallenged, frustrated that his potential is not being realized. In their different ways, Marx and Watson are experiencing a resonance of individuality, which the World State of *Brave New World* cannot tolerate. Both are in danger of being sent to Iceland, where they can cool off with others like themselves.

The most interesting character in *Brave New World*, John Savage, does not live in the "utopian" civilization, but on a New Mexico reservation, an outpost where "primitives," i.e., Native Americans, are housed. Savage is the product of an illicit, and normally sexual, love affair between Linda, originally a New Worlder, and Tomakin, no less than the director of hatcheries and conditioning, who has abandoned Linda and her son, exiling them to live on the reservation, while he continues to live the lie of the New World. Savage, now grown, longs to visit this civilization he has heard so much about from his mother, who continues to idealize it. So when Bernard Marx and Lenina Crowne visit the reservation on a vacation, learn about John Savage, and bring him back to the New World, the central movement of the novel begins.

Most critics agree that John Savage is modeled on D. H. Lawrence (Buchanan, Firchow), who died in 1930, with Frieda Lawrence, Huxley and his wife Maria at his bedside. Lawrence, who lived in Taos, New Mexico, while he was in America, was a great friend of Huxley's, an inspiration and, to some extent, an alter ego. Huxley labored under the view of himself as essentially a rational man, in the tradition of T. H. Huxley and Matthew Arnold, his forebears. He tried very hard to be modern, even experimenting with open marriage, but he kept returning to his persona of polymath and sharp-tongued critic of the age. Lawrence was his weak spot, a person in whom he could never completely disbelieve. Huxley saw genius and prophecy in Lawrence, Nietzschean irrationalism, and passionate extraversion, qualities he saw himself as lacking. He felt that Lawrence *lived* his life-worshipping philosophy, rather than merely thinking about things, and that Lawrence's belief in the power of blood-consciousness to cure the modern ills of nihilism and hedonism showed real moral courage. To use Campbell's language, Lawrence was for Huxley a mythic image, a living metaphor that was "transparent to transcendence," carrying the psychic projection of wholeness. If Huxley could integrate the passion and genius of Lawrence into himself, he would be whole.

But the power of such an image could be overwhelming, of course. So in *Brave New World*, Huxley's next novel after the death of Lawrence, we see, perhaps, in the fate of John Savage, who commits suicide when he finds the New World unbearable, Huxley's psychic energy pulling back from Lawrence and reinhabiting his own skeptical ego. We could, equally well, read the end of *Brave New World* as Huxley's way of grieving Lawrence, of expressing how it felt to him that such a man was no longer in the world, almost as if a part of himself had died.

John Savage tried to unite two worlds in himself, the reservation, where there was sex, violence, and naïve religious faith, and the New World, where antiseptic rationalism ruled along with narcissistic self-indulgence. He might have stoically endured this split life, more or less approximating the psychological condition of modern people, except for his own mythic images encountered in the plays of Shakespeare. He had found in *Othello, Romeo and Juliet*, and *The Tempest* images that were "transparent to transcendence"; in Shakespeare's characters and actions, Savage experienced passion shot through with intellect, intellect lived in the flesh. And so evolved his conclusion about the limitations of the New World: "But I don't want comfort. I want God. I want poetry. I want real danger. I want freedom. I want goodness. I want sin" (215). By this point in the novel, however, Savage has become a celebrity, a commodity. And failing to escape the unshakable paparazzi at a lighthouse, he hangs himself. The final image of the novel is one of ironic wholeness, defined by Savage's dangling feet slowly rotating through the four directions of the compass.

The hero's journey, for Campbell, which unites all mythologies East and West, is basically a dynamic archetype of spiritual renewal. It moves through a three-part cycle of departure-renewal-return. As Campbell says in a thousand ways, "A hero ventures forth from the world of common day into a region of supernatural wonder; fabulous forces are there encountered and a decisive victory is won; the hero comes back from this mysterious adventure with the power to bestow boons on his fellow man" (*The Hero's Journey* xv). It is for Campbell, as Phil Cousineau says in his introduction to *The Hero's Journey*, "a movement beyond the known boundaries of faith and convention, the search for what matters, the path of destiny, the route of individuality, the road of original experience, a paradigm for the forging of consciousness itself" (xv). *Brave New World* is Huxley's strongest statement about the forces discouraging modern people from experiencing the energy of that archetype, or experiencing it only in debased forms. And *The Perennial Philosophy* is his strongest statement of what could bring sanity back into the world, or, one could actually say, what inevitably always does bring sanity back into the world, eventually.

The Perennial Philosophy is the culmination of Huxley's intellectual development from the death of Lawrence until the end of World War II. During that time he joined the Peace Pledge Union, came under the influence of another strong personality, Gerald Heard, and became involved with the Vedanta Society in Los Angeles. But when his guru Swami Prabhavananda demanded absolute devotion and when Heard identified himself totally with the movement, becoming a guru in his own right, Huxley distanced himself and formulated his own relationship to the wisdom tradition. It is important to remember that Huxley never saw himself as a guru, a mystic, or an enlightened person. *The Perennial Philosophy* is an anthology of wisdom writings from East and West, arranged under headings like "God in the World," "Truth," and "Self-Knowledge," with extensive explanatory commentary by Huxley. In this work, Huxley makes the case for "a metaphysic that recognizes a divine Reality substantial to the world of things and lives and minds: (a) psychology that finds in the soul something similar to, or even identical with divine Reality; (an) ethic that places man's final end in the knowledge of the immanent and transcendent Ground of all being" (xii). The perennial philosophy was, for Huxley "the "Highest Common Factor" in the world's theologies. But the anthology is not a tract or a personal statement of conversion, and does not deserve the criticism leveled at it by C. E. M. Joad in the *New Statesman*, which accuses Huxley of being a "sour-faced moralist," guilty of intellectual whole-hoggery" (Murray 356). Huxley's anthology is objective, encyclopedic, and clear, colored with no more bias than William James's *The Varieties of Religious Experience*, with the difference that Huxley is offering the sense of these texts being good for the world. As Dana Sawyer succinctly states, "*Brave New World* had been Huxley's satirical description of the disease affecting humanity; *The Perennial Philosophy*— more than ten years in the making — was his view of an antidote. Today it is interesting to note that these two books, out of the fifty or so that he wrote, are the two that are continually in print, counteracting each other's presence as it were on the bookstore shelf" (Sawyer 126). Huxley had struck a balance between the perhaps unsolvable problems satirized in *Brave New World* and the perennially available means of combating them. Both are part of our eternal now.

The point of contact between these two works is the issue of the self and how it is experienced. In *Brave New World*, the state regulates all personal experiences, channeling them into controlled social occasions. Even orgies are orchestrated. And the Hourly Radio is continuously monitoring and reporting on all activities, so that individual experiences are represented, characterized and understood in public terms. There are no private moments, and all anxiety is alleviated with soma immediately, so that a general optimism prevails.

There is nothing mysterious about the self in the New World. The conflict that gives the novel its interest derives first from the anxieties of Marx and Watson, who have become more self-conscious than is good for them, and second from the full-fledged identity crisis of John Savage, ending in suicide. The turning point comes for Savage when his mother is dying in Park Lane Hospital and a nightmare troop of identical eight-year old boys comes to ogle. He is scolded by the nurses for disturbing their "death-conditioning" by weeping at his mother's bedside. Huxley has put his finger on an experience that perfectly captures the modern worry that people are becoming more and therefore less than human. The modern hospital, with its impressive technologies, godlike doctors, tactful bureaucrats, and visiting hours, is, too often, *Brave New World* in miniature.

In *The Perennial Philosophy*, Huxley ponders how ordinary people are seduced into identifying with whatever they regard as above them, and in this way lose themselves. In the chapter called "Mortification, Non-Attachment, Right Livelihood," he says, "(S)o long as the policy which gratifies the power lusts of the ruling class is successful, and so long as the price of success is not too high, even the masses of the ruled will feel that the state is themselves—a vast and splendid projection of the individual's intrinsically insignificant ego" (122). "*L'etat c'est moi*," has become the motto of the masses in *Brave New World*. This experience of the self as collective, inflated ego is rendered opaque by constant verbalization. In the chapter "Truth," Huxley says of our time, "Never have so many capable writers warned mankind against the dangers of wrong speech — and never have words been used more recklessly by politicians or taken more seriously by the public" (129). The experience of self that is promoted in *The Perennial Philosophy* is dharma, which means the individual law of one's own being conjoined with the law of righteousness and piety. Huxley explains, "a man's duty, how he ought to live, what he ought to believe and what he ought to do about his beliefs— these things are conditioned by his essential nature, his constitution and temperament" (153). Experiencing the self as dharma is not possible in the New World, where "being" means "doing," "having," "enjoying," etc., as defined by the state.

The experience of self in *The Perennial Philosophy* is paradoxical, being an experience of the individualized self as *nothing* and the underlying spiritual ground of which the self is a part as *everything*. But at this point it is necessary to make certain qualifications, if we are to take Campbell — and his chief inspiration, Jung — into account. For both Campbell and Jung there is an significant difference between Western and Eastern perspectives toward what we might as well call God. The goal of the Eastern wisdom traditions is to unite consciousness with spiritual reality; the goal of Western religions is a *relationship* with the divine (*Myths to Live By* 97). Jung is dubious about European faddish enthusiasm for Eastern wisdom. He implies that it is not only rudely condescending toward a great tradition, but also appallingly naïve. As he says in his foreword to Suzuki's *Introduction to Zen Buddhism*, "Zen shows how much 'becoming whole' means to the East. Preoccupation with the riddles of Zen may perhaps stiffen the spine of the faint-hearted European or provide a pair of spectacles for his psychic myopia," but the "sympathetic reader (should not) underestimate the spiritual depth of the East, or ... assume that there is anything cheap and facile about Zen" (557). And in his essay "Yoga and the West," Jung harshly admonishes, "Western civilization is scarcely a thousand years old and must first of all free itself from its barbarous one-sidedness. This means, above all, deeper insight into the nature of man. But no insight is gained by repressing and controlling the unconscious, and least of all by imitating methods which have grown up under totally different psychological conditions" (537).

For Jung, the Westerner who is "into" Eastern wisdom is most likely trying to bypass the painful and difficult task of coming to terms with his own personal unconscious. Western religion requires the individual not only to become conscious of his innate shortcomings, personal sins, and the sins of his people and forebears, it requires him to make *amends* for the wrongs of which he becomes conscious, even if it takes his whole lifetime. The stage of Jungian analysis having to do with the Shadow, essentially the same as Freudian psychoanalysis, is a lengthy, incremental assimilation to consciousness of repressed motives, some of which are shameful. Ultimately, Jung — and, I think, Campbell and Huxley — see these differences as those of the cultural clothes, and not the inner spiritual body. But it would be wrong to overlook the differences. As Jung says in his essay "The Psychology of Eastern Meditation," "At bottom the two confessions (Christian and Buddhist) are identical, in that the Buddhist only attains this knowledge ('that *thou* art the Buddha') when he is *anatman*, 'without self.' But there is an immeasurable difference in the formulation. The Christian attains his end *in Christ*, the Buddhist knows he *is* the Buddha. The Christian gets *out of* the transitory and ego-bound world of consciousness, but the Buddhist *still* reposes on the eternal ground of his inner nature, whose oneness with Deity, or with universal Being, is confirmed in other Indian testimonies" (575).

According to anecdotal evidence, Jung occasionally went somewhat further. Talking with Chilean poet Miguel Serrano, Jung described a visit he had made to India: "I was there some time ago, trying to convince the Hindus that it is impossible to get rid of the idea of the Ego or of consciousness, even in the deepest state of *samadhi*" (48). It is possible that Jung is being a bit mischievous here. Still, in Serrano's notes from his conversations with Jung we find one of the clearest statements Jung ever made of his concept of the "Self" (which he always capitalized), as he lays out a decidedly Western alternative to Eastern enlightenment. "So far," Jung says, "I have found no stable or definite center in the unconscious and I don't believe such a center exists. I believe that the thing which I call the Self is an ideal center, equidistant between the Ego and the Unconscious, and it is probably equivalent to the maximum natural expression of individuality, in a state of fulfillment or totality. As nature aspires to express itself, so does man, and the Self is that dream of totality. It is therefore an ideal center, something created" (50). In keeping with his Western heritage, Jung aimed for a rapprochement with the unconscious, just as, in *Answer to Job*, he read the book of Job as man's rapprochement with God. Both sides have to have their say, sometimes agreeing to disagree.

Practically speaking, Lawrence, Huxley, and Campbell are all in agreement with Jung. Lawrence objected to Huxley's "whoring" after the philosophies of the East, seeing them as temptations to lose oneself in abstractions. Lawrence had himself served as a kind of rough draft of a self for Huxley, but after Lawrence's death, Huxley had to look into his own experience for a sense of self closer to his own dharma. He found another rough draft for the self in Gerald Heard, but this too was in need of further revision. Ultimately, Huxley wisely gave up on solutions and went to work on his anthology, his final rough draft of a self to be added to whatever others the West may possess. Campbell's work, too, is a vast anthology. Not only in *The Hero with a Thousand Faces* (1949), but also in his four-volume *Masks of God* series (1959–68), he preserves hundreds of mythological stories, in his marvelous, spellbinding retellings, as a treasure trove of the world's experience of its own soul through the imagination of mankind. The title of one of Jung's most popular works, *Modern Man in Search of a Soul*, could well describe the agendas of all three, Lawrence, Huxley, and Campbell, in this sense: that the search for a replacement for or clarification of literalistic religion in the West is a work in progress, an important part of our eternal now.

Arguably, the idea of people losing their souls not by "gaining the whole world" (Matthew 16:26) but by modernizing themselves, goes back at least as far as Shakespeare, as suggested by Huxley's title. John Savage makes the novel's connection to *The Tempest* quite explicit, when, weeping over his dead mother, he sees the literal future in a mob of genetically engineered twins: "Like maggots they ... swarmed defilingly over the mystery of Linda's death" (190). Savage sarcastically quotes to himself Miranda's words in Act V of *The Tempest*, when she sees more men than she had seen in her whole lifetime on Prospero's island, as they are freed from enchantment. "How many goodly creatures are there here!... How beauteous mankind is! O brave new world...." (190). To which, Prospero replies understatedly but with a world of meaning: 'Tis new to thee" (604). Savage and Prospero cannot go back to a youthful view of the world like Miranda's as she begins her new life with Ferdinand. Savage commits suicide, and Prospero plans after his daughter's wedding to retire to Milan when "every third thought shall be (his) grave" (609).

In *Shakespeare Our Contemporary*, Polish director Jan Kott reads Shakespeare's play in a dark way, as though it could be Huxley's reading of the development of the Western world since the Renaissance. For Kott, *The Tempest* is not a play of "forgiveness and reconciliation with the world" (295), nor should it be produced as "an operatic fairy story" (298). Rather, it is "a great Renaissance tragedy of lost illusions" (329), a play that reflects the world of the last generation of humanists and equally speaks to our atomic age. Prospero's island is not an Arcadian retreat, but an apocalyptic theatrical vision of a ruthless world, where the Machiavellian forces set in motion by Antonio in Milan are repeated in modes that are variously lyrical, fantastic, and grotesque. According to Kott, Shakespeare "invariably depicts cruel nature, cruel history, and man who struggles in vain trying to get the better of his fate" (298). Thus Prospero could suggest Leonardo da Vinci, whose philosophical bitterness contemplated a world that was both ahead of and behind itself.

The play is full of references to the New World. "The times abound(ed) in great voyages," Kott reminds us, "newly discovered continents and mysterious isles, dreams of man floating in the air like a bird, and of machines that would enable him to capture the strongest fortresses" (299). Kott quotes Jean Fernel, a Renaissance humanist, who writes in 1530, "Our times have seen things not even dreamt of by the ancients.... The Ocean has been crossed thanks to the bravery of our sailors, and new islands have been discovered.... A new globe has been given us by the mariners of our times" (307). Gonzalo's naïve description of what a utopia would be like for him is taken, word for word, from Montaigne's "On Cannibals" (314), where Montaigne blames myopic Europeans for not being able to appreciate the noble savages of the New World. And he asks if eating other people is really worse than the European practice of having them drawn and quartered in a spirit of spectacle sport. Prospero's island might be a version of Bermuda, where an English fleet's flagship *Sea-Adventure* was wrecked in 1609 on its way to Virginia. In the midst of a heroic voyage toward the world's future, the travelers found themselves on a devil's island, where they heard voices all around them. It was for them a "garden of torment, or a picture of mankind's folly," not like a Renaissance utopia at all, but a late Gothic fantasy of Hieronymus Bosch (309).

Prospero may be read as the genius or spirit of the age who has to learn the hard way about its Machiavellian Shadow. Prospero had not been attending to the mundane treacheries of his historical time, but was steeping himself in the wonders of science and magic when his brother, seeing his chance, betrayed and exiled him. He had lost himself in mythic images and had forgotten their often disappointing cultural settings, just as Huxley was appalled when he visited India and saw its poverty. Those voyagers on the *Sea Adventure* did eventually get to Virginia, or many of them did, but while they were on that island we now call Bermuda they must have understood how easy it is in a world of wonders to be lost. The New World relied on slavery, after all, for some of its economic magic. What self did a slave experience when he or she was no more than a means to an end in the dominant culture's march toward future glory?

The citizens of *Brave New World* think their revolution has already come, that they are the improved version of humanity. Whereas, *The Perennial Philosophy* suggests that their "utopia," seen in light of the perennial wisdom of mankind, is neither "brave" (splendid), particularly "new," or anything that could be called a "world" (a coherent universe in which people live interdependently). It is, as *The Tempest* suggests, a condition of enchantment that lacks the power to change or even interpret history.

For Jung, Campbell, and for Huxley, the heroism needed to live in such a world requires the wisdom of the ages, but it also implies enduring a certain amount of despair, for which all the wonders of mythology, psychology, and literature, do not quite completely compensate. As Campbell says in the last paragraph of *The Hero with a Thousand Faces*:

> The modern hero, the modern individual who dares to heed the call and seek the mansion of that presence with whom it is our whole destiny to be atoned, cannot, indeed must not, wait for his community to cast off its slough of pride, fear, rationalized avarice, and sanctified misunderstanding. "Live," Nietzsche says, "as though the day were here." It is not society that is to guide and save the creative hero, but precisely the reverse. And so everyone of us shares the supreme ordeal — carries the cross of the redeemer — not in the bright moments of his tribe's great victories, but in the silences of his personal despair [391].

Works Cited

Buchanan, Brad. "Oedipus in Dystopia; Freud and Lawrence in Aldous Huxley's *Brave New World*. *Journal of Modern Literature* 25, no. 3–4 (Summer 2002): 75–89.

Calder, Jenni. *Huxley and Orwell:* Brave New World *and* Nineteen Eighty-Four. London: Edward Arnold, 1976.

Campbell, Joseph. *The Hero with a Thousand Faces.* Princeton: Princeton University Press, 1973.

_____. *The Hero's Journey: Joseph Campbell on His Life and Work.* Edited and with an introduction by Phil Cousineau. Shaftesbury, Dorset: Element, 1999.

_____. *Myths to Live By.* Toronto: Bantam, 1984.

Firchow, "Wells and Lawrence in Huxley's *Brave New World*. *Journal of Modern Literature* 5, no.2 (April 1976): 260–78.

Huxley, Aldous. *After Many a Summer Dies the Swan.* New York: Harper and Row. 1965.

_____. *The Perennial Philosophy.* New York: Harper & Row, 1970.

Jung, C. G. *Psychology and Religion: West and East.* 2nd ed. Vol. 11 of *The Collected Works of C. G. Jung.* Princeton: Princeton University Press, 1975.

Kott, Jan. "Prospero's Staff." In *Shakespeare Our Contemporary.* New York: Norton, 1974.

Murray, Nicholas. *Aldous Huxley: A Biography.* New York: St. Martin's, 2002.

Sawyer, Dana. *Aldous Huxley: A Biography.* New York: Crossroad, 2002.

Serrano, Miguel. *Jung and Hesse: A Record of Two Friendships.* New York: Schocken, 1966.

Shakespeare, William. *The Tempest.* In *Shakespeare: The Late Romances,* edited by David Bevington. Toronto: Bantam, 1988.

"Everyone Belongs to Everyone Else": The Influence of Brave New World on Cinema

By James Fisher

Aldous Huxley (1894–1963) endeavored to carve out a screenwriting career in the early 1940s. The scripts he contributed for a few films, most notably *Pride and Prejudice* (1940), *Jane Eyre* (1944), and *Madame Curie* (1943; uncredited), do not overtly reflect themes from his most enduring novel, *Brave New World* (1932). Although Huxley's brief Hollywood interlude fizzled, several of his works arrived on screen in adaptations by others. "The Giaconda Smile" became *A Woman's Vengeance* (1948) before being made into a television film in 1963 under its original title. "Young Archimedes" appeared on screen as *Prelude to Fame* (1950) and the *Devils of Loudon* was adapted as *The Devils* (1971), directed by Ken Russell. The attention paid to sexuality and drug use in *Brave New World's* dystopia virtually assured that it would not receive screen treatment during Hollywood's "Golden Age," an era when any overt depiction or discussion of sexuality and drug use was taboo. As censorship barriers crumbled in the 1960s, the possibility of adapting *Brave New World* to the screen became more possible, but by that time futuristic science fiction was so prevalent in movies and on television as to render a cinematic adaptation superfluous.

Huxley was part of a generation of writers who found progress potentially problematic. Born as the late nineteenth-century era of invention came to full fruition, and coming of age when new technologies brought forth horrors in World War I, Huxley shaped his satiric novel of ideas to reflect the inevitability of technological advancements, but also their corrosive effects on human life. In a sense, the novel is a warning, but one in which Huxley presents his concerns in an ironic voice and with a satiric gaze. For Huxley, technology obscures from view the mind-numbing conformity and anti-intellectualism of a life of ease. By the time *Brave New World* first appeared, World War I — era writers (German expressionists, for example) had already made the case that technological progress has a fiercely destructive potential, but Huxley's view of a technologically advanced futuristic society in which its citizens willingly accept luxuries in exchange for defining attributes of culture and individuality is presented with both philosophical clarity and considerable humor.

172

Huxley may well have found it amusing to see his novel on screen, for cinema itself was part of the flood of technological advances arriving with the twentieth century he was warning against. *Brave New World* has yet to be produced as a major feature film, but two different television adaptations (1980, 1998) appeared to decidedly mixed response from critics. Both films more or less retain Huxley's emphasis on the collision of technology and the natural world, but both tend to downplay philosophical questions and the subtle wit of the novel. Huxley's serio-comic depiction of a happy humanity living in a well-ordered utopia (what Huxley referred to as a negative utopia in which poverty and other forms of human suffering have been obliterated, leaving only ease and pleasure via sexual hedonism and drug use which can conveniently wipe away the blues), is retained. Also present are Huxley's lamentations over the loss of familial relations, individuality, art, literature, and spirituality, except for the mindless worship of the great Ford, the technological god whose theology of mass production replaces traditional belief systems.

In his foreword to the 1946 reprinting of *Brave New World*, Huxley writes of this loss of individuality and the difficulty of survival for human liberty in this technological juggernaut, noting that the theme of *Brave New World* "is not the advancement of science as such; it is the advancement of science as it affects human individuals" (v). For Huxley, the "really revolutionary revolution is to be achieved, not in the external world, but in the souls and flesh of human beings," a theme expanded on in many of the films inspired by *Brave New World*. "The people who govern the Brave New World," as Huxley writes, "may not be sane (in what may be called the absolute sense of the word); but they are not madmen, and their aim is not anarchy but social stability. It is in order to achieve stability that they carry out, by scientific means, the ultimate, personal, really revolutionary revolution." Both the 1980 and 1998 television adaptations exude Huxley's vision of social stability as a paradise turned nightmare, but both alter or eliminate thematic aspects and characters, as well as plot elements and much humor, from Huxley's novel.

The first of these television films, a nearly three-hour version of *Brave New World* directed by Burt Brinckerhoff from an adaptation by Robert E. Thompson, was initially broadcast on March 7, 1980. Starring Keir Dullea as Thomas Grahmbell (director of hatcheries), Bud Cort as Bernard Marx, Julie Cobb as Linda, and Kristoffer Tabori as John Savage, this adaptation faithfully follows the broad outlines of Huxley's plot, eliminating secondary characters and most sexual imagery. It also eliminates much of the material set on the reservation, particularly regarding Linda's decline and John's conception and childhood. As such, the character of Popé is dropped entirely and, after a brief visit by Bernard and Lenina, the reservation is abandoned as the adult John and an aging, disoriented Linda are carried back to London where, as in the novel, "the savage" attains celebrity status while Linda drifts into a soma-induced coma hastening her demise.

Brave New World presents obvious problems in making the transition to the screen, especially to television where boundaries regarding sex and drug use remain in force. Many of the novel's scenes, and much of its imagery, are problematic, particularly the one depicting naked children engaged in sexual experimentation, a scene that would pose a challenge even in the most permissive movie-going times, and, understandably, this challenge is avoided by both television adaptations.

Brinckerhoff's 1980 film makes other minor changes, expanding on Huxley's use of famous names for his characters. Lenina Crowne, for example, becomes Lenina Disney. No helicopters are shown, there are no panoramic views of this futuristic world society, and although the film accumulates power as it moves toward its tragic conclusion, initial scenes depicting Huxley's "brave new world" are unconvincing. The settings and costumes appear cheap and flimsy, the approximate equivalent of television sci-fi shows of that era, resembling more than anything an episode of *Star Trek*. Lighting is bright and flat, appropriate perhaps for interior scenes of a sterile society, but even in the brief interlude at the reservation, where evocatively shadowy lighting may have enhanced both Linda's disorientation and Lenina's fears, none is used and the reservation otherwise seems little more than an elaborate junkyard.

Acting in the secondary and small roles is similarly flat, exacerbating the one-dimensional nature of Huxley's characters. Critics have often found Huxley's *Brave New World* characters, with perhaps the exception of the two leading figures of Bernard Marx and John Savage, as either ill defined or underdeveloped, only present to permit the author a means of fully exploiting his themes. However, such a view overlooks a significant point: these characters are necessarily less dimensioned because the world they live in, and the society that has created them in a bottle, has reduced them to a near-robotic humanity, devoid of feeling and desire, programmed to do their jobs and enjoy their pleasures. Deviance from this norm is the only way Huxley's characters attain individuality, or distinction of character, which is why Bernard and Savage are the more fully developed personas. Understandably, this issue presents a problem for filmmakers and actors involved in presenting *Brave New World*, and it is a problem that undermines this particular film.

Leading roles are skillfully performed, particularly Bud Cort's dimensioned, wide-eyed interpretation of Bernard Marx and Kristoffer Tabori's John Savage, marred only by an unconvincing fake beard and some poorly edited sequences, particularly those on the reservation. Keir Dullea also does well as Grahmbell, lacing touches of absurd humor and malice into the character. Marcia Strassman is an appropriately attractive blank as Lenina and Julie Cobb is impressive as Linda, although as an attractive twenty-something she fails to make a fully convincing transition into the blowsy forty-something Huxley describes. Despite this, Cobb supplies the film's most affecting acting in Linda's death scene.

On the level of a 1980s made-for-TV movie, this largely faithful adaptation of *Brave New World* is better than average, but the modest and generally unimaginative visuals recreating Huxley's twenty-sixth-century London significantly hinder its overall impact. If ever a novel required a large budget, state-of-the-art cinematic technology, and highly imaginative visuals, *Brave New World* is that novel. A similarly modest television adaptation premiered on NBC-TV on April 19, 1998, profiting to some extent from two decades of improvements in movie magic. Despite the improvements, however, this adaptation of *Brave New World* inevitably falls short in the visual area. Improbably starring musical comedy performer Peter Gallagher as Bernard Marx, with Leonard Nimoy as Mustapha Mond, Rya Kihlstedt as Lenina, Sally Kirkland as Linda, and Tim Guinee as John Savage, under the direction of Leslie Libman and Larry Williams, this *Brave New World* is, like the 1980 version, superficially faithful to Huxley. Dan Mazur's and Davis Tausik's screenplay stresses Bernard's fascination with the Shakespeare–quoting John Savage, otherwise maintaining Huxley's major themes of artificial human happiness created through conformity and the ease resulting from technological advancement. Sequences are eliminated from the novel, especially depictions of the Bokanovskification process, and critics complained of this omission and a few relatively minor changes to both the beginning and end of the film. A strengthening of Lenina's character, presumably to lessen the "sexism" of Huxley's women characters, generated a mixed critical reaction, but others noted that this adaptation's strength emerges from the ways in which it accentuates aspects of Huxley's novel, including touches of ironic humor. Other changes, such as the identity of John Savage's father (no longer Native American) and a subplot about a Delta programmed to kill Bernard, are incorporated to little effect. The film's ending suggests that happiness can still be found in the world society, a significant distortion of Huxley, who stresses that hope for utopia, and the possibility of creating one, is a slippery slope; his pleasure-driven, conformist, amoral society is so bland that it becomes both frightening and funny. The "happiness" proffered is a false kind for Huxley. Depictions of sexuality transcend the more staid 1980 film, but the Brave New World's hedonism is seen only through flashes of scantily-clad dancers in Alpha bars, a conventional brand of eroticism which also seems counter to Huxley's ironic view of sex in his futuristic society as an insipid, loveless recreation, and in the more unsettling imagery of nude children encouraged in sexual experimentation.

Other changes to Huxley's novel in this adaptation are, from a strictly filmic point of view, effective. The one-dimensional characters of Huxley are given more defining characteristics, a problematic choice since Huxley's one-dimensionality points up the loss of individuality resulting from conformity. The casting of Gallagher as Bernard Marx is a significant change from Huxley's idea of the character, for he emerges as more a romantic hero than an outcast. This interpretation is also quite a departure from Bud Cort's "nerdy" Marx in the 1980 film, which is drawn faithfully from Huxley's description of the character. With a strengthening of Lenina's character, it undoubtedly made sense to reinvent Bernard in this direction, but this choice also forces an abandonment of Huxley's Bernard as a malformed Alpha mocked by his peers, an anxious loner until he brings John Savage home and attains instant celebrity. Clearly, the filmmakers felt it necessary to update *Brave New World,* perhaps in an attempt to make a classic novel seem more relevant, and although they may have created an effective entertainment, much of what made the novel a classic is distorted in the process. Some critics lamented the changes to Huxley's original, while others found them necessary and desirable, feeling that the movie captured Huxley's spirit without being constrained to follow the exact letter of his text.

The greatest distortion of Huxley, not only in these two television film versions, but also in many subsequent films inspired by *Brave New World,* is that all tend to depict Huxley's society darkly and grimly. With the exception of the interpretations of a few of the actors, these films largely miss the flavorful strain of satire inherent in Huxley's novel with its depiction of the banality of a mindless pleasure-seeking society and the unquestioning conformity that is its guiding principle.

The profound influence of *Brave New World* on cinema science fiction can be found in an incalculable number of movies from the 1930s to the present. Like H. G. Wells, whose futuristic imagery and utopian novel *Men Like Gods* influenced Huxley in the writing of *Brave New World,* Huxley's influence is far-reaching. A complete accounting of films inspired by *Brave New World* would demand a book-length study; however, several films, some in themselves influential, owe much to Huxley's novel in thematic possibilities, as well as in plot devices, characters, philosophical questions, and the visual potential of the Brave New World he imagines.

Unquestionably, any film with a futuristic sci-fi setting, from William Cameron Menzies' *Things to Come* (1936) to Steven Spielberg's adaptation of H. G. Wells's *War of the Worlds* (2005), owes something to Huxley, but it is perhaps best to trace the cinematic influence of *Brave New World* through films expressing elements of Huxley's ambivalence about the technological doctrine of progress, its impact on the development of societal values, and, most importantly, on the ways in which it alters individual human experience. This somewhat narrows the vast field of sci-fi films inspired, in part, by *Brave New World,* to several key films.

Filmmakers have most frequently explored Huxley's themes of continual pleasure as a replacement for freedom and the totalitarianism it encourages, subversion to social conditioning, mass-production principles applied to human life, and consumerism gone wild. In Huxley, with old religions abandoned, the new god is the great Ford. Christ's crucifix is no longer the dominant spiritual icon, Ford's Flivver, an early product of mass production, replaces it and what it represents radically changes the way its society functions. George Orwell's *1984*, written in 1947 in the wake of the catastrophes of Nazism, fascism, and the dawning of the atomic age, set his darker vision of the future, in which the total domination of Big Brother offers terror and militaristic might as the ultimate means of control. Huxley, somewhat more prophetically (and, one might argue, more benevolently), wrote before the cataclysms of the Second World War, and, as such, sees governmental control coming through mind-altering drugs, luxury, and subtle brainwashing. Many post–*Brave New World* films reflect this, as well as the notion of mass-production technology as providing the path to utopia. For Huxley, this absurd notion shapes the ironic, lightly comic tone of many passages in the novel; however, filmmakers sometimes overlook Huxley's approach in favor of a bleaker Orwellian vision, as late twentieth-century pessimism dominated. As the millennium approached, filmmakers increasingly merged Huxley's themes and aspects of his Brave New World with Orwell's apocalyptic viewpoints.

The classic 1966 film of Ray Bradbury's 1951 novel *Fahrenheit 451*, directed by François Truffaut, with a cast including Oskar Werner, Julie Christie, and Cyril Cusack, is a case in point. Orwellian gloom pervades in an isolated futuristic society in which the government, fearing the tendency of books to inspire independent thinking, has outlawed literature. Crews of firefighters burn books and the citizens of society are drugged into complaisance like those soma-riddled citizens of *Brave New World*. Bradbury's protagonist, Guy Montag, is one of these firemen, but when he becomes involved with Clarisse, who secretly hoards books, Guy reads them with the result that he begins to question the government's motives. In this development, the film leans more toward Huxley's vision, as Montag's intellectual fever reflects that of John Savage, an isolated humanist in an anti-intellectual, conformist environment. This future society is a thoroughly utilitarian dystopia, as suggested by one moment when the firemen are setting a house fire. Confronted by their captain, one of the firemen says, "This house has been condemned, it's to be burnt with the books immediately," to which the captain replies, "Burning the books is one thing, burning the house is another altogether." The house can be put to use, but books have no worth, in an ironic touch reminiscent of Huxley. Loss of individual liberties and adherence to a blind conformity resulting from drugs in *Fahrenheit 451* also owes much to Huxley, as does the portrayal of a faceless government suppressing free thought and dissent. Aspects of *Fahrenheit 451* can be found in a recent film, Kurt Wimmer's *Equilibrium* (2002), a work more obviously influenced by *Brave New World* than most, but one which also adopts an Orwellian darkness, offering few Huxleyesque ironic reflections on the future.

In *Equilibrium*, Christian Bale plays John Preston, a ruthless "Grammaton cleric" enforcing repressive laws in an apocalyptic post–World War III landscape. Clerics are part of an elite squad wielding high-tech weaponry to enforce oppression against prewar art, literature, culture, and those rebellious beings attempting to save the evidence of human thought and feeling. The survivors in this new society follow Father, a dictator not unlike the great Ford of *Brave New World*, who guides all thought via huge television screens streaming a continual loop of his dictums. Positing that the catastrophic violence which has nearly brought human extinction results from human volatile nature, Father concludes that cruelty stems from a fundamental human propensity for feeling. Stressing that "mankind could never survive by force," Father has outlawed feeling through force, a touch of irony Huxley would undoubtedly have appreciated. The full hypocrisy of Father's mantra becomes evident as cleric squads round up "feelers" and carry them off to be incinerated in a futuristic crematorium. Absolute obedience to Father's laws are assured by the fact that all citizens are required to take a daily dose of Prozium II, a soma-like mind-altering drug intended to block the highs and lows of human emotion. Whereas soma was a means to pleasure, Prozium, like the drugs of *Fahrenheit 451*, is intended to destroy any desire for resistance. Those resisting can only do so by ceasing to take their Prozium, a capital crime. Preston exhibits extraordinary skill at sensing the ways offenders think, including his own cleric partner whom he catches reading a forbidden copy of William Butler Yeats's poetry. Without hesitation, Preston exterminates him.

Preston also leads a raid in which a cache of forbidden artworks are found, including *Mona Lisa*, which have been hidden by revolutionaries opposing Father's oppressions. Preston coolly orders incineration of the art, but his own resolve begins to waver. When he skips his Prozium, Preston's emotions are aroused and he develops feelings of resistance, ultimately leading his own personal revolt against the government he has served. Recalling that four years earlier his wife was incinerated, Preston observes with mounting concern as his young son is brainwashed. A critical moment in Preston's change comes as his feelings are stirred by a young woman, played by Emily Watson, who has a secret room filled with artifacts of the past. She defends it fiercely, and futilely, against the clerics, and when Preston is unable to save her from incineration, he becomes a full-fledged revolutionary. In a sense, Preston's newly awakened dissidence is not unlike that of *Fahrenheit 451*'s Montag and, as such, Huxley's John Savage, and all are striving against a social order likely to overwhelm them. However, unlike Savage, Preston seems initially to believe in the social order, perhaps mostly a result of his daily doses of Prozium, and only his observation of the suppression and brutality of the leaders finally causes him to change his views. And, in the final analysis, he prevails, while Savage opts out through suicide.

Some critics chided *Equilibrium* for a lack of originality, finding it too similar to *Brave New World* and *Fahrenheit 451* in story and thematic issues, but it stands with films like *Fahrenheit 451*, *The Matrix* trilogy (1993, 2003), and *Minority Report* (2002), all grim portraits of technological suppression of human feeling. Along these lines is another film, one that brought George Lucas to prominence as a filmmaker. *THX 1138* (1970) grew out of an earlier version Lucas had written and filmed when he was a cinema student. Adapting it into a major film co-authored by Walter Murch, Lucas cast Robert Duvall as a man whose mind and body are under complete government surveillance. There is no freedom and he is trapped in a harrowing universe where even his thoughts are completely controlled. As with *Fahrenheit 451, Equilibrium, The Matrix,* and *The Minority Report, THX 1138* evokes a harrowing conception of a technologically based future. Another movie in this vein, *Logan's Run* (1976), directed by Michael Anderson from a novel by William F. Nolan and George Clayton Johnson, is set in the year 2274 in a society in which a life of total pleasure is offered in exchange for extinction by the age of 30. *Logan's Run* obviously drew on the soma-induced luxuries and sexual pleasures described in Huxley's *Brave New World,* but it otherwise falls far short of Huxley's inspiration as a result of superficial storytelling that fails to probe beneath the surface of its inherent moral questions.

Some of these films, especially *Equilibrium,* deserved more critical attention, but among acknowledged classics, Ridley Scott's *Blade Runner* (1982), adapted by Hampton Fancher from Philip K. Dick's novel *Do Androids Dream of Electric Sheep?,* exploits many elements of *Brave New World.* An indictment of the human desire to control nature through unchecked scientific manipulation is a Huxleyesque theme at the forefront of *Blade Runner.* Technology has led to the evolution of a disorienting, shadowy post-apocalyptic world in which human beings are separated from nature and their natural impulses; it is a world in which unseen governing forces reorder the meaning of "human." Materialism, scientific advancement, and economic forces dominate humanistic, spiritual, artistic, and philosophical concerns, with a sole character struggling to retain vestiges of humanity against a malevolent social order. Rick Deckard, played by Harrison Ford, is retired from the Los Angeles Police Department's Blade Runner unit, an elite force charged with terminating replicants, human clones originally created to work in space colonies away from Earth. Replicants, or "skin jobs" as they are derisively described by humans, rebel in a violent uprising and five escape to Earth in a plot similar to Karel Capek's pioneering 1921 play *R.U.R. (Rossum's Universal Robots). R.U.R.,* which depicts an uprising of robots (a word coined for this play) against their human creators, is frequently overlooked in examinations of Huxley, whose familiarity with Capek, a pacifist and socialist, is unclear; however, Capek's thematic protestations against the dehumanization inherent in technology and the impact of capitalist-inspired mass production directly parallels (and precedes) that of Huxley, although it is lacking in Huxley's satiric qualities or the depth of his philosophical questioning. Similar plot elements are central to Alex Provas's *I Robot* (2004), adapted from Isaac Asimov's book by Jeff Vintar, starring Will Smith and James Cromwell. *I Robot* is set in the year 2035 and follows a robot-hating Chicago policeman who must investigate the murder of Alfred Lanning, a scientist at U.S. Robotics. The crime may have been committed by one of Lanning's robots and the film thus raises questions about the relations of humans to their mechanical creations. The techno-based future depicted bears some resemblance to Huxley's but is also indebted to Capek, whose expressionistic futuristic society ties him to a post–World War I generation of expressionistic dramatists and filmmakers who constructed nightmarish cautionary tales of unfettered technological progress and forecast a future of machines or clones who turn on their creators.

R.U.R. touches on a theme central to *Blade Runner* and, of course, *Brave New World*. When Deckard is pressed into service to terminate the revolting replicants across a bleak cyberpunk cityscape, his mission leads him to confront the meaning of being human, a dilemma that derives from the struggles of both Bernard Marx and John Savage in *Brave New World*, if less overtly stated. A similar film, Richard Jobson's *The Purifiers* (2004), is set in yet another grim futuristic city wasteland not unlike that of *Blade Runner*. It depicts the creation of a separate urban society by martial arts clubs who have succeeded in ending crime and random violence. Despite some pasted-on quasi-political subtext, *The Purifiers* is little more than a martial arts film that falls short of the best of its genre as typified by Jet Li and Bruce Lee films. Superficially, *The Purifiers* calls to mind *Brave New World* but misses the mark in most departments.

Another film occasionally (and superficially) compared to *Brave New World* is *The End of Violence* (1996), written by Nicholas Klein and the film's director Wim Wenders, and featuring Gabriel Byrne and Andie MacDowell in a story of a Hollywood movie producer who makes violent action films but must take matters into his own hands when his wife is kidnapped. Comparisons to *Brave New World* in its depiction of a hedonistic society drawn to violent images are apt, but Andrew Niccol's *Gattaca* (1997) owes much more to Huxley, as well as Ray Bradbury. *Gattaca's* protagonist, Vincent Freeman, played by Ethan Hawke, is a genetically inferior man ostracized in his society, much as Huxley's Bernard Marx is in *Brave New World*. Born with a genetic heart condition, Freeman is denied a much-desired opportunity of space travel, which is reserved exclusively for the best human specimens, so he steals the identity of an athlete to achieve his desire. The intellectually curious Freeman exhibits characteristics of two Huxley characters, the aforementioned Bernard, but also John Savage in his intellectual yearnings, and Freeman's very name is an obvious statement of the compelling characteristic of many Huxley-inspired films, the human desire for knowledge and liberty despite constraints of an increasingly dehumanizing society. Connections can also be made between the film's Gattaca Corporation which, like Huxley's world society, is moving away from natural birth to a sterile society in which genetic engineering will eliminate those, like Freeman (and Marx), with physical or mental deficiencies.

Among contemporary filmmakers identified with futuristic science fiction films, Steven Spielberg stands out. His classic *Close Encounters of the Third Kind* (1977) and *E.T.* (1982) refreshed the science fiction genre through the creation of benevolent, intelligent (even childlike) aliens, and his version of H. G. Wells's *War of the Worlds* (2005), in which the natural world (a virus) kills murderously destructive aliens attacking the Earth, relates to Huxley in that sense only. However, Spielberg's under-appreciated *Artificial Intelligence: A.I.* (2001), adapted by Ian Watson from Brian Aldiss's short story "Supertoys Last All Summer Long," is, among recent films, the one owing most to Huxley's vision. Originally planned for production by Stanley Kubrick, whose classic sci-fi film *2001: A Space Odyssey* (1968) employs the Huxleyesque notion of malevolent technology, *A.I.* draws on fairy tales (like "Pinocchio") in an exploration of the dilemma of David, a highly advanced robotic boy abandoned by his human "mother." In *A.I.*, robots are referred to as "mechas" and David is among the first of his kind endowed with feelings. He develops a desire to be real so that he can win the love of his human mother, a woman agonizing over her real son, frozen in cryostasis awaiting a cure for his currently incurable disease. When the cure finally comes and the real son returns home, David's happy existence is shattered. Ruins of a more "primitive" past emerge in an obvious parallel with *Brave New World*'s reservation, as well as horrific scenes of the wreckage of the society, including violent sporting events in which discarded mechas are the victims. David's journey takes him to New York City, which is completely submerged in water from melted polar ice caps. David's heartrending search for the "Blue Fairy," who will make his wishes come true, ends underwater before her crumbling statue, a plaster remnant of Coney Island. Spielberg's mastery of state-of-the-art cinematic technology provides visions of a futuristic society owing incalculably to Huxley's imaginings of the impact of technology on human experience and, in fact, the fundamental meaning of humanness. Merging childhood terrors of abandonment with a society in which human feeling does not extend to synthetic beings, Spielberg's usually optimistic — even enthusiastic — outlook on technology is neglected for an uncharacteristically dismal depiction in *A.I.*, but this film emerges as one of his singular achievements. Most critics were not appreciative, but surely Spielberg will return to futuristic tales. His demonstrated skill in merging serious questions with human and humorous elements positions him as the filmmaker most likely to bring a masterful *Brave New World* to the screen. In the meantime, there is little doubt that Huxley's influence on film will continue into an unknowable future that can only be imagined, as he well knew.

Works Cited

Bedford, Sybille. *Aldous Huxley: A Biography*. London: Chatto & Windus: 1973.
Buckland, Warren. *Directed by Steven Spielberg: Poetics of the Contemporary Hollywood Blockbuster*. New York: Continuum, 2006.

Clark, Virginia M. *Aldous Huxley and Film*. Metuchen, NJ: Scarecrow, 1987.

Huxley, Aldous. *Brave New World*. New York: Harper Perennial, 1998.

James, Edward, and Farah Mendelsohn. *The Cambridge Companion to Science Fiction*. Cambridge: Cambridge University Press, 2003.

Lawrence, Matt. *Like a Splinter in Your Mind: The Philosophy Behind the Matrix Trilogy*. Malden, MA: Blackwell Publishing, 2004.

McBride, Joseph. *Steven Spielberg: A Biography*. New York: Da Capo Press, 1999.

Moylan, Tom. *Scraps of the Untainted Sky: Science Fiction, Utopia, Dystopia*. Boulder, CO: Westview Press, 2000.

Murray, Nicholas. *Aldous Huxley: A Biography*. New York: Thomas Dunne Books/St. Martin's Press, 2003.

Rowlands, Mark. *The Philosopher at the End of the Universe: Philosophy Explained Through Science Fiction Films*. New York: Thomas Dunne Books/St. Martin's Press, 2004.

Sawyer, Dana. *Aldous Huxley: A Biography*. New York: Crossroad Publishing, 2002.

Smith, Don G. *H. G. Wells on Film: The Utopian Nightmare*. Jefferson, NC: McFarland, 2002.

Telotte, J. P., and Barry Keith Grant. *Science Fiction Film*. Cambridge: Cambridge University Press, 2001.

Tillman, Aaron, and Harold Bloom, eds. *Aldous Huxley's* Brave New World. *Bloom's Modern Critical Interpretations*. New York: Chelsea House, 2002.

Woodcock, George. *Dawn and the Darkest Hour: A Study of Aldous Huxley*. New York: Viking, 1972.

About the Contributors

Angelo Arciero holds a PhD from the Department of Political Studies of University La Sapienza in Rome, Italy. He does research on political theory and philosophy, specializing in the field of the relationship between art and politics, with particular reference to the ideological debate of the 1930s. In addition to publishing several essays and a book about Orwell — *George Orwell. Contro il totalitarismo e per un Socialismo democratico* — he has edited a special issue of the journal *Igitur* on *L'Inghilterra e la sfida del totalitarismo 1930–1940*.

Bradley W. Buchanan, assistant professor of English at California State University, Sacramento, earned his PhD from Stanford University in 2001. He has published essays in *Journal of Modern Literature* and *Twentieth Century Literature*.

Robert Combs is the author of *Vision of the Voyage: Hart Crane and the Psychology of Romanticism* and articles on American dramatists. Combs has an essay in *Stephen Vincent Benét: Essays on His Life and Work*, edited by David Garrett Izzo and Lincoln Konkle.

John Coughlin is a Web application developer for Oakland University in Rochester, Michigan. He obtained his bachelor's degree in English from Oakland University in 1993.

James Fisher, chair, Theater–UNC Greensboro, has authored a half-dozen books, including *The Theatre of Tony Kushner: Living Past Hope* (2001) and the *The Historical Dictionary of the American Theater: Modernism, 1880–1930* (2008), co-authored with Felicia Hardison Londré. He recently edited *Tony Kushner: New Essays on the Art and Politics of the Plays* (2006) and he has edited six volumes of *The Puppetry Yearbook*. He has written essays for a variety of publications including *Modern Drama, Theatre Journal, The Mississippi Quarterly, The Southern Quarterly, Theatre Symposium, The Annual of Bernard Shaw Studies*, and many others. He is also the author of two plays and is a director, staging the first Indiana production of Tony Kushner's *Angels in America*, as well as many classic and contemporary plays.

Theo Garneau is a third year PhD candidate in English and graduate assistant at the University of Hawaii, Manoa. He holds a bachelor's degree in music performance from the State University of New York, Potsdam, and works professionally as a jazz and classical guitarist. He also earned master's degrees in

English and French literature from the University of Hawaii. In affiliation with the University of Hawaii's Center for Biographical Research, he is writing a biography of Hawaii-based alto saxophonist Gabe Baltazar, Jr., as his doctoral dissertation.

Angela Holzer, a graduate student at Princeton University, has published essays on Rilke and on the relationship of German intellectuals to Rome. She is currently working on her dissertation about the representation of ancient Rome in German philhellenism.

David Garrett Izzo has published 14 books and 57 essays of scholarship on twentieth-century British and American literature. He also published the historical novel *A Change of Heart*, about Huxley and his circle from 1929 to 1933. For more information: www.davidgarrettizzo.com.

Kim Kirkpatrick is assistant professor of English at Fayetteville State University in North Carolina, where she teaches literature, writing, and women's and gender studies. She attended Washington University in St. Louis, the University of Cincinnati, and Saint Louis University. Her interests include feminist science fiction literature, film, and television. She has written on Golden Age science fiction, cyperpunk, and *Buffy the Vampire Slayer*.

Gavin Miller is Leverhulme Early Career Fellow in the Department of English Literature, University of Edinburgh. He is the author of two monographs, *R. D. Laing* (2004) *and Alasdair Gray: The Fiction of Communion* (2005), and has published in *Journal of Narrative Theory, Scottish Studies Review*, and *Scottish Affairs*. His current project is a history of psychoanalytic psychiatry in Scotland.

Katherine Toy Miller has an MFA in creative writing (fiction) from the University of Arizona and a PhD in English (creative writing) from Florida State University. She is editing the annotated memoirs of Frieda Lawrence and adapting *Brave New World* into a screenplay, *Brave New World: The Third Way*.

Coleman Carroll Myron is a teacher of English at American Public University. Previously he taught at Fayetteville State University in North Carolina and Shippensburg University in Pennsylvania.

Scott Peller, an adjunct faculty member teaching African American literature at Wayne State University, earned his PhD from the Wayne State University Department of English in 2005. His dissertation, "Revising the Worker: Fordist Ideology and the Fictions of 'Proletarian' Counter-Hegemony," reveals the functioning of Fordism in proletarian fiction and film texts of the Depression.

Paul Smethurst, associate professor of English at the University of Hong Kong, was awarded his PhD at London University in 1996. He is the author of *The Postmodern Chronotope: Reading Space and Time in Contemporary Fiction*

(2000), and more than 20 essays on contemporary fiction and travel writing. He is currently working on three books on travel writing including a monograph, *Empirical Eyes and Mobile Worlds: Travel Writing and the Reinvention of Nature* (1760–1840).

Sean A. Witters, lecturer in English at the University of Vermont, is currently completing his doctoral dissertation, *Branding the Author: Literary Authenticity in America,* at Brandeis University.

Index